LOST
GARDENS

LOST
GARDENS

Foreword by Monty Don

JENNIFER POTTER
Photographs by Andrea Jones

For Robert and in memory of Vanne

First published in 2000 by Channel 4 Books, an imprint of Pan Macmillan Publishers Ltd,
Pan Macmillan, 20 New Wharf Road, London, N1 9RR, Basingstoke and Oxford.

Associated companies throughout the world.

www.panmacmillan.com

ISBN 0 7522 1873 5

9 7 5 3   2 4 6 8

A CIP catalogue record for this book is available from the British Library.

Special photography © Andrea Jones
Plans of the gardens by Michael Kerr

Designed by Blackjacks

Colour reproduction by Speedscan
Printed in the UK by Bath Press

LOST GARDENS

This book accompanies the television series *Lost Gardens* made by Flashback Television for Channel 4.
Executive producer: David Edgar
Series producer: Ann Booth-Clibborn

Frontispiece shows the restored Japanese garden at Gatton Park, Surrey.

CONTENTS

Foreword *by* Monty Don

Imagine you are in a hole 20 feet deep. Imagine you are sharing that hole with three mechanical diggers, four archaeologists, five tree surgeons and six members of a television crew. There are thirty more faces peering over the edge. Oh yes, there is also 2 feet of water in the bottom. The rain continues falling. Got the scene? Now, to really get inside the skin of *Lost Gardens*, imagine that this has absorbed your every waking moment of the past four days and that of a team of people for months, and that you are horribly aware that there is only a day and a half left to try and turn this mess into something approaching a well-researched, historically accurate recreation of a beautiful garden. Adrenalin tightens your stomach like a gathered leash. You are wet through, tired, cold, hungry and in way over your head.

And you are *loving* it.

This is the secret of *Lost Gardens*. We dig ourselves into one hell of a hole, literally and metaphorically, and then dig even harder to get ourselves out, having become totally absorbed in the stories of these remarkable gardens. It is hard, dirty, unglamorous work and none of us would miss it for anything. The scene I was describing came straight from my own experience of Eller How. The story of the garden that you will read in these pages is altogether a more measured account, but those of us involved in the actual excavation and rebuilding of that extraordinary creation were, for a few days, closer to the reality of the actual original experience of making the garden than anything else could be.

That experience ends up edited down to an hour's rich television, where finally we triumph over all odds and come out to a beautiful garden at the other side. That is perfectly true – sort of – but my own private film running in my head is slightly less glamorous. Penjerrick was a mudslide. Thacker's garden in Warwick and the officer's garden in Chatham were both bitterly cold. I put my back out on the first day of the lock-keeper's garden in Coventry. Dunira was magnificently crazy. Yet, at the drop of a hat, I would go back through every minute of filming them because we had that magical opportunity to live tracts of history through the actual stuff of history.

This combination of archaeology, human stories and the opportunity to recreate and rebuild with living materials is completely absorbing. Every garden has a story to tell and yet, unlike buildings, they can only exist in the present. It is not enough just to replant the space accurately and then solemnly observe the result as a frozen slice of time. Plants will not allow that. They cannot be fixed at some idealized moment. So the new garden that we restore is as much a modern, living thing as the original, and this is what really connects us to the past that everyone involved in *Lost Gardens* has tried so hard to recreate.

In the end, *Lost Gardens* is not really about gardens at all. It is not the mud, rain, nor the transformation of overgrown sites into beautiful and meticulously researched restorations, or even the recorded evidence of all that on television and in this book; it is about the stories that made them. *Lost Gardens* is about people. It is the terrible sadness of the corrosion of the splendour of the Macbeths' garden, it is the extraordinary breadth of interests of the Quaker Foxes at Penjerrick, the surprising richness of the life of a Warwick shopkeeper or tales of life for under-gardeners in the gardener's bothie at Gatton Park in the 1930s.

All gardens are made by people for people, and what we are uncovering, hidden beneath the brambles and weed trees and layers of soil, are their stories.

Introduction

AS MONTY SAYS in the foreword, this book comes out of a passionate belief that gardens tell stories – about the people who made them and the times in which they lived. Some of the very best stories lie hidden underground, in the tangled ruins of gardens that have somehow slipped off the map. Finding out who those people were and the dreams that inspired them is what this book is all about. Like the television programmes it illuminates, here are tales of passion, decay and rebirth, all pieced together with the wiles of detective fiction.

(above) Monty Don, garden historian Toby Musgrave and landscaper Ann-Marie Powell survey raised Tudor beds in Suffolk.

The programmes themselves were made with great skill and intensity to a format devised by David Edgar of Flashback Television. Monty Don led a team of experts whose job it was to tease out clues that landscaper Ann-Marie Powell could then realize on the ground. Despite all the careful preparation beforehand, every programme started off as an adventure as Monty and the presenters came to each site completely fresh, never having seen it before filming began. This was critical to the whole spirit of the programmes, which aimed to communicate the thrill of discovery, of history unfolding before your eyes, and the miraculous transformation of weed-ridden earth into a dimly remembered earthly paradise.

Inevitably, only a fraction of the many layers unearthed about each garden found their way into the finished programmes. So here, the programme-makers stand aside to let the gardens and their original owners and creators tell their own stories. From a boggy Home Counties woodland rises a thatched Japanese hut where a king and queen once sipped afternoon tea. A weary Tudor courtier brings a new young bride to his moated *pleasance*. Deep underground in the English Lake District, a fanatical Victorian breeds orchids and ferns. Further south, a prosperous shopkeeper enjoys a view of the races from his staunchly utilitarian pleasure garden. Primeval tree ferns weave into a Cornish wilderness garden, home to monkeys and a shining white cockatoo. More prosaically, pigs and chickens add fertility to the vegetables and bright flowers of a lock-keeper's cottage. A Georgian master craftsman smokes a quiet pipe as evening falls in a bustling dockyard. Tragedy unfolds its wings in a Scottish rose garden.

(below) Researcher Emma Geary delves into a lost Scottish rose garden.

These are just some of the characters and tales that have left their mark on the gardens we set out to discover and restore. While plenty of books and programmes deal with the grander landscapes of garden history, we were determined to include more ordinary gardens as well. Industrialists and royalty rub shoulders with shopkeepers and Quaker scientists; panelled rose beds and topiary with humble cabbages and heartsease.

A thread running through many of the stories is the excitement of plant-hunting and the introduction of new plant species – from the Apothecary's rose brought back in the saddlebags of the Crusades to Sir Joseph Hooker's blood-red Himalayan rhododendrons that found their way to a Cornish valley garden. The planting designs for each garden are illustrated here in plans drawn by Michael Kerr, whose expert plant knowledge enriched the programmes.

Recreating each of the gardens became a very personal odyssey for the whole *Lost Gardens* team. Monty talks about the insane thrill of digging down into the hillside at Eller How in Cumbria. The same garden is especially personal to me, too: many years ago my family rented Eller How for six months from Polish widow Clara Boyle. The garden then was truly lost under a mat of rhododendron scrub pierced by a Gothic folly tower, like the house in Hitchcock's *Psycho*. The stories Clara told about crocodiles and tropical water lilies in the blustery damp of the English Lake District lodged in my memory and began a fascination with ruined gardens that has never left me. When the archaeologists opened tunnels into the hillside, it was my childhood they exhumed as well as Victorian eccentric Henry Boyle's flamboyant obsessions.

Filming each programme took place over a concentrated five-day period, with a visit a few months later to see the changes that had taken place. Although restoring a garden will usually take much longer than this, the five days of each shoot helped to concentrate enthusiasm, resources and adrenalin. This meant huge progress could be made in a very short time – and gardens brought back to life that would otherwise have remained derelict or buried for many more years. The five days were backed up by months of patient research and exploration, helped by the many people who shared their knowledge, time and enthusiasm so generously – garden historians, county gardens trusts, archivists, experts, friends, owners – all the people thanked at the end of the book and many more besides. These lost gardens would not have been found without them. Equally, they would not have been put back without the heroic efforts of the many volunteers who lent their labour and skills just as generously.

If the story of each garden really began very much earlier than the films suggest, so, too, they continue to spin out their endings. After the first series was shown, Flashback received many letters from people who relived their own memories, or the memories of their parents and grandparents – about the Japanese garden at Gatton especially. Shortly before this book was finished, a photograph of Henry Boyle's long-lost fernery surfaced to prove our hunches right … and so the stories will continue to rewrite themselves.

'Ruins provide the incentive for restoration, and for a return to origins,' wrote American geographer J. B. Jackson in *The Necessity for Ruins*. 'The old order has to die before there can be a born-again landscape.' Lost gardens provide the same impetus, with the added richness that comes from a garden's privileged status. Planting a garden is the closest most people get to making the world in their image. By rediscovering these decayed and forgotten landscapes, our aim was to carry past hopes and dreams into the future and this book records the many stories we uncovered along the way.

(above) Eller How's folly tower from the author's family album.

(below) Monty examines the evidence on site with plantsman Michael Kerr.

chapter one

pleasure and produce for a victorian grocer

O N RISING GROUND overlooking the racecourse at Warwick lay a tangled patch of green. Though close to the city centre, the site was easy to miss, shut in by the houses of Linen Street and the vacant lot of Bread and Meat Close. But venture further into the scrub and you could lose yourself in a secret world of brambly hedgerows and makeshift doors beckoning you onwards.

Immediately the site presented a puzzle. Here the land had been divided into strips and gardened like allotments, without any houses attached. Already a number of these smaller gardens had been cleared and put to fresh cultivation. Yet dotted about the site were a handful of exquisitely ruined summer houses that pointed to a grander heritage than mere 'potato gardens'.

At the top of the hill, beside a gabled row of terraced houses, stood the finest summer house of them all. Two-storied with a chimney and elaborate bargeboards (sadly rotting), it was pure Gothic fantasy. Windows and doorway gaped blackly and the roof opened to

The derelict summer house broods over the site like an abandoned railway hut.

show a patch of sky. In the garden below the summer house, two neglected pear trees hinted at happier times. Otherwise, the place contained little of interest – a few clustering weed trees and a sloping rectangle of meadow grass choked with weeds.

This was the garden we had come to discover and restore. Apart from the ruined summer house, you would pass it by with scarcely a second glance.

Garden plots

The story of our garden began in 1845, when Edward Wilson of Exhall first divided the field known as Hill Close that had come to him through a complex family trust. (The main sources for each garden are listed on pages 186–188). The first evidence of garden layouts came six years later in a beautifully hand-coloured Board of Health map of 1851. This showed that the eastern part of the site (including our own plot) had already been laid out as gardens without any houses attached – twenty-two individual plots in all, shown in meticulous detail. The map's main purpose was to survey Warwick's urban landscape prior to installing a modern sewerage system and piped water supply. Overflowing privies and piggeries next to wells were of special interest as a primary cause of contaminated drinking water.

Hedges, paths, trees and garden structures – all were carefully recorded on the 1851 map. Most gardens had small buildings at the top of each site where their owners enjoyed the best views, surrounded by ornamental paths and flower beds. Our own plot was disappointingly plain, with no ornament beyond a central path and no hedge shown for its southern boundary. Quite possibly it had not yet been transformed into a garden.

By 1866, our garden had a summer house, although not in the same place as the one that survives today. We know this from a manuscript map of 1866 attached to a property deed for one of the other gardens. The map confirmed that the whole site was laid out by then into thirty-two separate gardens. (Over the years, some boundaries shifted as gardens were amalgamated or split into smaller parcels of land.)

In the same year – 1866 – the whole site was offered for sale at auction as 'highly valuable freehold building or garden land'. According to an advertisement in the *Warwick Advertiser* of 14 July 1866, the 4-acre-plus site was subdivided into thirty-five lots of garden ground, producing an annual rental of £76 12s. 'The land is enclosed from the street by a good brick-built wall and is laid out with suitable roads and other tenant accommodation. It also possesses a first-class site for building purposes.'

The Ordnance Survey map of 1886 was the first to show the summer house in its present position.

Despite this invitation to develop the site for building, the close remained as individual gardens. The land changed hands a couple of times and then most of the plots were sold off individually – some to existing occupiers, others to new freeholders. In her investigation of the finances surrounding the sales, garden historian and local councillor Christine Hodgetts has concluded that economics favoured the sale of the plots as individual gardens. The 1866 price of £367 per acre rose to an average selling price of £490 per acre when the plots were sold on during the first ten years.

The first edition 25-inch Ordnance Survey map for Warwick, published in 1886, showed the gardens in their prime. There were still over thirty plots, separated by hedges or fencing, all with well-established (and sometimes quite elaborate) path structures. Most had small garden buildings. A few had extensive glasshouses and at least one garden had been terraced. Trees grew on most plots – quite probably fruit trees laid out in regular patterns.

Excitingly, the 1:500 1886 map showed our own plot in great detail and established that by then a new summer house had been built in its current position. A path flanked by trees (including quite probably, the pear trees that have survived) ran up the centre to the summer-house steps. On either side of the summer house were further steps leading down to cellars. Two flower beds or small patches of lawn to north and south of the summer house completed the symmetry of the arrangement. A hedge or fence line marked the boundary with the northern plot, while the southern boundary still appeared to be open – perhaps to avoid casting shade. The summer house itself was built against a retaining wall, not shown for the plots on either side despite the change in levels between all these gardens and the bowling green above.

Although no information has surfaced so far to tell us how our garden was planted, inventories and sale notices for other gardens present a charming blend of utility and beauty. The inventory in a handwritten deed of 1870 between owner William Alfred Walker (woollen draper) and tenant Benjamin Chadband (confectioner) clearly defined the garden's character as part ornamental and part productive, with a definite leaning towards fruit:

> Summer Arbour. Pig stie. Wash tub. Cucumber lights and brick frame.
> 2 Asparagus beds. 1 Filbert tree. 2 Standard Rose trees. 4 Standard Plum trees.
> 3 Standard Apple trees. 2 espalier ditto. 1 Standard Cherry tree.
> 29 Gooseberry trees. 32 Currant trees. 2 Strawberry beds. All walks edged with tiles, gates and locks thereto, water tub, quick hedge. 1 row Sea-kale. Herbs.

In 1878, plot twenty-three (then occupied by gunmaker Mr S. Partridge) was put up for sale, 'an exceedingly prettily laid out garden with slated summer house, neatly arranged walks and choicely planted'. An inventory for plot eight in 1879 indicated that the summer arbour contained kettle, gas light and stove, iron and wood painted seats, inside and outside blinds,

spittoons and sundry glass. It also had a patent dry earth commode, vinery, fire hole, potting shed and greenhouse.

One of the most detailed inventories was drawn up in 1883 for a garden that contained equipment for mowing and rolling lawns and growing and displaying flowers as well as for cultivating vegetables such as sea kale, asparagus and cucumbers. A variety of seats were provided to enjoy the fruits of so much hard labour – cane seats, rush seats, elbow chairs, stools and an iron-and-wood garden seat. All these descriptions would help us reconstruct our own plot.

Sleuthing for dates

The manuscript map of 1866 and the Ordnance Survey map of 1886 established a twenty-year time span during which our summer house had been built. Could we be more precise about the date?

The records that gave us this vital information were the land tax assessments held in Warwick County Record Office. Land taxes and rates were first levied on the individual gardens in 1877 – before this time, a tax was recorded for the site as a whole. The records for 1878–79 named John Burford as the owner of our plot and Thacker as the occupier. Along with about two-thirds of the other gardens, the plot's rental or annual value was assessed at just £2. The highest valuation was £8 for the plot owned by the late Thomas Snape, solicitor. The next year, 1879–80, the records gave James Thacker as both owner and occupier, and the rental value had leapt to £6. This was just the clue we were seeking. As only a handful of other plots had been reassessed, the leap in value surely indicated that this was the year James Thacker built his fine new summer house.

So we now had a date for our garden, and a creator. The next task was to find out as much as we could about the man who built our summer house and the aspirations that impelled him to create a miniature pleasure garden here in Warwick.

Citizen Thacker

When James Thacker poured the pride and energy of ownership into his new plot in 1880, he was about forty years old and a partner in the High Street firm of Italian grocers and warehousemen, Thacker & Christmas. He lived with his wife Jane above the shop; they had no children. *Kelly's* trade directory for 1880 gave his address as Swan Street, which formed the corner with High Street where his shop was situated.

Front-page advertisements for the shop in the *Warwick and Warwickshire Advertiser* during the 1880s drew attention to its fine range of products, both imported and local. In November 1880, for instance, an advertisement promised the finest new fruits for the season – raisins, currants, sultanas, figs, muscatels, French plums, grapes and fancy fruits – as well as a large stock of cheeses, such as Cheddar, Warwickshire, Gorgonzola, Gruyère, Parmesan and Stilton. Early in 1884, the shop offered crystallized and dessert fruits, nuts, Huntley & Palmer's cakes, fancy biscuits in small tins and a large assortment of bonbons or crackers. By August of the same year, the family grocers had opened another shop in Coten End, Warwick, promising 'all Goods of the same Superior Quality and at the same Prices as at High Street'.

James Thacker died of a heart attack on 25 July 1907 while still a relatively young sixty-seven. His obituary in the *Warwick and Warwickshire Advertiser* confirmed his standing in the community. Born to a large family in Leicestershire, he learned his business as a grocer, then moved for a time to Grimsby and Coventry before settling in Warwick. Here he started out as a chief assistant (with Caleb Christmas) at the high-class grocers that eventually bore their names. A senior Justice of the Peace, prominent Methodist and staunch Liberal, Thacker was much involved in unobtrusive good works and civic duties until ill health forced him to retire from public life. Just before he died, he had arranged to go to a Liberal gathering by car 'and was looking forward with great glee to his first motor ride'.

All this portrays James Thacker as a solid middle-class citizen, highly moral in the best Victorian sense, though accustomed, through his business, to imported novelties and fancy foods. Married but childless, we could safely assume he was reasonably affluent and would therefore want the best for his garden – like the summer house that bore witness to his excellent taste.

Thacker & Christmas staff line the High Street, *c.*1912.

Our story unfolds

James Thacker continued to own the plot until his death in 1907. Land tax records show that he gave up active gardening here around the turn of the century when the occupier of his garden is shown as Walter Thacker, soon followed by coal merchant Samuel Hunt. Hunt bought the plot after Thacker died, by which time the assessed value had dropped to £3. He remained as owner-occupier until land tax assessment records stopped in 1931.

We were lucky to trace two brothers, Jim and Phil Durrant, whose parents had rented our plot for ten years or so from 1937. Their father ran a hardware shop and, like James Thacker, the family had no garden attached to their home. Both Jim and Phil clearly remember the garden of their boyhood, when plentiful fruit trees grew on either side of the central path. Mrs Durrant would bottle the fruit for the family's use, and Jim remembers the big Pershore plums his mother kept in the pantry.

The family used their garden a lot, especially on half-closing days, weekends and summer holidays, when they would pitch a tent on the lawn and sleep overnight. Mr Durrant grew root vegetables, peas, beans and raspberries on both sides of the path, which was bordered with flowers. He also kept bees in a hive. The mature fruit trees gave them Conference pears, Pippin and Bramley apples, and plums. The brick summer house had two cellars, each with a separate entrance on either side. One was used for the earth closet, the other as a fruit store. The main room upstairs was panelled with pine boards painted green and had a wooden floor and small cast-iron fireplace. Mr Durrant replaced the fireplace with a cupboard as they used an oil fire for heating.

In 1947, however, the owner of the site took it back and sold it on for development that never happened. After this, all the gardens sank slowly into decay until, in 1989, Warwick District Council obtained planning permission to develop the Hill Close site for housing. A few years later, concerned residents mounted a campaign to save the gardens, forming a Residents' Association and lobbying the council to enlist the support of English Heritage. Four of the summer houses (including our own) were listed Grade II in 1994 and, in December of that year, the gardens were added to English Heritage's register of parks and gardens of special historic interest. Now an energetic steering group is overseeing the revival of the Hill Close site as individual gardens. Our plot lies on development land just outside it.

(top) Mrs Durrant and a friend enjoy the garden from the summer house steps.

(bottom) Mrs Durrant's view recreated today looking down towards Warwick racecourse.

A lost world of pleasure

Before we could begin to put back James Thacker's garden, we needed to know more about the kind of place it was in its Victorian prime. In particular, why did people create detached gardens like these close to city centres, and how were they enjoyed?

These really are lost gardens in the widest sense. Not only have most disappeared to development, but so too has virtually any memory of detached *pleasure* gardens as opposed to purely productive gardens or allotments. Christine Hodgetts is one of the few garden historians to have made a special study of them. Another is David Lambert, conservation officer in England for the Garden History Society. Both are eloquent in their attempts to resurrect these forgotten gardens.

Before mass transport, most professionals, craftworkers and shopkeepers lived close to their work in town centres – or, like grocer James Thacker, directly above the shop. As their homes generally lacked gardens, separate 'garden plots' sprang up on urban fringes across much of Britain, where the better-off could rent or buy plots (typically an eighth of an acre), which they laid out as private pleasure gardens with hedges and fanciful summer houses and arbours, and planted with a mix of ornamental and kitchen produce. Old maps take the story back even earlier to the seventeenth and eighteenth centuries, showing that garden grounds like these, detached from their houses, were found even then on the outskirts of towns.

In Birmingham, where these gardens were especially popular, they became known as 'guinea gardens', after the annual rent charged for the smaller plots. (The rateable value for Thacker's Warwick garden was double this sum,

(left) Victorian bedding favoured bold splashes of colour like these asters edged with *Senecio cineraria*.

(opposite top) Bright annual nasturiums will self-seed each year.

(opposite bottom) Clinker paths give access to the vegetable plot.

even before he built his summer house.) Writing in the *Gardener's Magazine* in August 1831, the famous garden writer J. C. Loudon described himself astonished at the selection of hardy shrubs and plants grown in one such Birmingham garden occupied by a Mr Clarke, chemist and druggist. Loudon also painted a larger picture of the popularity of these gardens in and around the Midlands:

> The detached town gardens are situated in the suburbs of towns, generally collected together, and separated by hedges. There are upwards of two thousand of such gardens in the neighbourhood of Birmingham, a considerable number at Wolverhampton, some at Dudley and at Manchester, and a few even in the neighbourhood of that stationary town Buckingham… When a party possessing such a garden is about to leave it, the plants and trees, and the right of possession, are bought by the successor for a price which, at Birmingham and Wolverhampton, sometimes amounts to as high a sum as 60 guineas. Twenty guineas is the usual price given for a garden paying from a guinea to 30s. annual rental.

Ever the moralist and improver, Loudon wished that gardens like these were to be found near all towns, 'as they afford a rational recreation to the sedentary, and a useful and agreeable manner of passing the leisure time of mechanics and workmen of every description'. He would return to the subject in a later issue, admiring some detached town gardens near Lancaster

where vegetables, gooseberries and florists' flowers were grown 'to great perfection', even overturning his prejudice against large Lancashire gooseberries.

The relatively high rents charged for such gardens, their tall hedges and mix of ornamental with productive planting clearly distinguished them from ordinary allotments. Intended purely for growing kitchen produce, allotments or 'potato gardens' had grown out of the Enclosure Acts of the eighteenth to mid-nineteenth centuries as a sop to the landless poor who had lost their traditional access rights to common land. Detached pleasure gardens, by contrast, were justified on economic rather than philanthropic grounds. Quite simply, the parcels of land fetched a better price as gardens than as pasture. However, economics came to argue against gardens in favour of development and sites were swallowed up in the building boom of the Victorian age. Today, only a handful of sites survive in Warwick, Birmingham, Coventry and Nottingham.

Even where gardens survived, their character changed as wealthier residents migrated to the suburbs where villas came with gardens attached. A site like Hill Close inevitably lost its character of 'pleasure gardens' and became indistinguishable from allotments. Buildings encroached along the south side of Linen Street and into St Paul's Close and St Paul's Terrace. Two world wars supported this change and the gardens slowly decayed. By the late 1980s, when the council obtained planning permission to develop the land for housing, only a few local memories remained to indicate the site was anything special.

Class, fashions and morals

The final piece in the jigsaw, before we could begin reconstruction, was to place our garden within its late Victorian context.

Class was a factor that profoundly affected garden styles and, therefore, the garden we were setting out to recreate – that of a prosperous, well-respected tradesman. The new (posthumous) 1871 edition of J. C. Loudon's ever-popular *An Encyclopaedia of Gardening* continued to classify British gardens according to their owner's status, starting with cottage gardens, rising up through street gardens, smaller suburban gardens, tradesmen's villas and suburban or citizen's villas, and culminating in the grand heights of mansions, demesnes and royal palaces. Under cottage gardens, the encyclopaedia declared that, 'Tradesmen and operative manufacturers, who have a permanent interest in their cottages, have generally the best cottage-gardens; and many of them, especially at Norwich, Manchester and Paisley, excel in the culture of florists' flowers.'

Local horticultural competitions, too, commonly distinguished between the entries of gentlemen, or their professional gardeners, and those of the lower classes. Warwick had its own Amateurs' and Cottagers' Society with an annual show restricted to bona fide amateurs, cottagers and allotment holders living in the borough. Even growing flowers *at all* could become a matter of class. In 1857, author George Glenny posed the question, 'Should cottagers grow flowers?' His answer was at best a qualified 'maybe': 'The idea of tempting poor men to grow Pansies, and Pinks, and Carnations, by awarding them prizes, seems to us downright wicked, or, at least, thoughtless and preposterous.'

One writer who appreciated the new class of urban lower- and middle-class amateurs, passionate about their gardens and avid for instruction, was Londoner Shirley Hibberd. A popularizer of science as well as horticulture, he brought a breath of real-life experience to his many gardening books. Two were especially helpful for restoring James Thacker's Warwick pleasure garden: *The Amateur's Kitchen Garden* of 1877 and *The Amateur's Flower Garden* of 1871 (we used the revised edition of 1878). Also useful was his earlier work, *The Town Garden* (second edition 1859).

In matters of Victorian garden design and style, the main battle lines were drawn between advocates of formal, architectural gardens and those who preferred a wilder, more natural style. But for a small town plot like James Thacker's, this argument was fairly irrelevant. The nature of his garden – part productive, part ornamental – dictated a comparatively plain overall plan where neatness and ease of cultivation were the main priorities.

James Thacker was more likely to follow Shirley Hibberd's practical and down-to-earth advice on laying out a kitchen garden: 'The ground should be rectangular, slightly sloping to the south [ours slopes away to the west], divided into convenient sized plots, with good walks of sufficient width between; it should be effectively drained; the soil a deep

(opposite) In Thacker's day, steps led down to an earth closet and basement storeroom.

(below) Also known as 'Black-eyed Susan', *Rudbeckia fulgida* remains a favourite for colourful borders.

loam; there should be sheltering plantations on the north and east, substantial boundary walls on all four sides, and a suitable extent should be screened off by means of hedges or walls, to serve as frame ground, and rubbish yard, and a place of shelter for pot plants and other nursery purposes.'

Much more open to debate was how Thacker might have planted the ornamental part of his garden. Again, the choice was between a formal planting style, incorporating seasonal bedding and perhaps even the latest craze – carpet bedding – or a more informal, relaxed 'cottagey' planting of perennials and annuals, which was

then considered old-fashioned although it was slowly regaining favour. We chose to tread a middle course, relating our garden to what we knew of Thacker the man.

Seasonal bedding schemes had been popular throughout Victorian times. By 1880, however, the vogue for brightly coloured summer bedding had peaked and gardening writers were urging simplicity in the plant varieties and colours used. This is how Shirley Hibberd described his own bedding scheme at Pentonville, London, which had two small circular beds planted separately in the spring with hyacinths and tulips. 'When the bulbs were removed I filled up the

beds with potted perennials, such as geraniums, pelargoniums, calceolarias, fuschias, pansies, verbenas, and heliotropes, preferring always to have *few sorts*, but abundance of *plants*, so as to produce rich masses of simple colours, rather than a spotted harlequinade of every tint of the rainbow.'

One new fashion we felt would definitely be out of place was carpet bedding using low-growing foliage plants and succulents like sempervivums. Although the style had been gaining popularity throughout the 1870s, a good Methodist like Thacker would surely have judged it too extravagant. A columnist in the

Gardeners' Magazine of 12 June 1880 argued hotly that while such beds might be acceptable for men of wealth wishing to 'give one the impression that some of the hearth-rugs had been scattered about the lawn', they were far too costly for the middle classes or for displays in public parks financed with public money.

When it came to plants, the Victorians loved novelty and new varieties – a trait that fitted well with Thacker's business as an importer of novelty goods and foreign delicacies. Garden catalogues of the time positively bristled with new introductions. *Carters' New, Rare, and Choice Plants for 1880* listed pages of new coleus, zonal geraniums, dahlias, roses and flowering bedding plants of all kinds. (The same went for vegetables, although whether all these varieties really were new was doubtful. Shirley Hibberd slyly drew attention in *The Amateur's Kitchen Garden* to 'a trading firm, that for several years in succession offered the British Queen pea every year under a new name'.)

Dahlias (both new and old) were special Victorian favourites. They came in three classes: show, fancy and bedding or border dahlias. An article in the *Gardeners' Magazine* of 2 April 1881 praised the virtues of the latter: 'The border dahlias, more especially the single and pompones are of immense value for supplying cut flowers for indoor decorations during the summer and autumn.'

We also wanted to make room in Thacker's garden for the old favourites (annuals and perennials) we felt sure he would have enjoyed. A correspondent in the *Gardeners' Magazine* of 11 December 1880 admiringly described a lady's flower garden that had discarded 'ordinary bedders' in favour of annuals: those plants 'generally called "everybody's" flowers, because all who have a garden might grow them, but they do not because they are not now quite fashionable.' The inspiration for this garden came from 'a glimpse of the many pretty flowers that she saw growing wild in the hedgerows'.

Vegetables formed an essential part of the Victorian garden – even small town gardens. William Paul's *Villa Gardening* (third edition, 1865) defined a hierarchy of vegetables to be grown according to available space: 'A small piece of ground will suffice for growing Peas, French Beans, Cabbages, Broccoli, Cauliflowers, Celery, Herbs, and Salads; if you have room, Sea Kale, Asparagus, Cucumbers, and Melons should also be grown; while, if space be limited, Potatoes, Turnips, Carrots and Onions may be advantageously purchased.'

Two Victorian 'luxury' vegetables we felt James Thacker would have favoured were sea kale and asparagus.

Shirley Hibberd discussed them in a chapter of his kitchen-garden book, arguing that their requirements were not as extravagant as generally assumed: 'for although these are certainly not to be regarded as vegetables suitable to the circumstances of a cottager, they may be produced in plenty, and of the finest quality, in any middle-class garden.' He considered their chief requirement was for a deep soil, well-drained and, if possible, 'made fat with manure'. Artichokes, on the other hand, Hibberd dismissed as 'scarcely worth growing' (along with cardoons and maize), although he was prepared to admit that they added an element of 'beauty and interest'.

Perhaps interestingly, given their current popularity, herb gardens had fallen out of favour by mid-Victorian times. Shirley Hibberd made a point of recommending one tailored to his class of readers. His ideal was a sandy bank, ornamental and private, 'so situated that the ladies of the household may be able at any time, without difficulty, to obtain small quantities of such herbs as they require'.

This was the background to Thacker's Victorian paradise – a neat, orderly sort of paradise that combined beauty with utility. We felt sure that everything he did in his garden – whether digging, planting, sowing, reaping or just enjoying the view – would have given him the moral pleasure that was so important to the way the Victorians approached gardening. As one correspondent to the *Gardeners' Magazine* of 3 April 1880 observed, 'It is impossible to overrate the advantage to a town community of gardens in which men of all classes – rich, poor, and middling – may find amusement in practical horticulture.' Even so, most writers of the time assumed their readers would employ a gardener for the really rough work; Hibberd, for instance, supposed his reader would 'regard the handling of the spade as *infra dig*'.

(above) Feathery asparagus makes a fine display.

(right) Dahlias reached a peak of popularity in the mid-nineteenth century: here is *Dahlia* 'Bishop of Llandaff'.

Plotting the restoration

Our restoration aim was to put back James Thacker's original garden of 1880, the probable year when he built his new summer house. The plan was based on maps and documents relating to our plot and its creator, supplemented by what we knew of other similar gardens in Warwick and elsewhere, and about Victorian garden styles and plants in general. It proved a fascinating mix.

The layout was fixed for us by the Ordnance Survey map of 1886, with the summer house at the top built into the retaining wall, a straight central path flanked by trees, and smaller lawns or beds close to the summer house. We added narrow paths to aid cultivation; and we chose to divide the garden into three parts, with pleasure lawn near the summer house, productive garden across the centre and more lawn towards the bottom. In this we were guided by the memories of the Durrant brothers, whose father had also kept a beehive. Shirley Hibberd had, in fact, warned against mixing fruit trees with vegetables because trees would keep sun and rain off the earth and cultivation would inevitably disturb the tree roots. We knew from the map, however, that by 1886 at least, trees had stretched the length of the plot.

The summer house provided the garden's focal point and its best view out of the garden. Although the structure had decayed badly, enough remained to dictate the style and manner of its restoration. Our primary aim was to restore the fabric of the building and make it properly weathertight, matching materials and construction methods to the original. For this we brought in skilled building conservators under the direction of a historic building consultant. The only detail we added was a roof finial designed by the consultant. As the summer house is a listed building, we

(opposite) A rose arch creates a romantic entrance to James Thacker's recreated pleasure garden.

(right) Spikes of lavender spill out from narrow borders.

consulted closely throughout the restoration with Warwick District Council's conservation architect.

Archaeology gave us the material for paths and edging. We used clinker for the bottom part of the central path and for the narrower paths, and imitation stone flags for the top path leading to the summer house. Discovering the clinker was a surprise, as it seemed to sit uneasily with the finery of the summer house. Traces of a mortar base near the summer house suggested that at least the top part had been paved.

Victorian literature discussed edging at length. Shirley Hibberd recommended clipped box, ivy, triangular tiles or, for the kitchen garden, simple planks of wood. Most edging tiles he judged 'objectionably frail'. We used reclaimed blue edging tiles along both sides of the central path to match those found on site. Around the dahlia beds and climbing roses planted by the entrance to the summer house we used dwarf box, and wooden planks for the secondary paths.

Decisions about hedges were determined by what we found on site, and by local memories. The late Arthur Measures, founding chairman of the Warwickshire Gardens Trust, remembered especially the height of the original hedges and the wonderful seclusion they gave. For the sides we used a traditional mix of privet and hawthorn, popular since Victorian times. For the bottom entrance we used roses and an archway supporting honeysuckle and more climbing roses. The privacy hedges like these afforded was an essential part of the gardens' special character as pleasure gardens.

The site itself dictated our handling of the ornamental garden, which was concentrated at the top around the summer house, with another lawn, beehives and a rustic seat at the bottom. The flower borders on either side of the central path were also part of the pleasure garden.

Even though several Victorian gardening books warned against lawns in small town gardens, we felt sure James Thacker would have laid one in his hideaway. He would have taken to heart Shirley Hibberd's advice that it would need trimming at least once a fortnight and should not be turned into a thoroughfare.

Presenter and garden historian Toby Musgrave's decision to incorporate fleur-de-lis beds into the two top lawns

provoked fierce discussion. Although the source was impeccable (a scaled design in Hibberd's *The Amateur's Flower Garden*), and the planting period-correct (cineraria, lobelia, pansies and asters), it is at least debatable whether Thacker would have introduced beds and bedding into his small town plot. Hibberd on the whole favoured simplicity and explained in the text that he had copied his fleur-de-lis designs from the forefront of a lawn in a fine and large 'old-fashioned garden'.

A bed to one side of the summer house was devoted to dahlias and the borders along the central path filled with a charming mix of cottage-garden perennials and annuals grown largely from seed. The contemporary sources we used to help build our plant list included two plant catalogues of 1880 – *Sutton's Amateur's Guide in Horticulture* and *Carters' New, Rare, and Choice Plants for 1880* – as well as contemporary gardening journals and books. A line of old-fashioned sweet peas growing up rustic tripods separated the top lawns from the vegetable garden.

Fruit was very important to all these gardens. Against the back west-facing wall we planted a fig, with gooseberries and currants in beds in the productive garden. Another bed was devoted to rhubarb, forced with the use of chimney pots. We replaced the trees now missing from the 1886 map with apple and pear.

For vegetables, we interplanted the asparagus with broad and runner beans. We also planted one bed with potatoes, two with artichokes (for their ornamental value at least) and made a nursery bed for mixed vegetables. One bed we set aside exclusively for herbs, concentrating on Mediterranean varieties that would have been familiar to an Italian warehouseman like Thacker, such as basil, lavender, fennel, chives, oregano and rosemary.

(left) Rustic tripods for sweet peas mark the boundary between pleasure and produce.

(opposite) Toby's cut-out beds, taken from Victorian writer Shirley Hibberd, sparked controversy.

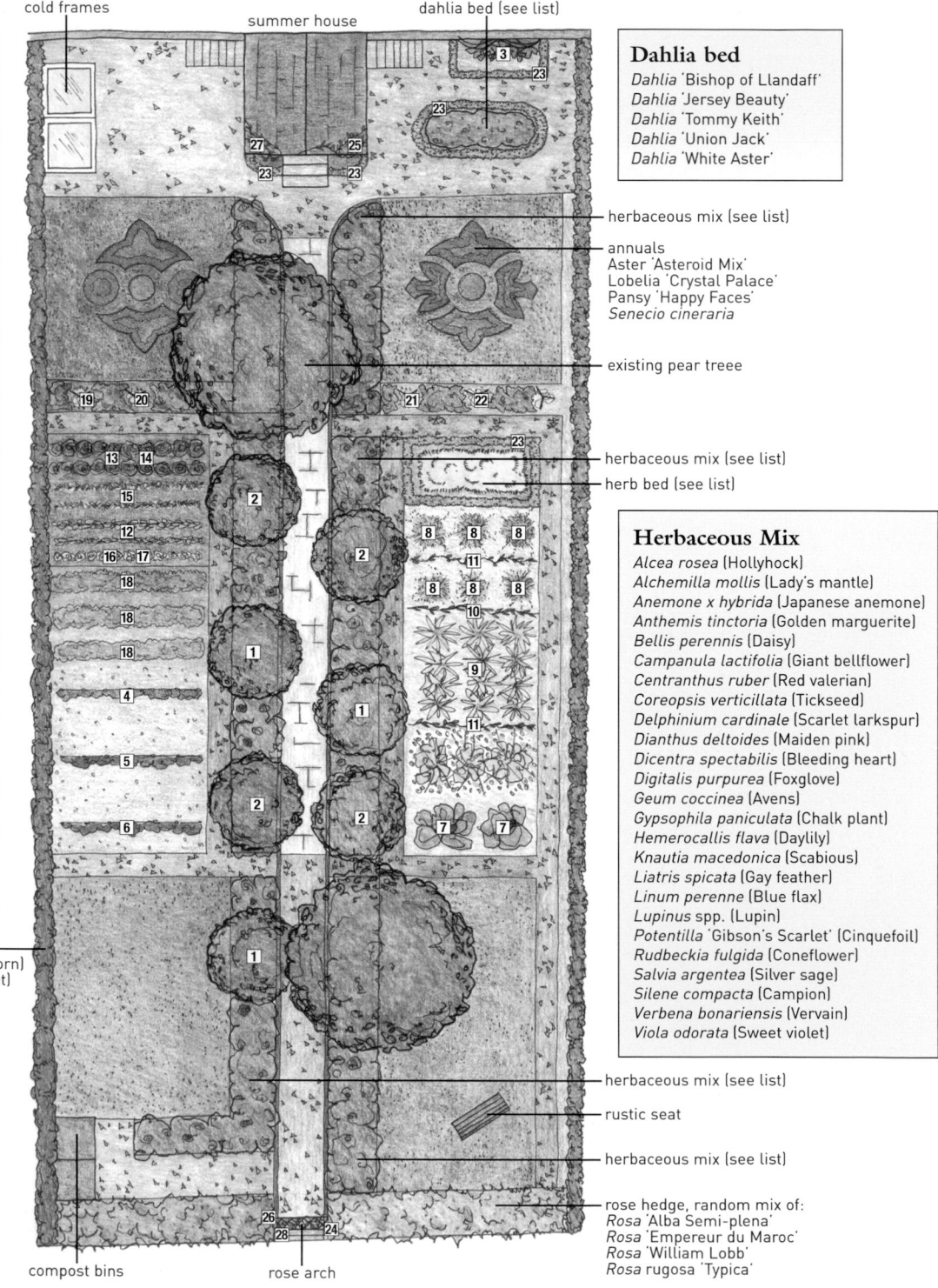

Key

Fruit
1 Apple
2 Pear
3 Fig
4 White currant
5 Red currant
6 Gooseberry
7 Rhubarb

Vegetables
8 Asparagus
9 Artichokes
10 Broad Bean
11 Runner Bean
12 Spinach
13 Cabbage
14 Cabbage
15 Carrot
16 Lettuce
17 Lettuce
18 Potato

Annuals
19 *Lathyrus odoratus* 'Violet Queen' (Sweet pea)
20 *Lathyrus odoratus* 'Cupani's Original' (Sweet pea)
21 *Lathyrus odoratus* 'Matucana' (Sweet pea)
22 *Lathyrus odoratus* 'Painted Lady' (Sweet pea)

Border edging
23 *Buxus sempervirens* (Box)

Climbers
24 *Lonicera periclymenum* (Honeysuckle)
25 *Rosa* 'Celine Forrestier'
26 *Rosa* 'Crimson Rambler'
27 *Rosa* 'Gloire de Dijon'
28 *Rosa* 'Mme Alfred Carrière'

perimeter hedge, alternate *Crataegus monogyna* (Hawthorn) and *Ligustrum vulgaris* (Privet)

Herb bed

Basil
Chives
Dill
Lavender
Mint
Oregano
Parsley
Rosemary
Sweet fennel

cold frames

summer house

dahlia bed (see list)

Dahlia bed

Dahlia 'Bishop of Llandaff'
Dahlia 'Jersey Beauty'
Dahlia 'Tommy Keith'
Dahlia 'Union Jack'
Dahlia 'White Aster'

herbaceous mix (see list)

annuals
Aster 'Asteroid Mix'
Lobelia 'Crystal Palace'
Pansy 'Happy Faces'
Senecio cineraria

existing pear treee

herbaceous mix (see list)
herb bed (see list)

Herbaceous Mix

Alcea rosea (Hollyhock)
Alchemilla mollis (Lady's mantle)
Anemone x hybrida (Japanese anemone)
Anthemis tinctoria (Golden marguerite)
Bellis perennis (Daisy)
Campanula lactifolia (Giant bellflower)
Centranthus ruber (Red valerian)
Coreopsis verticillata (Tickseed)
Delphinium cardinale (Scarlet larkspur)
Dianthus deltoides (Maiden pink)
Dicentra spectabilis (Bleeding heart)
Digitalis purpurea (Foxglove)
Geum coccinea (Avens)
Gypsophila paniculata (Chalk plant)
Hemerocallis flava (Daylily)
Knautia macedonica (Scabious)
Liatris spicata (Gay feather)
Linum perenne (Blue flax)
Lupinus spp. (Lupin)
Potentilla 'Gibson's Scarlet' (Cinquefoil)
Rudbeckia fulgida (Coneflower)
Salvia argentea (Silver sage)
Silene compacta (Campion)
Verbena bonariensis (Vervain)
Viola odorata (Sweet violet)

herbaceous mix (see list)

rustic seat

herbaceous mix (see list)

rose hedge, random mix of:
Rosa 'Alba Semi-plena'
Rosa 'Empereur du Maroc'
Rosa 'William Lobb'
Rosa rugosa 'Typica'

compost bins

rose arch

LOST GARDENS

Restoration

In many ways, James Thacker's lost Victorian pleasure garden was one of the easier sites to restore, both on paper and in practice. We had a reasonably detailed map, good background information on the creator and a site that had gently decayed over time without suffering active destruction. But the controversy over the motif flower beds in the top lawns illustrates the difficulty of restoring a site without a detailed planting plan and plant list. Some garden historians argue against restoration at all unless detailed plans can be found.

Without doubt, the hardest part of the whole operation was the restoration of the listed summer house. In this we were able to draw on the dedication and skills of building conservator John Ward and his team, advised by historic-building consultant John Goom. Their aim was to match the quality of the original in materials and workmanship. They also left telltale clues about their work for any future repairers.

After all the debris had been cleared, the first task was to repair the floor. This involved fitting new joists on a like-for-like basis to replace the old ones that had all decayed and

New tiles for the listed summer house match the old in colour and texture.

rotted at the ends. As the original floor had obviously been laid as the building went up, the problem now was to fit the new floor without damaging the finished brickwork. John's solution was to enlarge the joist pockets to the rear of the building so that his team could slide in the joist for the full depth before returning it to the original position. Fitting the joists around the hearth was especially tricky. The joints used for the new joists (known as tusk tenon joints) matched the original construction, as did the replacement softwood timber used. The only new precaution was to pressure-treat all timbers first. Because wood is now supplied in metric rather than imperial measurements, John and his team had to saw and plane all the new floorboards to match the size of the originals.

Next came the roof, which was open to the skies and so needed a complete overhaul. John estimated there were just

enough undamaged old tiles to cover one side of the restored building. He located a source of new clay tiles (some 1,000 altogether) in the correct buff colour, but they had pegs instead of the original nibs. Rather than mix old and new tiles together, John's solution was to use them on separate sides of the roof. (With more time, he reckons he would have been able to find a precise match for the originals.) Holding the tiles in place was lime mortar. This would traditionally have been strengthened with hair from English cattle, but as these are now all short-haired, the conservators used imported yak hair instead.

Remaining tasks on the summer house included fitting new door and window frames, and glazing and repairing the curlicued bargeboards which give the building its Gothic air. All this work meant that John Ward and his team were not able to tackle the building's interior. This was a pity as the original structure was as fine inside as out.

Although the garden of our plot was not as brambly or overgrown as some of the others on the Hill Close site, its meadow grass was none the less riddled with perennial weeds. The ideal solution (except in fully organic gardens) would be to treat the weeds with a translocated weedkiller that is absorbed by the leaves and then moves down into the roots – glyphosate is the chemical usually used. Best applied in summer when weeds are in active growth, it does not persist in the soil so you can replant as soon as the weeds have died. But this would have taken more time than we had available as at least two to three weeks are needed between application and replanting, and more than one application is usually necessary for really persistent weeds. In the end, we were forced to rely on energetic hand-weeding, much as James Thacker himself might have done, so the weeds may return to haunt us. We also aped the Victorian fascination with fertility and added huge amounts of horse manure, especially to the asparagus beds.

Gardening catalogues from the 1870s and 1880s guided our planting lists.

Our criterion for sourcing the plants was that all varieties must have been available before 1880, the date of our restoration. For annuals, bedding plants, herbaceous perennials and vegetables, we sent our proposed list to Suttons Seeds, having used their 1880 catalogue to help compile the list. They could supply only four varieties as plants: cineraria, aster, pansies and lobelia. As they explained, varieties have changed considerably since 1880 and most modern bedding plants are now bred to be drought- and pest-resistant for the patio. Remarkably, though, they were able to offer seeds for forty-five of the pre-1880 plants on our list.

Finding materials and finishing touches, such as glass frames and chimney pots, is relatively easy for Victorian gardens. Most towns have reclamation yards that recycle garden ornaments and materials such as paving slabs and edging tiles. For the programme, we were also able to borrow some of the ingenious gadgets and tools the Victorians loved so much. The rustic tripods were made specially for us to a traditional design.

A Victorian paradise reborn

Just two months later, we returned to find a garden James Thacker would surely have recognized. The open gate under a rose-covered arch beckoned invitingly. With its fanciful bargeboards painted a delicate green, his summer house gathered the garden around it like a flowery skirt. While much of the planting needed at least another summer to fill out properly, it had already burst into colour, with fine heads of hollyhocks, delphiniums, artichokes, scabious and bright cut-outs of summer bedding. The vegetables were fattening well, too, and the herbs lent their Mediterranean scents to the summer air.

Thacker would doubtless have employed a jobbing gardener for many of the routine tasks, but he would still have enjoyed rolling up his sleeves and getting his hands dirty with good, honest toil. The vegetable garden must have given him special pleasure, as must harvesting the fruit that Mrs Thacker may well have bottled just as her successor, Mrs Durrant, did in the 1940s.

Together with the other gardens in the close that local residents are slowly transforming back to treasured gardens, James Thacker's reminds us that towns and cities throughout Britain once bloomed like this. Men, women and children from all classes came here in their free time to escape the drudgery of work and enjoy the benefits of fresh air in a living, growing environment. We can imagine James Thacker and his wife sitting on their summer-house steps at the end of a summer's day, admiring their garden and taking in the view down to Warwick racecourse.

'Contact with the brown earth cures all diseases, mitigates all troubles and anxieties, smoothes the wrinkles that city cares have engraved on the face; and restores, even in the later days of a man's life, some touches of the joy that made gold and honey and music.' So wrote Shirley Hibberd about the joys of vegetable gardening. Gardens were rarely as cherished as these.

chapter two

a tudor courtier's delight

SHELLEY HALL in Suffolk is a magical place. Abandoning the main roads thundering on towards Ipswich and the North Sea ports, you enter the twisting lanes of Constable country. At the hamlet of Shelley, the driveway passes the church then crosses a stretch of open parkland before sweeping round some magnificent old yews close to the main house. The hall's brickwork and chimneys are clearly Tudor, but this is a building of jumbled shapes and corners that has grown (and shrunk) organically.

The garden we had come to investigate lay in front of the hall, facing east – a square grassy platform, about the size of four tennis courts, completely surrounded by a reedy moat and reached by a narrow brick bridge. Garden and bridge were off centre, aligned to a door at the hall's northern end, suggesting that a whole wing had disappeared. Along the northern edge of the moat was a line of straggling yews, planted close together for a hedge, but since allowed to grow into huge misshapen trees. Close by was a tall poplar, leaning dangerously, and a handful of recently planted trees and shrubs. Otherwise, apart from emerging spring bulbs, the moated platform was windswept and bare.

We knew the moat had once enclosed a garden because of one very significant piece of information: a written survey of 1519 (revised in 1533) that described the garden with its fish ponds and stews (where fish were kept alive for the table) and a dovecote to the south of the ponds. Although it contained no actual plan, the survey was quite emphatic about the garden's existence: 'The site of the manor of Shelley as it is built, set and lyeth in Shelley within the park of Shelley, that is to say in the east part of the same park with a garden on the east side of the same site of the manor which garden is built with stywes and ponds. And also it is moated on every side, And a dove house is built on the south side of the said stywes and ponds.'

The survey also gave us the identity of Shelley's owner and possible builder of house and garden: royal courtier Sir Philip Tilney, who died in 1533. The survey appeared in a manuscript book compiled mid-century for Sir Philip's son Thomas, showing the extent of his Shelley lands.

Strangely, however, later maps gave no hint that the moated platform continued in use as a garden. While they confirm the moat itself survived, the platform is always shown as empty and treeless – on the tithe map of 1838, for instance, and on later large-scale Ordnance Survey maps.

A Tudor courtier

We gleaned more information from documents relating to the Tilney family, who commissioned the 1519 survey. The Tilneys acquired the manor of Shelley in 1517. We know this from a document called the 'Feet of Fines of 1517', which registered the transfer of the manor of Shelley to the Tilneys through a group of trustees. The document does not say whether the manor came with a house but six years later, in 1523, Sir Philip Tilney is shown paying taxes at Shelley Hall and at nearby Framlingham Castle where he was steward of the manor. The size of his tax bill at Shelley – over £200 – made him a considerable landowner and confirmed that a house must have been built by then.

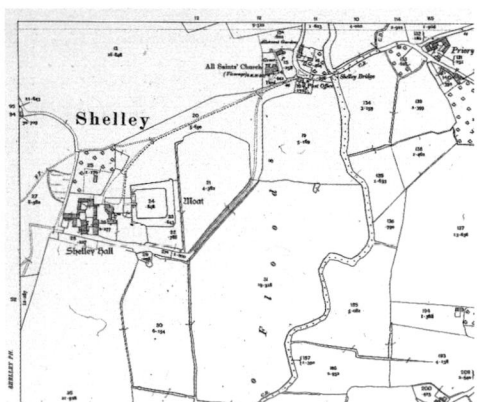

(above) Ordnance Survey maps show the moated garden lying empty to the east of the house.

(main) The Tilney family arms featured a mythical griffin with a lion's body and eagle's head and wings.

Sir Philip Tilney was a minor courtier of the first Tudor king, Henry VII, and then of the much more flamboyant Henry VIII, who came to the throne in 1509. Tilney's family connections were good: his sister Agnes married the second Duke of Norfolk and a Tilney cousin was grandmother to Anne Boleyn. Among his royal appointments, Sir Philip was Knight of the Sword at the marriage of Henry VII's son, Prince Arthur, to Catherine of Aragon in 1501 (she would later become Henry VIII's first wife, after Arthur's death). As treasurer of the English king's Scottish expedition of 1513, Tilney was present at the Battle of Flodden, at which the Scottish king James IV and most of his nobles were killed.

Tilney may well have built the hall and its garden in honour of his young third wife, Elizabeth Jeffery, who gave him three daughters in addition to the three sons surviving from his first two marriages. (One of their daughters went on to marry the Archbishop of Canterbury's half-brother; another attended Lady Jane Grey at her execution.)

He must have loved and honoured her because, when he died in 1533, he bequeathed her in his will his Shelley mansion, 'with all the gardeynes, orchardes, pondes and all other comodyties thereto belonging. Also the parke with all

Tudor gardens included plants for cooking, distilling, strewing, curing ills, and delight.

An Elizabethan tragedy

Two more Tilneys feature in our story. In 1561, Sir Philip's great-grandson (also called Philip) entertained his kinswoman Elizabeth I at Shelley Hall at a cost of £128 3s 3½d. This included some £30 for stabling, a similar amount for the kitchen, £19 for the buttery and £10 for presents – these were often 'gifts' of the queen's property for which she none the less expected payment (at nearby Helmingham she left behind her lute, for instance.) Queen Elizabeth (daughter of Tilney relative Anne Boleyn) was in her late twenties. Enjoying a time of relative stability, she set out on progresses to make contact with her subjects and to escape the pestilence of the city. Suffolk was then the centre of the woollen trade and therefore of economic importance.

At the time of the queen's visit, Philip's wife Anne was nearly eight months pregnant with their only son, Charles. A quarter of a century later, the family's triumph turned to tragedy when Charles converted back to Catholicism and was arrested for his part in a conspiracy to kill the 'illegitimate' Protestant queen and replace her with the 'true' queen, Catholic Mary Queen of Scots.

Like most loyal subjects, the Catholic Tilneys would have adopted the Protestant faith following Henry VIII's Reformation. Although the country had veered back towards Catholicism during the short reign of Elizabeth's elder sister, Mary I, Elizabeth herself upheld the Protestant faith as the state religion.

Charles was accused of meeting and plotting with a group of friends in St Giles and Clerkenwell in London in a plot that became known as the Babington Conspiracy. He pleaded not guilty and asked to be tried 'by God and honest men'. At his trial, he defiantly proclaimed himself a Catholic, 'for which I thank God most heartily' and, after judgment, humbly asked the court to see that his friends paid off his London debts 'for discharge of my Conscience'. Three days before his twenty-fifth birthday, Charles Tilney was convicted of high treason and taken with his co-conspirators to St Giles in the Fields where he was hanged, drawn and quartered.

the profutts and pleasures of the deer and connyes [rabbits] fedings. Allwaye provided that she doo no waste nor spoyle of woodd nor decaye of howses.' In other words, Elizabeth could keep Shelley for life, as long as she looked after the estate and its properties.

According to Sir Philip's will, Elizabeth and his first-born son, Thomas, were to share out his plate (apart from a gilt cup bequeathed to second son, Philip) and she was given his gold chains and jewels. After Sir Philip's death, she married Francis Framlingham (who died in 1544) and then Lionel Tollemache of Helmingham Hall. When Elizabeth died, Shelley and its lands reverted to her stepson Thomas Tilney – the same Thomas whose revision of the original 1519 survey had first alerted us to Shelley's lost garden.

Could this tragedy mark the beginning of Shelley's decline? After Philip's death, Shelley passed to another branch of the family through an uncle. Shelley Hall itself was sold in 1627 and slips quietly out of sight. The moated garden may have simply reverted to pasture, hiding its Tudor past under the Suffolk loam.

Exploring below ground

To discover the secrets of Tilney's garden, we needed to look more closely at the ground itself. Archaeology has become a vital probe in discovering and restoring gardens that have slipped into decay. Field archaeology is usually tried first, walking the land (or inspecting it from the air) to see what its humps and bumps can reveal. We knew this couldn't help us find Shelley's lost garden because the moat had been dredged in the 1980s and alluvial silt spread like butter across the whole platform. The only answer was to look beneath the surface, first with the aid of a geophysical survey and then by excavation. This is usually a technique of last resort because digging can also destroy the evidence you uncover.

The different types of geophysical surveys share the same aim: to locate and plot buried objects in the same way that an X-ray reveals the bones beneath your skin. We chose to conduct a resistivity survey, which measures the soil's resistance to the flow of an electric current. Different soils respond in different ways. Areas like silted-up ponds (which we knew had once existed within the moat) conduct electricity better and so show up as areas of low resistance. Hard, dense features, such as paths and buried foundations, record a much higher resistance. When you take readings across a whole site and plot your findings on a map, these hard features begin to appear.

The results were better than any of us had hoped – almost too good, in fact, because we knew that our plan to recreate a garden here could not be allowed to disturb valuable archaeology. The survey revealed a formal layout of four paths radiating from a central square. These divided the garden into quarters aligned with the bridge and the entrance into the hall. We couldn't tell at this stage if the central square indicated more paths or the foundations of a solid structure. The pattern looked Tudor, apart from two additional lines that broke the symmetry. The survey had also picked up two distinct areas of low resistance (possibly ponds and stews or flower beds) and a further area of higher resistance that might indicate some sort of structure. Were we dealing with several layers of garden perhaps?

To explore further, we needed to excavate the site and enlisted the help of Edward Martin and a survey team from Suffolk County Council's archaeological service. Martin is

A young honeysuckle clambers up the central arbour.

the county's recognized expert on moats and author of a brief article on Shelley that had first drawn our attention to the 1519 survey. The archaeologists hand-dug five trenches about a metre (3 feet) wide and 4 metres (13 feet) long, each carefully positioned to examine possible features identified by the geophysical survey. At the same time, four auger holes were sunk to recover soil samples for pollen analysis.

Putting all the results together was tremendously exciting. The first trench immediately cleared up the mystery of the stray 'paths' disturbing the garden's Tudor symmetry. These were, in fact, Victorian field drains and could be discounted from our plans. Evidence from the second

trench in the area of low resistance was sadly inconclusive (these were our hoped-for ponds or flower beds), while the third trench tentatively identified a path running along the inside edge of the moat. The fourth and fifth trenches came up with archaeologist's gold, confirming the geophysical results about radiating paths and a central square.

Trench four excavated the path leading from the bridge to the centre. Underneath a top layer of moat dredgings, the archaeologists found the remains of a wide gravel and shingle path, 36 centimetres (14 inches) below the surface and aligned precisely with the bridge. The fifth and final trench at the centre promised to be even more exciting.

Here the archaeologists discovered chalk and tile fragments similar to those found in the path trench. Below this was a layer of crushed chalk, mortar and fine crushed brick – quite possibly a small structure and perhaps the remains of the dovecote mentioned in the survey of 1519.

Just as crucially for our restoration plans, neither archaeology nor pollen analysis uncovered any garden features or remains later than Tudor, so we could concentrate on recreating a garden from this period. Also, as the original Tudor garden was safely buried under at least 36 centimetres of silt, we were given the all-clear to recreate the garden, as long as we dug no deeper than 20 centimetres (8 inches) into the topsoil.

(above) Archaeology is about to uncover the Tudor garden buried beneath the surface.

(left) When fully grown, the nut tunnel will lead visitors through darkness into light.

Dowsing and divining

We had one more investigative technique to try: dowsing. This was carried out for us by Ted Fawcett, one-time chairman of the Garden History Society and founder of the Architectural Association's garden conservation course. Dowsing has its supporters and detractors. Although its scientific basis remains unproven, it can bring interesting results. Dowsers use forked hazel twigs or metal rods that twitch or twist when they pass over buried objects or underground water, apparently in response to magnetic forces. Experienced dowsers can sometimes read enormous detail into a site, as Ted did at Shelley without access to any of the other results.

Starting at the southern edge and walking methodically up and down the site, Ted marked his findings directly on the ground with canes and later interpreted these for us as a plan. Like the geophysical surveyors and the archaeologists, he found the central path from the bridge, with a structure at the centre which he interpreted as statue bases. On the eastern edge he found two large rectangular pools or beds, and to the west a series of twelve smaller oblong beds in a couple of rows. From the rhythmic twitching of his hazel rod, he concluded the garden had been surrounded on three sides by hedging and on the fourth by a wall. At the edge of the moat on the eastern side he found evidence of two more structures, which he interpreted as fishing pavilions.

The bridge to the moated garden survives from Tudor times.

(left) Through the nut tunnel, the garden takes shape.

(below) Author Jennifer Potter helps out with planting.

(bottom) Presenters Toby Musgrave and Twigs Way fill the raised beds.

From medieval to Tudor fashions

We had the bones of a garden and knew something of its creator. Next we needed to add the brush strokes of early Tudor fashions.

Officially, the Middle Ages ended in England with the battle of Bosworth Field in 1485, when the Lancastrian Henry Tudor defeated the Yorkist Richard III and so brought to an end the Wars of the Roses and thirty weary years of fighting. Henry Tudor had spent fourteen years in exile, first in Brittany (then a vassal state of the French king) and later travelling with the French court. He would have brought back to England his knowledge of French ways and fashions in French gardening, which were themselves influenced by the radical ideas of the Italian Renaissance. Fashions do not fit quite so neatly with history, however, and medieval garden features continued well into the time of the Tudors.

Of the many different types of medieval garden, the small enclosed 'herber' is the most familiar, often placed beneath the sleeping quarters of royalty and nobles. Tightly surrounded by walls, hedges, fencing or trellis, this garden was a place of quiet delight and courtly encounters. Its elements were simple and constant: fruit trees, turf seats, shady arbours around the edges, a flowery mead of turf scattered with wild flowers and sweet-smelling herbs, perhaps a fountain. Larger gardens often had a separate area of raised beds, invariably square or rectangular, planted with herbs and flowers, and maybe topiary shrubs and turf. Though most surviving early paintings and representations of gardens are European rather than British, it seems likely that simple herbers were the norm in medieval Britain as elsewhere, meeting the nobility's needs for a place apart from the rigours and sour smells of medieval life.

By the early 1520s, when royal courtier Sir Philip Tilney planted his garden in honour of his new wife, the confidence and humanism of the Renaissance was beginning to break down the walls of these enclosed, inward-looking spaces, but many of the old elements survived. As garden historian David Jacques explained in

A rose and a pea illuminate an early sixteenth-century pattern book.

a recent issue of *Garden History* devoted to Tudor gardens, royal and noble gardeners in early Tudor England increasingly borrowed their grammar from French and Italian models while retaining many of their old familiar words. So features such as raised beds, arbours and mazes survived within a new structure of individual compartments, each surrounded by trellis and sometimes low hedges. This division into compartments was the gardens' main novelty. Only later, as Tudor England burst into the great flowering of the Elizabethan age, did individual elements reflect the finery and conceits of court life.

One site that gave us a useful model was the royal garden at Richmond Palace in Surrey, remodelled by Henry VII and made ready for the wedding celebrations of Prince Arthur and Catherine of Aragon. As Knight of the Sword at the wedding, Sir Philip Tilney would have known the garden well. Dutch painter Antonius van den Wyngaerde sketched the garden some fifty years after it was laid out. You can still make out the medieval elements of rectangular beds and a maze, organized neatly into compartments.

A handful of Tudor portraits offer tantalizing glimpses of distant gardens, like the *c.*1545 painting of Henry VIII's family at Whitehall. Open doorways give a view of rectangular planted flower beds set

This moated garden with arbour and rectangular beds comes from Stubbes' *Anatomie of Abuses* (1583).

with heraldic beasts on painted poles – a feature we judged too royal for the garden of a mere courtier.

For help in our recreation, we also turned cautiously to books. As the first popular gardening books in English did not appear until the mid-sixteenth century, several decades after our garden was created, we looked for features that may have survived from the start of the century.

An early author is Londoner Thomas Hill (also known by his pseudonym Didymus Mountain), whose interests ranged across comets, sympathetic magic and the interpretation of dreams. Hill's gardening manuals began with *A Most Briefe and Pleasaunt Treatyse*, first published *c.*1558 and republished in 1568 as *The Proffitable Arte of Gardening*. Borrowing freely from Greek and Latin sources, Hill was a

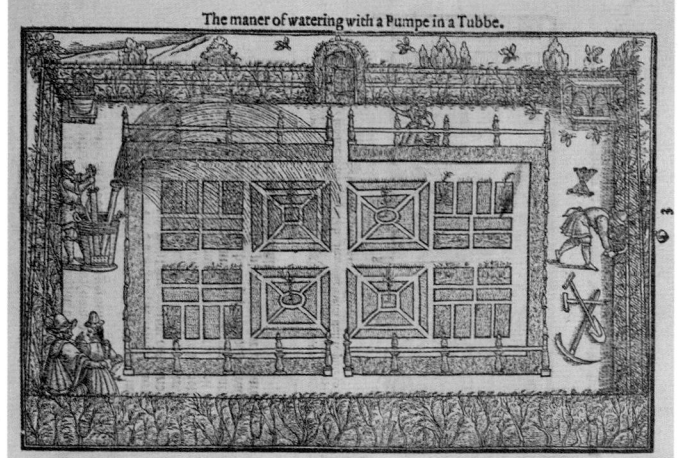

The maner of watering with a Pumpe in a Tubbe.

highly practical writer who liked to get his hands dirty. He peppered his text with good, solid advice – on hand-weeding, for instance, and ingenious tips for hedging – mixed in with his now quaintly outmoded magical beliefs. For example, he recommended sowing flatulent lentil seeds to save seed beds from wind damage, on the grounds that like repels like.

We borrowed from Hill's most famous work, *The Gardeners Labyrinth*, published posthumously in 1577. As this date is very much later than Sir Philip's garden, we avoided any obviously Elizabethan ideas and stuck instead to garden features that Sir Philip might have seen and enjoyed at court. In his garden at Shelley, we wanted to push the boundaries of garden design and show him responding to some of the new ideas.

One feature we took from Hill was a simple knot garden of raised beds cut into geometric shapes. The first English knot appeared like an open rose on the title page of *A Most Briefe and Pleasaunt Treatyse*. Placed at the heart of a small, mid-century manor house garden, it marked the advent of Renaissance symmetry borrowed from the grander gardens of France and Italy. A more complicated knot to be woven in either hyssop or thyme appeared in *The Proffitable Arte of Gardening* and several more examples in *The Gardeners Labyrinth* – all looking as if they have stepped right out of an embroiderer's pattern book.

Hill did not go into any detail about the construction and cultivation of these knots. This could suggest they were just coming into fashion and were therefore beyond his immediate experience. In any case, they would not have found their way into a Suffolk manor house garden as early as 1520. Gardens *were* changing, though, and it seems probable that the rectangular raised beds of the Middle Ages were beginning to reshape into more complex geometric patterns like the ones we introduced at Shelley.

A riot of Tudor colour

We know more about early Tudor plants than we do about design, partly because of the extraordinary survival of some very early plant lists and partly through the patient detective work of garden historians such as the late John Harvey. The best list for Shelley's garden is the 'Fromond list' compiled very soon after 1525. This is a fascinating alphabetical list of herbs 'necessary for a garden', compiled for Surrey landowner Thomas Fromond (who died in the early 1540s) and entered in a cookery book. It is followed by different classifications according to use, such as herbs for potage, for sauce and for distilling. Two of these groups relate specifically to pleasure gardens – 'herbes for savour and beaute' and plants 'for an Herber'. Among this last group are trees (almond, bay, peach, pine and plum), shrubs (gooseberry, gourds, white roses, vine) and herbaceous plants (campion, columbine, cornflower, hellebore, lilies, peonies, safflower).

Blue spires of hyssop enliven the maze.

The raised beds and arbour planting at Shelley include many old cottage garden plants that survive today, mixed in with herbs for cooking, medicine and strewing, plus some ornamental vegetables and wild flowers. From the Fromond list we took chives, columbine, borage, marigold, camomile, globe artichokes, pinks, sweet bay, lilies, basil, roses, rue, sage, thyme, valerian, viola, campion and quince. Fromond omits a number of border plants popular in Britain since at least the fourteenth century – plants such as the flag iris, lavender, strawberry, woodruff and water lilies for the pond. These we added by looking at other early lists, such as those of Master John Gardener (c.1350) and the botanist Friar Henry Daniel (c.1375).

Another fascinating source for Shelley's garden was an early sixteenth-century pattern book of trees, plants and shrubs in the Bodleian Library at Oxford. Clare Putnam has published a selection as the *Flowers and Trees of Tudor England*. The full manuscript contains ninety-four gloriously colourful paintings of trees, plants and flowers, as well as smaller pictures of houses, landscapes, birds and household objects. Plant names are given in English rather than Latin, and the painted flowers show the Tudor love of colour and decoration. This collection gave us hops, pinks, iris, lavender, roses, the Madonna lily (*Lilium candidum*) and hyssop.

Intriguingly, the Bodleian manuscript has a twin that belonged to Lord Tollemache of Helmingham Hall until the 1960s – the same family into which Sir Philip Tilney's widow later married. Could Elizabeth Tilney herself have used this 'book of beauty' to identify the herbs and flowers in her own garden at Shelley?

As for planting styles, early Tudor gardens marked the transition from formal planting in rows of the same species to more informal mixtures of herbs, flowers and vegetables. The Tudors liked to play a great number of colours against each other. Spacing between plants was wider than today, leaving much more soil visible. Thomas Hill is full of good advice about the planting of flowers, roots and herbs. 'Rose-trees are commonly planted in a plot by themselves,' he says in *The Gardeners Labyrinth*, '(if you have roome enough) leaving a pretty space betwixt them for gathering.'

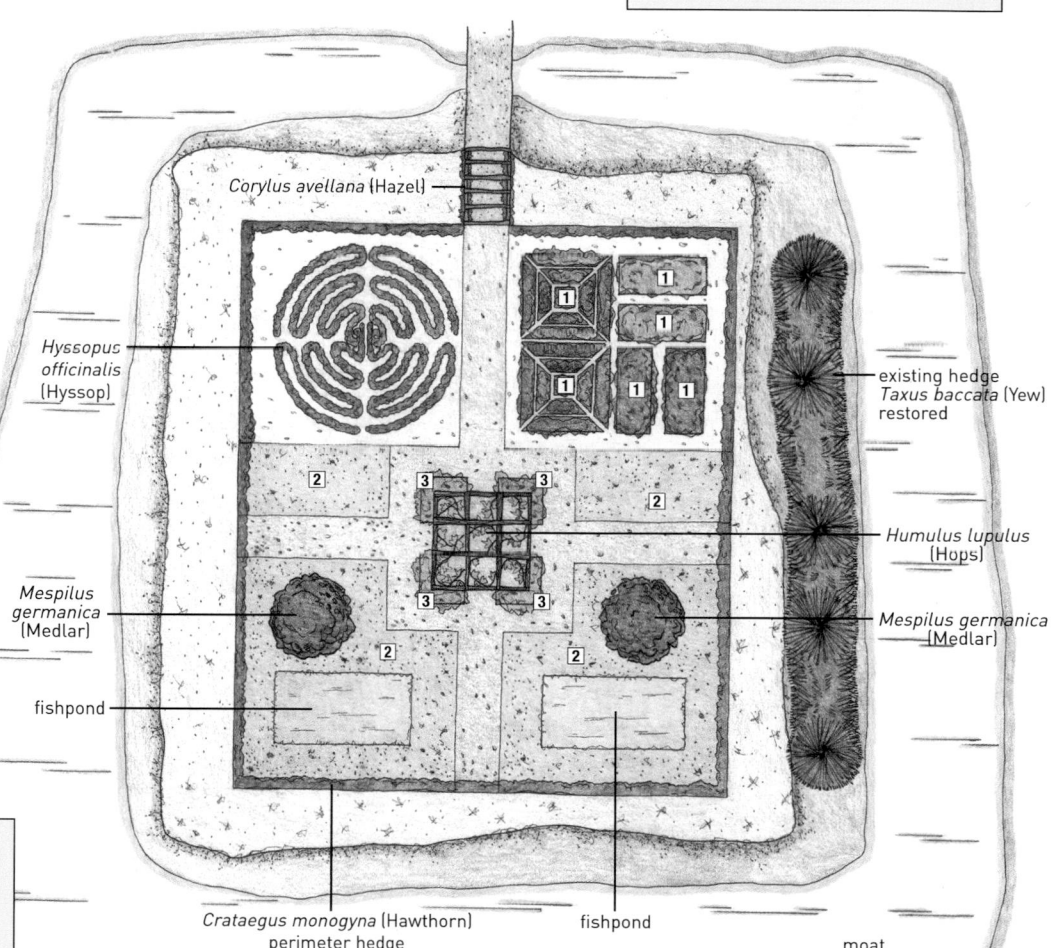

Corylus avellana (Hazel)

Hyssopus officinalis (Hyssop)

Mespilus germanica (Medlar)

fishpond

existing hedge
Taxus baccata (Yew)
restored

Humulus lupulus (Hops)

Mespilus germanica (Medlar)

Crataegus monogyna (Hawthorn)
perimeter hedge

fishpond

moat

Tudor husbandry

A mid- to late-Tudor author who gives a vivid flavour of gardening and agricultural practices of the time is Eton- and Cambridge-educated Essex man Thomas Tusser, who farmed for a time in Suffolk. His books (in excruciating doggerel) include *A Hundreth Good Pointes of Husbandrie* (1557 – with an extended edition of 1571 'lately maried with a hundrethe good points of Huswifry') and *Five Hundred Pointes of Good Husbandrie*, 1573.

Tusser describes in detail the tools used in husbandry, and provides a calendar of rural and domestic tasks. By January, for instance, the garden should be dug and manured and cleared of weeds and stone. March and April, by contrast, are the months when the housewife should be sowing the kitchen garden with produce for strewing and for the pot. The housewife would also be responsible for growing simple, medicinal herbs:

> Good huswives provide, ere an' sickness do come,
> Of sundry good things, in her house to have some:
> Good aqua composita, and vinegar tart,
> Rose-water, and treacle, to comfort the heart.
> Cold herbs in her garden, for agues that burn,
> That over strong heat, to good temper may turn,
> White endive and succory, with spinage enough,
> All such, with good pot herbs, should follow the plough.
> Get water of fumitory, liver to cool,
> And others the like, or else go like a fool.
> Conserves of barberry, quinces, and such,
> With sirops, that easeth the sickly so much.

The globe artichoke appeared in a plant list discovered in a Tudor cookery book of *c.*1525.

White clusters of yarrow (*Achillea millefolium*) lighten the planting.

A garden for a new wife

We were now ready to bring together all the evidence we had. Our plan was to recreate Sir Philip Tilney's garden of 1519 – the garden of a Suffolk gentleman and royal courtier, fit for his new wife. Wherever possible, we based the design on site and documentary evidence, filling in any gaps by looking at other gardens of the period. Technically this is re-creation rather than restoration, a task made even more difficult by the scarcity of visual or written evidence about English gardens of the time.

All three site investigations clearly established the bones of Sir Philip's original garden, which show the new Tudor division into compartments, separated by wide gravel paths. Marking the boundaries between the compartments we used low hyssop hedging rather than medieval trellis work.

Around the perimeter we planted a traditional hawthorn hedge (*Crataegus monogyna*) with espaliered cobnut (*Corylus avellana*) forming an entrance tunnel. 'The most commend-able inclosure for every Garden plot,' said Thomas Hill, 'is a quick-set hedge, made with brambles and white thorne.'

Deciding how to fill the individual quarters was more difficult. All we knew for certain was that the garden contained ponds and stews. At the centre was a structure of some sort, possibly the dovecote mentioned in the 1519 survey, although this could have stood just outside the moat.

The moat itself was a key feature defining the garden's character. Moats are still common in the Suffolk landscape as they are in neighbouring Essex. Appearing in England from about 1150, most were built between 1200 and 1325. These early moats generally enclosed houses and were viewed as status symbols, though some were defensive and most helped to improve drainage. Keeping fish was another function, and providing water for household tasks like washing. Moats as garden features usually came later and continued to be built into the mid-sixteenth century. They were both ornamental and practical, protecting tender plants and young trees from deer and grazing animals, and providing delightful walks and garden spaces.

Moats could also add drama to the landscape. One early approach route to Shelley, described in the 1519 survey as a 'goodley entre', passed through the new orchard, then dropped down below the moat. Here a causeway between two narrow stretches of water linked the hall with a church built by Sir Philip. As the tithe map of 1838 shows, the moat was connected to these other drainage channels, which would have kept the water fresh. We don't know how the sides of Shelley's moat were planted – most probably with willows and rushes along the banks. The Tilneys would almost certainly have bred fish in the moat – bream, perch, pike and roach were all on the late medieval menu, as well as swans and wildfowl.

Archaeology suggested that the central structure might well have been the dovecote of the 1519 survey. In early Tudor times, a dovecote was both ornamental and practical; the cooing of doves was a popular symbol of romantic and religious love. The birds were also eaten and their dung was valued as manure – the very best manure according to Thomas Hill, because of its 'mighty hotnesse'. But practical reasons and the lack of firm evidence ruled out a dovecote at Shelley. We opted instead for a simple rustic arbour as the garden's centrepiece. Here the Tilneys might have grown hops and vines and sat in the shade to enjoy their garden.

Hill provided down-to-earth advice on building an arbour. 'The herbar in the garden may be framed with Ashen poles, or the Willow,' he wrote in *The Gardeners Labyrinth*, 'either to stretch, or to be bound together with Oziers, or wyers, after a square form, or in arch manner winded, that

(right) Following Thomas Hill's advice, we provided a central arbour planted with hops.

(opposite) The hyssop maze is planted, then raked with gravel.

the branches of the Vine, Mellon, or Cucumber, running and spreading all over, might so shadow and keep both the heat and Sun from the walkers and sitters therunder.' For planting, he also recommended rosemary and fragrant climbers such as jasmine and red roses, 'that the owners friends sitting in the same, may the freelier see and behold the beauty of the Garden, to their great delight'.

At least we knew there had definitely been ponds and stews in the garden. Like the dovecote, these were both ornamental and practical. When guests were expected, live fish would be brought from the moat or nearby river to the stew pond, which acted as a larder, keeping them fresh for the table. As ornamental features, the ponds were also delightfully cooling and showed how landscapes were designed for pleasure even then.

But the ponds had already been backfilled by the time of later maps so we couldn't be certain of their precise location. Both the geophysical survey and dowsing agreed on one possible site, in the north-eastern quarter, but they offered conflicting sites for a second. In the end, we followed the dowser's report and created rectangular fish ponds in each of the two eastern quarters. These we raised slightly to avoid disturbing any buried Tudor remains.

The ponds were set in turf scattered with herbs and wild flowers like a medieval flowery mead. Of all the elements in Shelley's garden, the flowery mead is the most obviously old-fashioned. Like turfed seats, it was fast disappearing from the courtly garden, but we felt it suited the ageing Sir Philip as he courted his young wife. All the herbs and flowers used were known in Tudor times: ox-eye daisies and bird's-foot trefoil, ragged robin and salad burnet, campion, vetch and yarrow.

In the south-western quadrant, we planted a maze like the one shown in van den Wyngaerde's sketch of Richmond Palace. Inspired by Christian symbolism, a maze in medieval Britain traced the pilgrim's tortuous route through life towards salvation at its heart. Mazes appeared in the stone floors of the great medieval cathedrals and as flat turf mazes outdoors: you can still see a late survival on the common at Saffron Walden in Essex. The Tudors began to plant low-growing herb mazes as garden features. Thomas Hill included two examples in *A Most Briefe and Pleasaunt Treatyse*, one based on a circle and the other on a square.

For planting a maze, Hill recommended, 'Isope and Tyme, or winter Savery and tyme. For these do well endure, all the winter through grene. And there be some, whiche set their Mazes with Lavender Cotton, Spike [spike lavender], Maierome, and such lyke.' We chose hyssop, introduced to Britain from the Mediterranean and valued for medicine, cooking and strewing 'to beautifie and refresh the house'.

The final quarter was filled with raised beds, which were the staple of productive and ornamental gardens right through medieval times and well into sixteenth-century Tudor England. They appear in woodcuts of monastic herb and kitchen gardens, and in early town maps, such as the famous 'Agas' map of London of the mid-sixteenth century. The beds were entirely practical, keeping the growing area separate from surrounding paths, aiding drainage, soil fertilization and weeding, and bringing all plants within reach of medieval watering cans, or primitive sprinkler systems like those Thomas Hill included in *The Gardeners Labyrinth*.

We took our design for the simple knot garden from an illustration in *The Gardeners Labyrinth* that included both rectangular and more 'modern' beds in the same garden. We also copied the wooden sides to the raised beds from Hill, who recommended that beds should be 2 feet high or just a foot in very dry gardens.

Recreating the Tudor garden

Even before we got to work properly, at Shelley, as elsewhere, we had to check the site for wildlife. The legislation is quite specific: you are not allowed to disturb bats or nesting birds, for instance, and some species of wildlife enjoy special protection. At Shelley, our main concern was great crested newts: their discovery in the moat would have brought work to an immediate halt while we applied for a special licence or brought in a contractor licensed to deal with them. No newts were found so work could go ahead as planned after we had sent in a mole charmer to save any moles (and our future garden) from disturbance.

Recreating the early Tudor garden at Shelley was, in many respects, physically easier than restoring many other gardens in the series because we started with a virtually clean site. Clearance involved little more than felling the dangerously leaning poplar, removing recent tree and shrub plantings and uprooting the many spring bulbs for planting elsewhere. We also removed the turf, as much of the garden would be overlaid with gravel.

We cut back the line of ragged yews into a 3 metre (10 foot) windbreak. Although the yew was known in Britain in 1520, these would not have been part of Sir Philip's original garden. But in our view, this didn't justify their removal. Instead, we preferred to help them regenerate and so continue to protect the site for future generations.

Getting access to the site presented some problems as the original Tudor brick bridge was not sturdy enough to support the weight of modern machinery. Our solution was to bring in a temporary bridge and route site traffic over a metal trackway. The archaeologists'

(opposite) Thomas Hill's geometric raised beds come back to life.

(below) The ragged yews will soon be cut back, and the poplar felled.

insistence that we dig no deeper than 20 centimetres into the alluvial topsoil naturally affected the way we approached many tasks, but we were pleased that our recreated garden would help to preserve the buried remains of the original Tudor garden.

Once the site was clear, we were able to proceed with work on the separate garden compartments and the central paths that divided the garden into quadrants with a square at the centre. Where gravel was to be used as the main surface material (on paths and in the maze area), we first laid a porous landscape fabric to help suppress weeds. The two ponds were raised slightly (in line with the archaeologists' restrictions) and lined with PVC instead of the more traditional puddled clay. To construct the hyssop maze, the landscapers first marked the simple design on landscape fabric stretched flat over the whole area, then planted out small pots of hyssop at 30 centimetre (12 inch) intervals. Finally, a layer of gravel was raked over the surface, leaving just a hint of green where the plants would bush up over the summer.

Although we built the central arbour ourselves, we brought in a traditional craftsman to construct the nut tunnel for the entrance. The techniques used have survived from Tudor times: selecting forked and arched timbers from a wild hazel coppice and lashing them together with willow. Along the sides of the tunnel we planted espaliered cobnut.

(above) By the first summer, the hyssop maze has pushed through the gravel.

(opposite top) Great flower heads of globe artichoke provide a fine display as summer ends.

(opposite bottom) Willow binds the hazel uprights of the nut tunnel.

When grown, this will give visitors the medieval experience of stepping through darkness into a bright, secret garden, shut away from the world. Altogether, nearly 750 hawthorns were planted to form a perimeter hedge on all four sides.

For the landscape team, one of the most awkward assignments was constructing the geometric raised beds to the design in Thomas Hill's *The Gardeners Labyrinth*. The boxes were some 30 centimetres (12 inches) in height and we filled them with a rich mix of soil, compost and organic horse manure. Although Tudor planting was becoming more informal, our finished beds were probably planted more closely than the beds you see in Tudor wood-cuts and illustrations. We continued to plant and water as darkness fell on the final day.

A Tudor love story

Now that Shelley's recreated Tudor garden has taken root, it is possible to imagine a world-weary Sir Philip Tilney, in the last decade of his life, enjoying the garden with his new bride.

The first signs of spring come with the catkins of the nut tunnel, followed by heart-sease and strawberries, the delicate pasque flower, columbines and iris. By late spring, quince and hawthorn have burst into flower, as have many of the wild flowers in the flowery mead. But the garden's true glory comes with the full bloom of summer. Pinks, sparkling blue borage and bright yellow flower heads of cotton lavender compete with the pure white heads of sweetly scented Madonna lilies. Hops and roses crowd around the arbour: the crimson Apothecary's rose mixes with the white petals of *Rosa alba* and the pale pinky red stripes of 'Rosa Mundi'. Then, from midsummer into autumn, the hyssop maze sends up its slender spikes of dark blue flowers, as the great purple flower heads of the globe artichoke (a novelty when the garden was first made) dominate the raised beds.

Ten years before Sir Philip created the original garden, Stephen Hawes wrote his great love poem *The Passetyme of Pleasure, or the history of graunde amoure and la bell Pucel*. In it he describes the pleasure of a garden much like Shelley's:

> Than in we went, to the garden gloryous
> Lyke to a place, of pleasure most solacious
> With flora paynted, and wrought curyously
> In divers knottes, of marveylous greatnes …
>
> Amiddes the garden, so muche delectable
> There was an harber, fayre and quadrant
> To Paradyse, right well comparable
> Sette all about, with floures flagrant …

Here, indeed, was paradise.

chapter three

a taste of edwardian japan

eNTERING ANY OF OUR SITES for the first time is always a special moment, evoking childhood memories of stepping into a lost domain. Here at Gatton Park in Surrey, the experience was doubly strange because the patch of woodland we had come to investigate looked so *ordinary*.

This grand estate, which has a history stretching back to before the Domesday survey, is now owned by the Royal Alexandra and Albert School, a state boarding school. The school's main hall, with its massive Corinthian portico, sits on a ridge with glorious views (if you ignore the tarmacked tennis courts) down across rolling green fields towards a Capability Brown lake edged with woodland. It is a view that seems timeless and very English.

Our lost garden lay to the west of the main hall, where the path dropped down past a reedy lake into a swampy hollow choked with weed trees. The water looked silted and stagnant, full of branches and debris and packed around with bog-loving sedges. Light penetrated this forgotten corner of the estate only in winter when invading sycamore, ash and alder trees shed their leaves on to the rotting woodland floor.

But if you kept your senses alert, you might begin to pick up clues that here was no ordinary woodland. The planting gave the first hint of an oriental theme, with scattered clumps of bamboo, a dead cherry tree, even a ginkgo half strangled by choking ivy. Remnants of paths circled the bog, buried under years of leaf mould. Rummaging among the rhododendrons on the far side of the swamp, you might have noticed a flattened plateau pocked with holes. And there, poking out of the mud, was a stone plinth – clearly a base of some kind, perhaps a statue or a lantern.

When we first arrived at the site, we were privileged to have with us an exhaustive report on the whole estate, prepared for the school by landscape architect Sarah Couch. This gave us many leads that proved invaluable for our research, as did the mountain of evidence collected by the school itself. But we were concentrating on just one small corner of the estate and so, inevitably, there were gaps we needed to fill and facts to cross-check before we could properly return this patch of Surrey woodland to its lush Edwardian design.

(opposite) Clumps of *Iris sibirica* once again crowd the pond.

(below) Boggy woodland hides the clues to an oriental past.

Layers of history

Gatton Park's history is long and there are traces of settlement here dating from Roman and even Iron Age times. By the thirteenth century at least, the manor of Gatton had a house of some importance and, at its peak, the estate swelled to over 2,000 acres.

Closer to our own times, Gatton's evolving landscape can be plotted in maps that reflect the great changes in garden styles and tastes. John Rocque's Surrey survey, published *c*.1762, records formal gardens close to the house and a stretch of water shaped like a boathook. This was soon to be swept away by Lancelot 'Capability' Brown – then England's foremost landscape gardener – who created a leg-of-mutton lake fed by two smaller ponds and a serpentine stream. His work of the 1760s is shown in a beautifully hand-coloured survey of *c*.1790.

The first 25-inch Ordnance Survey map of 1877 shows the water much as Brown left it, with two ponds and a stream (now officially called the 'Serpentine') feeding into the larger lake. Our own site – between the fish pond and the Serpentine – is indistinguishable from the rest of the woodland bordering both sides of the stream. A virtually identical map was redrawn for the sale catalogue of 1888, when the whole estate was put up for sale by the heirs of the seventh Lord Monson. Gatton Park was then bought by the key figure in our story, Jeremiah Colman (later created a baronet, Sir Jeremiah Colman Bart), whose uncle had founded the world-famous family mustard firm, J. & J. Colman.

Colman's impact on the Gatton landscape, and our own site in particular, can immediately be seen by comparing the 25-inch Ordnance Survey map for 1913 (revised in 1911) with the earlier edition. Under Colman, the baldly named 'Fish Pond' became 'Engine Pond'. A clearly marked waterfall connected the pond with the head of the Serpentine,

where the stream had been reshaped into a wiggling double-appendix crossed in two places by paths, at least one of which was marked as a footbridge. The paths wandered around the west of the stream, then snaked past Engine Pond to join the ornamental grounds up towards the house. Other small garden features dotted about the grounds included an enclosed rectangular pool north of Engine Pond and another pond surrounded by paths in the old Cedar Walk to the east of the house.

So what sort of garden did Jeremiah Colman create at the head of the Serpentine? Remnants of oriental planting and the reshaping of the stream all pointed to a Japanese theme. This would fit the date: sometime between Colman's purchase in 1888 and 1911, when the garden was surveyed for the Ordnance Survey map of 1913. Throughout this time, Japanese gardens were all the rage, even if most aped the trimmings rather the spirit of the true Japan.

Excitingly, we were able to pinpoint the date even more precisely with the help of Japanese garden expert Jill Raggett. Hunting through old copies of the *Surrey Mirror and County Post* she came across a long article in the 20 May 1910 edition recording the annual visit to Gatton of a local gardeners' society, the Redhill, Reigate and District Gardeners' Mutual Improvement Association. After all the speeches and tea, the gardeners were led round the grounds. And there we had it: they showed special interest in 'the Japanese garden', created in the winter of 1909 to 1910 by as many as thirty unemployed labourers. Arranged 'on true Oriental lines', the garden would prove a 'most artistic addition' to Gatton's many beauties. This was surely our boggy woodland, where surviving bamboos and the strangled ginkgo hinted at its oriental past.

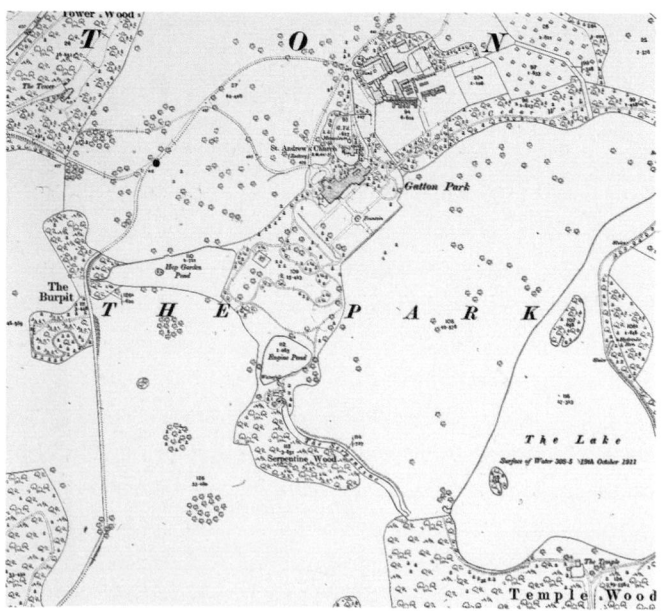

The woodland's full beauty was revealed in two contemporary gardening articles that were to prove invaluable for the restoration that followed. On 6 November 1913, the *Journal of Horticulture and Home Farmer* published a three-page article on Sir Jeremiah Colman's many improvements at Gatton Park. The author, Gerald Butcher, described the steep undulating lawns to the west of the mansion, adorned with an Indian temple, a fine old cedar of Lebanon and an old English garden (once a rose garden) with a rectangular lily tank planted around with thyme and surrounded by a neatly clipped yew hedge. Butcher then went on to describe the charms of the Japanese garden:

> A few more steps, and we come upon the Japanese garden, where a rustic
> bridge spans a ravine, and here and there wooden Japanese lanterns are seen.
> By the water's edge Forget-me-nots, Water Buttercups, Primroses, and all
> kinds of bog plants, bamboos, and sedges grow, while aquatics in variety
> thrive in the pools. The water is supplied from a lake near by, tumbling over
> jagged rocks into the deep pools, whence it winds its way to other falls and
> pools, between Maples, Oaks, Chestnuts, Willows, Cherries, and Yews.
> This Japanese garden is one of the most charming spots to be found at
> Gatton. It was made a year or two ago by unemployed labour recruited
> from the surrounding district.

If Butcher was seduced by the spirit of Colman's Japan, the *Gardeners' Chronicle* of 11 September 1915 was much harder to please, slyly referring to it as a *water* garden, 'since one oriental lantern does not make a Japanese garden'. All the same, the author wrote approvingly of its many charming effects. 'It was devised four or five years ago,' he explained, 'with the view of masking the sluggish effect of the stream which connects the lower fish pond with the great lake. It is evident that the work has quickly matured. This is due partly to the shelter given by the wood from the prevailing wind, and also to the rich alluvial soil which had accumulated on the site.' The author also commended the careful supervision of detail, 'for a water garden needs constant attention if it is to retain its intended attraction'.

Best of all for our purposes, the *Gardeners' Chronicle* included two photographs of the garden. The first showed a stone Japanese lantern in the foreground placed near the still waters of the stream. The planting mixed oriental bamboos with typical reedy marginals. In the middle distance, a rustic thatched hut with open sides stood on a low, planted mound, with a view of parkland grass and tree clumps beyond. The second (full-page) photograph showed another stone lantern angled over the water, its top quite obviously installed upside down. Water lilies floated gently across the surface and the planting was again aquatic rather than specifically Japanese.

(above) Photographs in *Gardeners' Chronicle* of 1915 provided vital evidence.

(opposite left) The meandering stream first appeared on the Ordnance Survey map of 1913.

(opposite right) Black stems of *Phyllostachys nigra* add drama to the perimeter planting.

A mustard baronet

Now that we knew a little bit about our site, it was time to gather more information about the owners of Gatton Park, especially the garden's creator, Sir Jeremiah Colman Bart.

Landscaped by Capability Brown in the 1760s, the whole estate had been bought in 1830 by the fifth Lord Monson, supposedly for the votes of the two MPs this tiny parish returned to Westminster. Gatton was then among the most rotten of rotten boroughs – a privilege that ended soon afterwards with the passing of the first Reform Act of 1832. Lord Monson started to construct a fabled marble hall, but died before it was finished. The house and grounds suffered some neglect in the decades that followed.

Colman was just twenty-nine when he acquired the Lower Gatton estate in 1888. After Cambridge, he had worked for the family business, soon becoming a partner and later chairman. He had many other business interests as well (he was chairman of the Commercial Union Assurance Co. Limited, for instance), held public offices such as High Sheriff of Surrey and was one of HM Lieutenants of the City of London. Philanthropy was another side to his character that reflected his liberal and nonconformist background. In 1885 he married Mary, third daughter of Mr J. Short McMaster.

Jeremiah Colman had one obvious disadvantage in high society: he made his money from trade at a time when land, not commerce, was the mark of a gentleman. Gatton Park gave him the country seat a gentleman needed to shine in the world, and he soon set about improving the hall and its 550 acres of gardens, pleasure grounds and park. For this he turned to landscape gardener Henry Ernest Milner. Although virtually forgotten today, Milner was then one of the country's foremost landscape practitioners. As chairman of the International Horticultural Exhibition of 1892, his flair for showmanship reached dizzy heights when he hired Buffalo Bill

(left) The aquatic grass, *Glyceria maxima* 'Variegata' shows off its attractively striped leaves.

(opposite) Sir Jeremiah and Lady Colman in later years.

and his Wild West Show to create a bridge between sharpshooting and serious horticulture.

At Gatton, Milner opened up views and repaired Capability Brown's fast-maturing landscape. It must have looked very similar to the gently tamed and undulating views that Milner included in his disappointingly dull book of 1890, *The Art and Practice of Landscape Gardening*. In true Edwardian fashion, Colman then began to plan a series of small 'theme' gardens on the parkland fringes to flaunt his tastes and his gardeners' skills. As well as the Japanese garden, these included an 'Old World' rose garden, an Italian garden, and a rock and water garden created by the firm of James Pulham & Son. Advising him on at least some of these garden compartments was Milner's son-in-law and professional heir, Edward White.

Colman's real passion was orchids, which he bred and showed at the Royal Horticultural Society, Vincent Square. Wherever he went in the world, his head gardener sent him a fresh orchid for his buttonhole. His collection (described with great admiration in the *Gardeners' Chronicle* for 11 July 1896) extended to cool-house and stove-house orchids. He registered more than 300 hybrids, many with 'Gatton' in their name, and for more than forty years worked on a book that he eventually had privately printed entitled *Hybridization of Orchids: The Experiences of an Amateur*. His passion for horticulture was rewarded with the Victoria Medal for Horticulture.

Gatton remained Colman's home until his death. He took an active part in local affairs and organized splendid celebrations for special events like the coming-of-age of his only son (another Jeremiah) and wedding anniversaries. When appointed High Sheriff of Surrey in 1893, he opened the park for a village fête. The day's programme included a cricket match (another of Colman's passions), an interlude of juggling clowns and mind-reading dogs, and a grand fireworks display to celebrate the marriage of HRH The Duke of York and HSH Princess Victoria Mary of Teck. The evening ended with a goodnight message in fireworks from the high sheriff.

Aided by his wife, Colman enjoyed a reputation as a philanthropist and benefactor to many good causes. The couple took pains to include estate workers and their families in their celebrations, along with the district's children and the 'aged poor'.

But there was a harsher side to living and working on a great estate that we heard about from former employees and their descendants. Homes went with the job and families had to leave when employment ended – even when the workers went off to war. The church organist was sacked when he developed pernicious anaemia and received just one month's salary after twenty-five years' service.

By the end of his life, Colman was becoming disillusioned with the creeping urbanization that sucked the parish into nearby Reigate. In 1934, a disastrous fire destroyed much of the hall and its art collection and although rebuilding began immediately, the hall was planned for eventual use as an institution. The great country house had run out of steam. Sir Jeremiah died on 16 January 1942 and part of the estate was put up for sale. After the war, the Royal Alexandra and Albert School bought the hall and some 250 acres. For several decades, the landscape fabric slowly drifted into decay but now the school has ambitious plans for its renewal.

Japan mania

Before we looked more closely at the design of Sir Jeremiah Colman's Japanese garden, we wanted to put it in context. Why would an Edwardian landowner want to create a corner of Japan in a Surrey woodland? And how did our garden fit with others of the time?

The craze for anything Japanese had accelerated throughout the second part of the nineteenth century, ever since Commodore Perry's gunboat diplomacy in 1853 had forced Japan to open its doors to the West for the first time in two centuries. The excitement was like opening a treasure trove as Japanese art, artefacts, ideas and tastes first trickled and then flooded into the West.

International exhibitions across Europe stoked the fervour for all things Japanese. London's International Exhibition of 1862 featured a Japanese Court crammed with lanterns, pagodas, ornaments, textiles and household wares to satisfy the interest of the public. Other exhibitions followed in Paris (1867), and then Vienna (1873), after which the miniature Japanese village was later whisked to the grounds of London's Alexandra Palace. The interest was not restricted to Europe – a Japanese village, complete with inhabitants in national dress, toured the United States in the 1890s, showing off the art industries of Japan.

In 1910, six months after Sir Jeremiah built his Japanese garden at Gatton, Shepherd's Bush in London saw the opening of the Japan-British Exhibition with artefacts of all kinds and two Japanese gardens built by Japanese gardeners. Even plants (and fish) were brought over specially from Japan, although many of the plants suffered from drought and subsequently died.

Fine and decorative artists and craftworkers throughout Europe quickly responded to the appetite for Japanese themes. Claude Monet painted Madame Monet in a kimono – one of his very few figure compositions and distinctly un-Japanese in style. He was also an avid collector of Japanese prints and added a graceful Japanese bridge to his garden at Giverny. In Britain, Japanese motifs could be seen in works by Whistler, Beardsley and Rennie Mackintosh.

Christopher Dresser's book *Japan: Its Architecture, Art and Art Manufactures* (1882) spread the taste for Japanese paraphernalia such as fans, screens and prints. On stage, Gilbert and Sullivan's comic opera *The Mikado* poked gentle fun at the Japanese craze. When performed at the Savoy Theatre, London, in 1885, the programme included an advertisement for Liberty art fabrics with models in Japanese dress. The trade was not entirely one-way:

a steady stream of Japanese visitors came to Tyneside and Northumberland to view warships and guns to help build the Imperial Japanese Navy.

Meanwhile, throughout Britain, gardens fell prey to the Japanese vogue, prompted in part by excitement at new plant introductions. Among the first British plant hunters to reach Japan in the 1860s was John Gould Veitch of the famous dynasty of nurserymen, with nurseries in Exeter and the King's Road, Chelsea. (Harry Veitch was present at the 1910 visit to Gatton's Japanese garden by the local Gardeners' Mutual Improvement Association.) Despite being shipwrecked en route and losing all his possessions, the young Veitch quickly threw himself into garden-visiting and plant-collecting, the latter sometimes by the simple ruse of sending his man to buy them from the nearest Japanese nursery some 24 kilometres (15 miles) away in an area still closed to foreigners.

Extracts from Veitch's letters appeared in Britain's gardening press. From his tiny room in a Buddhist temple in Nagasaki, he wrote that he was as comfortable as he possibly could be and found the priests kind: 'They take great interest in my plants, scarcely a day passing without their bringing me some novelty in their eyes. I always receive their presents and

thank them very much, although I generally throw them away afterwards.' Veitch's Japanese introductions included *Lilium auratum*, several magnolias (*Magnolia stellata, M.* × *soulangiana* 'Nigra'), primulas (*Primula amoena, P. cortusoides* and *P. japonica*), and a number of new conifers – the prize of them all being the beautiful Japanese umbrella pine,

Sciadopitys verticillata, described by Veitch as 'the finest tree in Japan' and planted by us at Gatton.

Veitch was followed by Robert Fortune in the same year and though they managed to avoid bumping into each other, many of their plants shared a passage on the same steamer home. Fortune visited Japan again the following year to see the spring

Gatton's new bridge copies the original from an Edwardian catalogue.

flowers. Despite the mildness of his adventures (he, too, bought many of his introductions from Japanese nurseries), he declared himself well pleased with his discoveries. These included *Arundinaria fortunei*, *Lonicera japonica* 'Aureoreticulata'

and the male form of *Aucuba japonica*. European and British plant collectors, including Veitch's son James Herbert Veitch and E. H. 'Chinese' Wilson, continued to visit Japan into the next century.

As new, exotic plants were creeping into the nurseries, so the gardening press was beginning to notice Japanese garden design, even if its symbolic principles were often misunderstood. On 17 March 1866, the *Gardeners' Chronicle* ran a short report on landscape gardening and the relationship between nature and art. It praised the ingenuity of urban Japanese gardens in overcoming their cramped spaces with tiny streams crossed by bridges, paths winding around groups of artificial rocks and 'a whole race of plants suitable for their decoration... many of them till lately unknown even to our gardening world'.

By the end of the century, books were beginning to appear that showed the British gardening public real Japanese gardens. Easily the most influential was Josiah Conder's *Landscape Gardening in Japan*, published in 1893, two years after his earlier book on Japanese flowers and floral arrangement. Sir Jeremiah Colman must have been familiar with both these works. Conder was an architect who joined the Public Works Department in Tokyo and later became a lecturer at the Imperial University. His book on landscape gardening was the first authentic do-it-yourself guide to the principles and practice of Japanese gardening. Two other works that brought images of real Japanese gardens to the British public were Edward Morse's *Japanese Homes and Their Surroundings* (1888) and *The Flowers and Gardens of Japan* by the Du Cane sisters, with text by Florence and charming illustrations by Ella.

Not all writers praised the Japanese style. Although an enthusiast for Japanese plants, in his book *The Bamboo Garden* former diplomat A. B. Freeman-Mitford dismissed the Japanese garden as 'a mere toy that might be the appanage of a doll's house... There is a dwarf forest of stunted Pines, with a Lilliputian waterfall running into a tiny pond full of giant gold fish... It is all spick and span, intensely artificial, a miracle of misplaced zeal and wasted labour'.

Generally, however, the novelty of Japanese gardens found favour and sparked a rash of imitations in late Victorian and Edwardian Britain that have now mostly vanished. Some, like Hinchingbrooke in Cambridgeshire, had a thatched tea house and miniature lake, much like Gatton. Others bristled with Japanese artefacts: like Lowther Castle in Cumbria and Sir Frank Crisp's Friar Park, Henley-on-Thames (Crisp also built a scale model of the Matterhorn elsewhere in his outrageous garden.) Eccentric garden writer E. A. Bowles began to compile a Japanese scrapbook, now a prized possession of the RHS Lindley Library. Colman knew many of these other aficionados of Japanese gardens through membership of the same Royal Horticultural committees.

Especially influential at the time – and particularly helpful to our restoration – was Leopold de Rothschild's Japanese garden at Gunnersbury House in west London, created

(above) Ella Du Cane painted 'real' Japanese gardens for *The Flowers and Gardens of Japan*.

(opposite) A stone lantern marks a pond-crossing.

at the beginning of the century by his gardener James Hudson. Hudson's lecture on the making of the garden was reprinted in the *Journal of the Royal Horticultural Society* in 1907. It gave us a very useful plant list that included specimens we planted at Gatton, such as Veitch's Japanese umbrella pine and the Japanese white pine, *Pinus parviflora*.

Most of these gardens – like Gatton – adopted the dress and trimmings of the Japanese style without appreciating that real Japanese gardens expressed a whole philosophy and attitude to life. Just a handful from the period stand out for their authenticity, such as Tully in Ireland and Tatton Park in Cheshire, both created by real Japanese gardeners in the early 1900s and both surviving to this day. Despite its artificial and controlled appearance, a Japanese garden takes its cue from nature and the natural world. Ultimately, its aim is to take the viewer beyond the physical into a symbolic reading of the landscape. An article of 1914 caught this spirit when it concluded, 'Study reticence, the "something left over", which leaves room for suggestion. A garden without suggestion is no real garden. Be ever careful to transcend artificial rules and enter as far as you can into the real spirit of Nature.'

The view from the tea house under the arch of a surviving plum yew.

Designer clues

Before we could begin to plan our restoration in more detail, we wanted to resolve the vexed question of design. We knew that the garden was constructed by unemployed labourers, but who prepared the original plan?

There were two probable contenders. The first was Edward White, son-in-law of H. E. Milner (who had earlier worked for Colman at Gatton) and head of the firm Milner White. A guide to Gatton published in 1914 credited him with much of the later work in the gardens. Although the firm has now closed, we managed to trace the surviving partner who had the firm's client books from 1913 – three years after our garden was made. It was an exciting moment when we discovered that the client books listed Sir Jeremiah Colman of Gatton Park for August 1914. But this didn't necessarily mean White had also worked on the Japanese garden.

An equally strong contender was the nursery firm of V. N. Gauntlett & Co. Limited, then based nearby at Chiddingfold, Surrey, and renowned as a supplier of hardy Japanese plants. Although the nursery has now closed, the RHS Lindley Library has a stack of old catalogues that contained detailed plant lists and descriptions; photographs of imported garden ornaments, such as lanterns (in bronze, stone, iron, marble and wood), storks, pagodas, gates and basins; and whimsical advice on design. 'In a subtle, mysterious way,' began one catalogue, 'the mystic spell of the flowery land has been cast over our English Gardens. This spell has touched the quiet slumbering beauty of the Old English Garden, *and with its fairy wand has transformed it into a living picture*.' (The italics are theirs.)

The catalogues offered the design services of Mr N. Gauntlett and, crucially for us, one catalogue (undated, but about *c*.1910 or 1911) listed Sir Jeremiah Colman as a patron of the nursery, along with the late King Edward VII, the governments of Australia, India and South Africa and the entire gardening establishment, starting at the top with assorted princesses, duchesses, dukes and earls, and descending through lords and ladies to mere baronets like Sir Jeremiah and a handful of (vaguely titled) reverends. Did Mr Gauntlett direct Colman's unemployed labourers during the winter of 1909 to 1910 as the garden was laid out?

Plotting the evidence

We were now ready to bring together all the elements of our research – in archives, documents, maps, photographs and on the site itself – to form a restoration plan. Our aim was very clear: to put back, as far as possible, the garden Colman created in 1909–10 and developed over some twenty to thirty years. We were not trying to 'improve' the garden's authenticity. Created some six months before the Japan-British Exhibition with its truly Japanese gardens, this was an Edwardian vision of Japan rather than the real thing. We also had to think about how the school might maintain the garden into the future.

(this page)
Silene dioica (Campion).

The basic layout came from the latest historic Ordnance Survey map for the Colman era (1933), because this showed the garden as Colman left it. The 1913 Ordnance Survey map was also key, as this was the first to show the altered flow of the waterway between Engine Pond and the Serpentine.

A careful site survey recorded by garden archaeologist Lesley Howes established the exact location of many of the garden's hard landscape features, such as hoggin paths (some of which were shown on the map) and lantern bases. Miraculously, although the thatched tea house had long since rotted away, the post holes survived under the rhododendrons. You could put your hand into the holes and feel the smooth sides where rustic posts had once stood. This part of the restoration process is rather like forensic detection: sifting the scene of a crime for the tiniest pieces of evidence and then building up a picture of what actually happened. Surveys are also vital for recording plant survivals from the original design.

For guidance on the garden's overall style and spirit, we turned to Josiah Conder's *Landscape Gardening in Japan*. This large-format book, illustrated with hundreds of drawings, devoted separate chapters to the main features of Japanese gardens. Of all the different garden types discussed, Gatton was closest to the 'pond-and-island' style, its hillocks and small pools symbolic of mountainous islands rising out of the ocean. In more literal examples, carefully pruned evergreen trees and shrubs would be used to evoke windswept trees and clouds. According to Conder, 'when fresh running water can be easily obtained, it is usual to introduce streams into a garden, arranged to wind through the grounds in an irregular and interesting manner.' Conder's book contained a number of possible models in which sinuous ponds dotted with flat stepping stones curl around meandering hillocks. He also provided much useful detail on tea houses, lanterns, cascades, stepping stones, paths and arbours.

For the planting plan, our aim was to use plants that were appropriate, of the right period and ones that would

Template for a large water garden from Josiah Conder's *Landscape Gardening in Japan*.

thrive. Where possible, we tried to position them according to photographs or surviving planting. We also had to think of the school's needs. They wanted a range of habitats to meet their developing environmental interests and a garden that was reasonably easy to maintain. So, for instance, we used sedge and ground-cover plants in place of manicured lawns.

We had a mass of sources to help us to compile our lists – contemporary photographs and descriptions, plants still surviving on site, Gauntlett's nursery catalogues after 1909 and suggestions from books and articles of the time, especially *Landscape Gardening in Japan*, and James Hudson's descriptions of planting at Gunnersbury. Contemporary journal descriptions indicate that many native plants were used. Our planting list probably included more truly Japanese plants than the original. The type of soil (alkaline, boggy and not terribly well drained) dictated many of our choices.

For the garden's artefacts – so vital to its Edwardian Japanese spirit – we were able to turn to photographs and descriptions in contemporary gardening magazines and guides to Gatton, as well as family albums showing the garden soon after its creation. (Sadly, no one is ever shown walking in

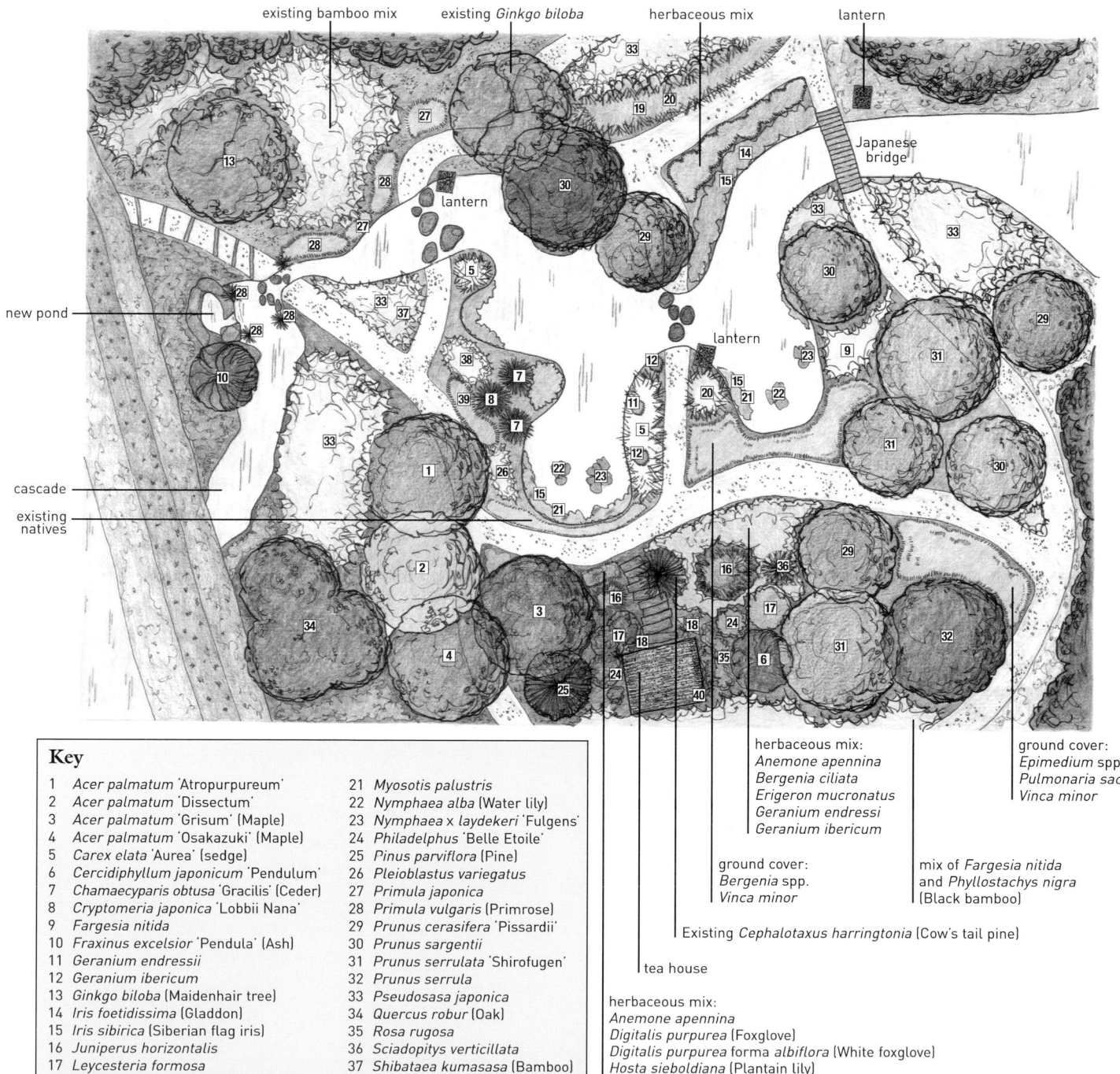

existing bamboo mix

existing *Ginkgo biloba*

herbaceous mix

lantern

Japanese bridge

lantern

lantern

new pond

cascade

existing natives

tea house

Key

1	*Acer palmatum* 'Atropurpureum'	21	*Myosotis palustris*
2	*Acer palmatum* 'Dissectum'	22	*Nymphaea alba* (Water lily)
3	*Acer palmatum* 'Grisum' (Maple)	23	*Nymphaea* x *laydekeri* 'Fulgens'
4	*Acer palmatum* 'Osakazuki' (Maple)	24	*Philadelphus* 'Belle Etoile'
5	*Carex elata* 'Aurea' (sedge)	25	*Pinus parviflora* (Pine)
6	*Cercidiphyllum japonicum* 'Pendulum'	26	*Pleioblastus variegatus*
7	*Chamaecyparis obtusa* 'Gracilis' (Ceder)	27	*Primula japonica*
8	*Cryptomeria japonica* 'Lobbii Nana'	28	*Primula vulgaris* (Primrose)
9	*Fargesia nitida*	29	*Prunus cerasifera* 'Pissardii'
10	*Fraxinus excelsior* 'Pendula' (Ash)	30	*Prunus sargentii*
11	*Geranium endressii*	31	*Prunus serrulata* 'Shirofugen'
12	*Geranium ibericum*	32	*Prunus serrula*
13	*Ginkgo biloba* (Maidenhair tree)	33	*Pseudosasa japonica*
14	*Iris foetidissima* (Gladdon)	34	*Quercus robur* (Oak)
15	*Iris sibirica* (Siberian flag iris)	35	*Rosa rugosa*
16	*Juniperus horizontalis*	36	*Sciadopitys verticillata*
17	*Leycesteria formosa*	37	*Shibataea kumasasa* (Bamboo)
18	*Lilium longiflora, candidum & regale*	38	*Sasa palmata* forma *nebulosa*
19	*Miscanthus sinensis* 'Gracillimus'	39	*Vinca minor* (Lesser Periwinkle)
20	*Miscanthus sinensis* 'Zebrinus'	40	*Wisteria sinensis*

herbaceous mix:
Anemone apennina
Bergenia ciliata
Erigeron mucronatus
Geranium endressi
Geranium ibericum

ground cover:
Bergenia spp.
Vinca minor

ground cover:
Epimedium spp.
Pulmonaria saccharata
Vinca minor

mix of *Fargesia nitida*
and *Phyllostachys nigra*
(Black bamboo)

Existing *Cephalotaxus harringtonia* (Cow's tail pine)

herbaceous mix:
Anemone apennina
Digitalis purpurea (Foxglove)
Digitalis purpurea forma *albiflora* (White foxglove)
Hosta sieboldiana (Plantain lily)
Hosta sieboldiana var. *elegans*
Primula rosea
Primula denticulata 'Superba'
Sisyrinchium striatum

it although we know from former gardeners that Colman and his wife often came here with guests.) One particularly fulsome guide to the estate was written in 1914 by garden writer T. G. W. Henslow, whose book *Garden Architecture* (1926) included a chapter on Japanese gardens in which he praised Gauntlett's Japanese Nurseries.

Contemporary photographs gave us good models for our stone lanterns. Two were tall and fairly similar (but not identical), the third was set on a curved base and known as the 'Valley' shape. They would probably have been ordered from catalogues and assembled by estate workers on site. Gauntlett's nursery supplied imported stone lanterns, though none in their catalogues matched ours exactly. While lanterns were essential to a Japanese garden, Conder notes that they were lit only rarely, producing at best a 'dim and mysterious glow' that looked especially effective over water. At least one contemporary report mentioned wooden lanterns at Gatton and these we know were available from Gauntlett's nursery. They are not shown in any of the contemporary photographs, however, and were not included in our restoration plan.

We were also unable to track down a source for Colman's thatched tea house. This may have been built by estate carpenters, using local materials. The management report had already located the source for the Japanese bridge in a catalogue for the Bedford works of J. P. White in the collection of the Lindley Library. (The same firm also supplied a rose arbour for a different part of the estate.) A former gardener remembers the bridge painted red, which was a feature of Chinese rather than Japanese gardens, but the Edwardians often confused the two. The original J. P. White bridge was supplied oiled in wrought oak or teak, stained in sawn oak, or painted any colour in deal with a slatted oak floor.

(left) New granite lanterns were hand-carved in China to match the originals.

(opposite) A master thatcher roofed the open-sided tea house on site.

Heaven-falling and so on. We knew the school had moved the outlet pipe when they repaired Engine Pond, but our budget would not stretch to putting this back. In the end, we tried to create a Japanese version of the dripping well shown in a family photograph of 1901, with a new top pool cascading down to another pool crossed by stepping stones and then falling further to the existing channel. Again, an illustration in Conder gave us our blueprint.

From blueprint to real garden

The major problem we faced during the five days of restoration was transforming a tangled boggy woodland back into a tranquil, ornamental pond-and-island garden. This involved two principal tasks: opening the site by clearing all the secondary weed trees; and dredging more than half a century's worth of mud and accumulated debris from the woodland floor. For this we needed experts and Gatton's own enthusiastic volunteers, supplemented by skilled helpers from groups like the Surrey Gardens Trust. It was a daunting prospect.

Altogether, the tree surgeons removed more than a hundred self-seeded trees that had grown up in the sixty-odd years since the garden was abandoned. First, school children had helped to identify eight trees that were clearly part of the original plan and would add maturity to the new garden. These included the gingko, which was brought back to life by stripping off its choking collar of ivy.

Dredging the sludgy stream was to prove much more difficult. After clearing wood and debris lying close to the surface, aquatics expert Glyn Onione and his team had hoped to remove the remaining silt by spraying it with water and siphoning out the resulting suspension, but there was simply too much debris matted together in the thick mud. The only answer was to call in the mechanical diggers and even they, at times, struggled with the enormity of the task. Dredging continued through to the end of the fourth day of filming – far longer than originally planned and not helped by persistent rain that turned the site into a

There may also have been two other crossings, joining paths on either side of the water. One gardener remembered three bridges but only one was definitely marked on the map, plus another crossing that may have been formed by stones sunk into the water. In the end, we decided to create three sets of stepping stones in Kentish ragstone – two near the cascade and the other directly opposite the tea house. Our crossings zigzag slightly like the ones in Conder, 'the whole being arranged with a studied irregularity for both comfort in walking and artistic effect.'

Lack of evidence meant that we had to guess the form of the cascade from the Engine Pond into the Japanese garden. Conder describes an extraordinary number of variations: thread-falling, right-and-left falling, side-falling, folding-falling, front-falling, stepped-falling, wide-falling, quagmire. There were, none the less, some moments of pure joy – like discovering a stone lantern toppled into the mud near its protruding base and submerged under the thickening slime. We even found the brass wick-holder intact.

Once the shape of the original waterway began to emerge from the slime, we were able to think about creating the network of paths shown in photographs and on the map of 1913. We laid hoggin for the surface, as used elsewhere on the estate. A common material for paths in the eighteenth and nineteenth centuries, hoggin is a mixture of gravel and clay, extracted together and compacted on site to give a naturally solid surface. Though it can look stridently orange when first laid, it soon mellows to a pleasant sand colour.

Just as in Sir Jeremiah Colman's original garden, what really transformed the space were the Japanese artefacts – the thatched tea house especially. This was constructed on site by a master thatcher using materials that matched the original photographs exactly: a structure of rustic poles roofed with bundles of water reed laid in courses from the bottom up. A fine ridge pattern was created from wheat straw and split hazel.

The bridge was made specially for us to the original manufacturer's design. The wood was pretreated softwood, stained a darker colour. We had intended it to be accessible for wheelchairs,

(opposite from top to bottom) Pat Pay of the Royal Alexandra and Albert School is helped by dedicated volunteers.

(below) Age will soon weather the artefacts that define the garden's Edwardian-Japanese spirit.

but a slight mix-up in the specification meant that it is now a very tight fit. Restoration involves thinking about the needs of visitors today as well as the demands of the past.

Determined that our stone lanterns should match the original photographs, we first looked for off-the-peg imported models. When this failed we found a company able to send designs and dimensions to China where they were hand-carved specially for us from solid granite. Of course, when they eventually arrived, they looked startlingly new, much as Sir Jeremiah's must have done in 1910. Well aware of the problem, in *Landscape Gardening in Japan* Josiah Conder proposed mimicking the patina of real antique lanterns from temples and shrines 'by attaching, with a gummy solution, patches of green moss, and by fixing to them decayed leaves by means of bird-lime, or by smearing them with the slime of snails; after either of which processes they are kept in the shade and frequently wetted.' We preferred the more modern solution of cow dung mixed with yogurt.

The final – and most enjoyable – task was planting. At the end of five days' filming, in and out of rain, we could tackle only the water margins and the higher ground around the tea house, leaving the rest of the ground to dry out. Plenty of marginals and aquatics went around the stream – sedges, rush, Siberian flag iris, bog arum, marsh marigold and water

lilies last seen floating serenely in photographs of the garden in its heyday. The tea-house mound included a few more obviously Japanese plants, such as Japanese anemones, a katsura tree (*Cercidiphyllum japonicum* 'Pendulum'), and the umbrella pine. The remaining areas were planted later, with more plants added by the school so that, even by the end of the first summer, Sir Jeremiah Colman's garden once again delighted visitors with its flowers and tranquillity.

Memories relived

The magic of Gatton's transformation was movingly captured in the visit of an old estate gardener who lived in a neighbouring county in a home for retired gardeners. Arthur Hooper, ninety at the time of his visit, had been one of four or five gardeners looking after the Japanese garden in the 1930s. He could clearly remember Sir Jeremiah and Lady Colman entertaining their guests in the tea-house, even royalty. When visitors arrived, the gardeners had to make themselves scarce. 'This garden had to match up to

(above) Glossy green and yellow leaves of the vigorous bamboo, *Sasa palmata* forma *nebulosa*.

(left) Yellow heads of flag iris appear from mid-summer.

anything the king or queen could do,' he recalled of his old employer. 'He couldn't bear to be bested.'

One of Arthur's jobs was to remove the pollen sacs from the stamens of white lilies to keep the colour pure. He planted miniature acers and many varieties of primulas down by the water's edge. Despite the chalky soil, Colman wanted lots of rhododendrons, which were planted in deep holes filled with ericaceous compost. They would grow for a few years then need replacing.

As Arthur revisited the garden he had tended more than sixty years before, his eyes lit up as he remembered the overhanging trees that gave the garden dappled shade, and the acers that set it on fire in the autumn with their magnificent colours. 'It isn't a new garden,' he said with evident delight, 'it's a very old garden. But it's come back to life. To me, it brings back memories of years and years ago. I didn't think I would ever have these memories stirred again, but here they are, in front of me. It's a joy to be back,' he declared. 'If I was younger I would want to take over this garden and run it myself, it's got that much of an appeal.'

(above) As in Colman's day, planting is wild and watery rather than authentically Japanese.

(right) The thatched hut where a king and queen took tea.

chapter four

tunnels and tropics in lakeland

ELLER HOW sits high above the Cumbrian town of Ambleside, at the head of Lake Windermere. Solidly built of local stone and slate, it's the last house on the steep road up from the town before the fells begin. A stony track continues up towards Sweden Bridge, commemorated in Victorian postcards and still a celebrated sight for hikers on their way up Scandale Fell.

The garden here was immediately different from others in the series: it looked a little wild, perhaps, but hardly lost. Through the main gates, a short drive swung round to the house. From the terrace there were fine views down across the town, with a glimpse of the distant lake. Beyond the house, the garden opened up with two round ponds joined at the middle and ringed in summer with giant clumps of the royal fern, *Osmunda regalis*. A rustic bridge crossed the pond at its pinched waist to the far bank, which was planted with choice rhododendrons and climbed steeply to the garden's most striking feature – a brooding Gothic folly of a tower, perched precariously on a mound by the boundary wall marked by a line of fine, ancient beech trees.

Stone and slate steps led down from the tower into the wildest part of the garden, brambly woodland choked with a rampant yellow-berried raspberry. A fat-trunked Japanese cedar, *Cryptomeria japonica*, pointed to the woodland's ornamental character, as did a fine Wellingtonia, *Sequoiadendron giganteum*, surprisingly unbuffeted by Lakeland winds. Towards the bottom gate was a solid stone octagonal summer house roofed in local slate. It looked Victorian with some later glazing, but vernacular structures in local materials are notoriously difficult to date.

Between the summer house and the pond lay the area we had come to investigate – a gloomy hollow filled with logs, leaves and garden rubble. A self-seeded ash grew roughly in the middle. Ringed with mostly nondescript evergreens and cut into the hillside leading up to the tower, the hollow looked the least interesting part of the garden. You could easily overlook the few clues lying close to the surface: a slimy concrete rim poking up through dead leaves; below it a rough stone arch, too small for a doorway but clearly part of some ornamental feature; a line of rusting lead embedded in the earthen wall.

(opposite) The folly in local stone and slate, towers over the hillside garden.

(below) Hidden behind gloomy evergreens, this unremarkable hollow guards its secrets well.

A fabled past

Eller How had already made one fleeting appearance in the literature about Victorian gardening eccentrics. In the 1930s, Polish widow Clara Boyle had published a memoir about her much older husband, diplomat Harry Boyle, who gained fame under Lord Cromer as 'Boyle of Cairo'. Her book, *A Servant of the Empire*, recalled Harry's wild, untutored childhood here at Eller How where his father, Henry, had created an extravagant garden on the edge of the fells. Clara was a noted fabulist, however. As we couldn't be certain that her stories were true, we set about uncovering the evidence for ourselves.

Maps and deeds together chart the building and early years of Eller How. The site appears on the tithe map of 1838 for the township of Ambleside above Stock as a triangle of arable farmland on the edge of the fell, owned by John Mackereth (a good local name) and farmed by John Wilkinson. Called Eller Rigg, it floated in a white sea of unproductive land.

John Mackereth sold the land in 1851 to Mrs Elizabeth Reid, who sold on two plots to Thomas Bell, the local chemist. Both Reid and Bell were connected with protofeminist and political economist Harriet Martineau, who had settled in Ambleside and established one of the very first building societies, which Thomas Bell chaired. Martineau's

special interests included drains and workers' cottages.

Eller How was built in 1851 by a local builder as a small country house. For ten years, it was occupied by Anne Jemima Clough, sister of the renowned Victorian poet Arthur Clough who died tragically young in Florence. Later the first principal of Newnham College, Cambridge, Anne Jemima opened Eller How as a ladies seminary for the daughters (and a few sons) of local tradespeople and farmers, introducing advanced ideas of child-centred education. One of the pupils was Mary Arnold, who later gained fame as the novelist Mrs Humphry Ward. For all its apparent isolation, Ambleside was fast becoming an intellectual centre, with a special focus on education. Until his death in 1850, the poet Wordsworth lived at nearby Rydal Mount; the Arnolds at Fox How; and John Ruskin over at Brantwood in Coniston.

During the Clough years, the gardens at Eller How were fairly plain with a broad gravel terrace bordered on each side with flowers, a Japanese quince trained up the house, steeply sloping lawns, shrubs, trees and fine views towards Lake Windermere. The pupils did physical exercises every day and romped in the garden when the weather was fine.

As one remembered later, 'I wonder if any band of girls ever studied in a prettier environment than we in our cosy schoolroom at Eller How. One window looked out upon the Stock Ghyll wood, and there were two or three trees which almost touched the glass. The other looked straight on to the beautiful lake and the green slopes and hills beyond.'

After the deaths of her mother and brother, Anne Jemima left Ambleside in 1862, the same year that young Henry Boyle from Staffordshire married Cornish doctor's daughter Eleanor (Nellie) Adams Hocking. The

pair spent several months travelling before coming to lodge at Ambleside. According to the deeds, Boyle bought Eller How on 16 September 1863 for £1,060. He also bought at least two adjoining fields and immediately started transforming the land to the west of his house into a garden.

Henry Boyle was the grandson of Zacharias Boyle, who amassed a fortune in the Potteries and whose son John was a partner in the first Wedgwood factory. Very little of the wealth came through to Henry, however. Cambridge-educated, in line with his status as minor gentry, Boyle emerges as a true Victorian dilettante and eccentric – a passionate landscape gardener and inventor, but utterly impractical with money and unable to live on his limited means. The deeds to Eller How tell a sorry tale as Boyle is forever remortgaging his property and buying it back, only to sell it on again for more money. When things became too bad, the house was let to tenants while Boyle, Nellie and their son Harry (born in 1863) took lodgings elsewhere, living for several years in London. The census never records Henry Boyle's residence at Eller How as the house was rented out in 1871 (to a clergyman's widow) and again in 1881 (to Mrs Adelaide Wordsworth), and stood empty in 1891, before the Boyles returned home from London. Annual trade directories confirm the Boyles' frequent absences from the ranks of Ambleside's principal families.

Ordnance Survey maps clearly record Boyle's transformation of his beloved garden. The first 25-inch Ordnance Survey map of *c*.1860 shows the garden at the end of the Clough years – a fairly standard arrangement with a carriage drive sweeping up from the road. Next to the house stood a large, bare field ringed mostly with conifers, and a few deciduous trees on the northern boundary (the beech trees, surely, that still stand).

The relatively slow pace of rural development meant that the second large-scale Ordnance Survey map for the area was not published until 1898, after a resurvey the previous year. The house and adjacent field were now joined into a substantial garden with all the features that can be seen today – egg-timer ponds, tower, flights of steps, summer house, lower lawn. Paths meandered gently around the garden, now shown as wooded with a mix of deciduous trees and conifers that must have included the Wellingtonia and the Japanese cedar.

And there, in the gloomy hollow we had come to investigate, was a substantial glass structure, rectangular in shape and sited some way below the tower. Intriguingly, by the next Ordnance Survey map of 1913 (revised in 1911–12), the structure had grown even larger with the addition of a longer, thinner rectangle across the top. The hatching on the map identified the structure as glass, but what, exactly, was it?

(opposite) Beyond the tower, the garden opens onto the fells.

(top right) This Ordnance Survey map of 1913 shows the enlarged glasshouses below the tower.

(right) The wild garden takes root.

Tropical gifts from Kew

The first hint that Clara Boyle might have been telling the truth about her father-in-law's prowess as a gardener came from the archives at the Royal Botanic Gardens, Kew. Referring to Henry as 'a born landscape gardener', this is how Clara described his passion: 'He specialized in rockeries and tropical plants; and in order to grow the Victoria Regia, he made a pond, egg-boiler shape, and twenty-eight feet deep, which was heated by gas. It was, and still is, surrounded by the finest Royal Osmunda ferns in the district.' Later in the same passage she gave us the clue that was to confirm at least part of her story: 'Henry was in constant touch with Kew Gardens,' she wrote proudly, 'and the directors were personal friends of his; they often sent him rare plants which they could not rear, and in consultation with them, he carried out many interesting botanical experiments.'

Henry's contact with Kew may not have been 'constant', but its 'Inwards' and 'Outwards' books record plants sent in by Boyle and out to him from Kew, for the very years he was creating his flamboyant garden at Eller How. The first date Kew records for plants sent to them by Boyle is 1 April 1868, when he sent mainly marginals and aquatics, including several water lilies. More plants followed in April, September and again in November of the same year, this time including some bamboo plants and seeds of an indecipherable plant from the New Jersey swamps. The next April, he sent lotus seeds, but, sadly, against the whole entry someone has written 'Dead' in a fine copperplate hand. More plants followed in the 1870s and 1880s, by which time the Boyles had moved to London, where they stayed for a period of about twelve years.

Most exciting of all were the plants Kew sent to Boyle in May and December 1868 and April 1869. As well as bamboos, filmy ferns, an exotic canna lily and aquatics like the water lettuce, *Pistia stratiotes*, and the beautiful red water lily, *Nymphaea rubra*, these included (in both 1868 and 1869) the giant Amazonian water lily, then called *Victoria regia* and now known as *Victoria amazonica*. Far too tender to survive ordinary Lakeland temperatures, this tropical water lily could only be over-wintered in a heated pool or grown as an annual. The fern-ringed pond claimed as its home by Clara was surely much too large to heat, so where had Boyle grown it? And was he successful in the attempt?

Both these questions were answered – at least partially – by a newspaper report in the *Kendal Mercury* of 4 September 1869 about the flower show organized by the Ambleside and Lake District Floral and Horticultural Society. Clearly no gardener, the correspondent spent most of his long and very wordy column describing the lady visitors. Tucked away towards the end was our man Boyle: 'Some exotic liliums [presumably the writer meant water lilies rather than botanical *Liliums*] contributed by Mr

(left) Henry Boyle, whose gardening passions brought him to the edge of ruin.

(opposite) *Blechnum spicant.*

(below) Old photographs of Boyle's fernery came unexpectedly to light after this book was written.

Henry Boyle, Ellerigg, Ambleside, were exhibited, and possessed the somewhat special merit of having been grown in the open air, in a tank heated from hot-air pipes. One specimen called the Victoria Regina [sic] displayed some really rare skill in successful cultivation and was an object of general admiration.' Whether or not Boyle won a prize was never made clear 'owing to the unaccountable neglect in the transmission to us of the official list'. Yet Boyle's feat really was remarkable. His adventurer brother, Frederick, later claimed in a book about orchids that relatives of his (which presumably meant brother Henry) were first and second in the country to coax the giant tropical water lily into flower in the open air.

If Clara had been at least partly right about the links with Kew and the tropical water lilies, might Eller How's garden, in fact, be as rare and special as she claimed? 'There were also grottoes,' she wrote, 'roofed with "stalactite" stones and adorned by coloured glass windows, and underground ferneries where tree ferns and orchids grew, and a tower, built by his own hands, on a high mound reached by flights of stone steps, and connected with the ferneries by underground passages.' Tree ferns grow best in shade, but if they were really grown underground they would need a glass roof to admit light. Could this be the answer to the puzzle of the glass structure shown on the late nineteenth- and early twentieth-century Ordnance Survey maps for the dull hollow we had come to investigate? And was this where Boyle also grew his orchids? The private Armitt Library in Ambleside still has Henry Boyle's copy of *The Orchid Grower's Manual*, inscribed with his name and later donated to the library by his son Harry.

Fern mania

Henry Boyle was by no means alone in his enthusiasm for ferns. The Victorian passion for them gripped society like a collective mania from the 1840s through to the 1870s, when it died as suddenly as it had arisen, a victim of its own success. When fern-collecting had become commonplace it lost its snob appeal, except for the true enthusiast.

Before the 1830s ferns were not seen as especially attractive, but then several factors conspired to turn an erudite hobby into a craze. Difficulties in propagating ferns were at last overcome, and a chance discovery of fern seedlings growing inside a sealed bottle led to the invention of the Wardian case, named after its inventor, Whitechapel doctor Nathaniel Bagshaw Ward. It was perfect for growing ferns indoors or for transporting plant specimens on long journeys. Not surprisingly, the craze for fern-collecting and fern-growing was fanned by the abolition of the glass tax in 1845 and improvements in the manufacture of sheet glass which reduced the cost of the glass ferneries that soon sprang up across the country. At the same time, the fern became a leading motif in decoration, satisfying the Victorian taste for exquisite ornament.

A succession of books from the late 1830s onwards kept the flames alive. Notable among these were Thomas Moore's *A Handbook of British Ferns* (1848, by the curator of the Botanic Gardens, Chelsea) and B. S. Williams' *Hints on the Cultivation of British and Exotic Ferns* (1852). Prolific Victorian garden writer Shirley Hibberd included ferns in his *Rustic Adornments for Homes of Taste* (1856) and later devoted a whole volume to *The Fern Garden* (1869). All these authors offered a huge range of models to suit every taste, whether for ferneries that were natural or artificial, modest or extravagant, temperate or tropical, dark or light.

The closest contemporary parallel to the underground fernery described by Clara Boyle is the sunken glazed one constructed in the early 1870s by A. B. Stewart at Ascog Hall on the Scottish Isle of Bute. Current owners Wallace and Katherine Fyfe recently restored this magnificent Victorian relic with help from Historic Scotland and the Royal Botanic Garden, Edinburgh. They were guided in their restoration by a glowingly detailed report in the *Gardeners' Chronicle* of 25 October 1879 by fern author B. S. Williams. He described the span-roofed structure, rounded at both ends, its iron framework resting on short walls. Backed by trees and shielded by a bank of shrubs in front, the unheated fernery was protected from the cold, showing only its roof to the outside world. 'To reach the entrance of this charming and natural-looking fernery,' wrote Williams breathlessly, 'we go down a flight of rustic stone steps, which have rockwork on either side, well planted with Ferns and alpine plants. Then a most surprising sight presents itself ...'

Williams went on to describe the 50-foot vista of ferns, rocks and water enlivened by the sound of water trickling over rocks. Planting was mostly exotic, verging towards the subtropical despite the lack of winter heating. Tree ferns included *Dicksonia antarctica;* the

(opposite left) Sporing tree frond.

(opposite right) *Asplenium scolopendrium.*

(below) *Osmunda regalis* 'Cristata'.

silver tree fern, *Cyathea dealbata*; a pair of *Dicksonia squar-rosa*; and the fine, black-stemmed New Zealand tree fern, *Cyathea medullaris*. Also worthy of special note were some *Todeas* and a number of British ferns. A meandering path paved with beach pebbles tempted the visitor to explore further towards a bridge and waterfall at the far end. 'Ferns also luxuriate in this spot, which is especially beautiful, so varied in character, with its rocks and the water tumbling down among them, and dotted with Ferns below, especially the Todeas; these, and indeed most of the Filmy Ferns, have the appearance of being set with crystals on their fronds, which seem so cool and refreshing to the eye.'

Ascog Hall is not the only fernery to hint at what we might find at Eller How. The *Gardeners' Magazine* of 23 December 1876 carried a report by Henry Harland of magic grottoes and show ferneries which used different-coloured panes of glass in their roofs – clear, rose, yellow, white, blue and (most successful for fern-growing) green. Problems with growing ferns under red and blue glass were surmounted on gala occasions 'by inserting cheap plants here and there in pockets made for the purpose'.

Lakeland menagerie

There were precedents, too, for Clara's most fantastic claim, that Henry had built 'another, smaller, pond in the ferneries, heated by a boiler, and connected with the larger pond, and here he kept some young crocodiles until they grew too big even for his liking.'

Throughout the nineteenth century, before the trade in wild animals was controlled, there were tales of sea captains bringing exotic animals into the country and selling them on as pets. Boyle's crocodiles are matched by polar bears in Paignton and giraffes in Gloucestershire. C. H. Keeling, author of some thirty books and pamphlets on private zoos and the keeping of unusual animals, knows of the Boyle story, but has never written about it because he has been unable to find conclusive proof. We had no luck, either, although the crocodiles (which were anyway much more likely to have been alligators) have passed into local legend. A retired neighbour who knew Clara Boyle well tells the story of the late John Mackereth (quite possibly a descendant or relative of the Mackereth who once owned the land), who recalled his grandfather's story about being taken by *his* father to see Boyle's crocodiles. The boy was held over the wall in the lane below the house to look into the tunnels where Boyle kept his

crocodiles. According to another local memory, two crocodiles were kept in a heated pond, but the gardener forgot to turn down the heat and they were boiled alive – 'especially unfortunate to happen to people called Boyle!'.

Certainly the evidence we were collecting suggested that Henry Boyle had a special interest in heating. To the newspaper report of his outdoor tank heated by hot air must be added the rusting pipes discovered throughout the garden. A retired agricultural lecturer contacted us about an invention by Boyle that might have made the fortune of a more worldly man. In 1872, Boyle filed a patent in London for a chicken-egg incubator, one of the earliest English machines on the market, which set extremely high standards of accuracy with its novel temperature controls. An advertisement for Boyle's Patent Incubator (priced from £12 12s to £25) appeared in an 1874 copy of the poultry industry's journal, the *Fancier's Gazette*. Readers could write for further information to Henry Boyle, Ambleside, Westmoreland, or see the machine in operation at an address in Bloomsbury, London. It seems that the egg incubator grew out of Boyle's experiments to maintain constant warm temperatures in his orchid house or fernery, for which he had first designed the new thermostat.

A truly wild garden

Even though our interest at Eller How was centred on the curious hollow below the tower, we wanted to establish the garden's wider context. Ordnance Survey maps show informal tree planting and a network of paths. These appear in greatest detail on a deed map of 1889, one of the many times Boyle remortgaged the property. The style of his garden is overwhelmingly natural and, although Boyle was clearly his own man, it is possible his ideas were influenced by the great Victorian garden writer, Irishman William Robinson, who published *The Wild Garden* in 1870.

In the polarity between art and nature, Robinson stood firmly in the natural camp. *The Wild Garden* was a counterblast to the Victorian obsession with gaudy displays of tender bedding that had rooted out all the old cottage favourites and left flower beds bare as soon as the first frosts struck. Though he also championed British natives, Robinson's definition of 'wild gardening' was quite specific. He meant the naturalization of hardy exotics 'or making wild innumerable beautiful natives of many regions of the earth in our woods, wild and semi-wild places, rougher parts of pleasure grounds, etc., and in unoccupied

(left) The wild garden stretches up to the tower.

(opposite) *Geranium ibericum.*

places in almost every kind of garden.' Although Robinson tried to argue that his system for planting hardy exotics in natural drifts could work equally well in forgotten corners of otherwise neat villa gardens, his style was best suited to the kind of terrain that Boyle commanded at Eller How – rocky, luxuriant, untamed. And Boyle, like Robinson, enjoyed experimenting with exotics.

Boyle would have found *The Wild Garden* an invaluable prompt. A small, pocket-sized book, the first edition was divided into four parts. A brief explanation of the author's purpose was followed by a comprehensive annotated list of hardy exotics for naturalization in British gardens and a further grouping by type of site, with a final section on gardening with British wild flowers. Boyle may well also have read later editions that expanded on Robinson's enthusiasm.

A Gothic tower of friendship

Before planning our restoration in any detail we wanted to fill in some remaining gaps in our knowledge of the Boyle family, and Henry in particular. The stone tower gave us invaluable clues about Henry Boyle's circle of friends, as many of their names were carved in stone and set into the facade of the folly tower. It was like a visitors' book in stone, each name accompanied by a date (mostly from the 1870s). Boyle's circle included connections to Lakeland's literary society: Wordsworth's son (also called William) and his step-granddaughter (Mima Quillinan); poet Matthew Arnold and his sister, Frances; members of Ambleside's educational elite, such as Harriet Martineau and Charlotte Mason; wives and daughters of premier families, such as the Redmaynes at Brathay Hall and the Le Flemings at Rydal; and Boyle and Hocking relatives.

Clara Boyle suggests in her book that Henry Boyle was an intimate, too, of John Ruskin's circle at nearby Coniston. Although Ruskin's diaries and letters never mention Boyle by name, they did share a close friend in Mrs Julia Firth of Seathwaite Rayne, Ambleside, whom Ruskin called 'one of the ablest and kindest of my women friends'. Ruskin was by now very famous and used Brantwood as a retreat. It is possible that Boyle was on the fringes of his society and may have met the great man without Ruskin considering the meeting important enough to record.

The later Boyle years

Money problems continued to darken family life for the Boyles, however. As recorded by Clara, on 15 June 1879 Nellie Boyle wrote in her diary: 'The dear garden so exquisite now, the laburnums magnificent, and the rhododendrons fast coming out; I wonder how much longer we shall enjoy this sweet home.' They had, in fact, just over a year until their problems became so acute they were forced to sell off the entire contents of the house and find another temporary home.

The sale was advertised in the *Westmorland Gazette* of 9 October 1880. Filling nearly a full column, the announcement poignantly listed the contents room by room. Nothing from the garden was sold, but there were two indoor Wardian fern cases, one measuring 2 feet by 4 feet; a number of books; and a collection of more than 2,000 moths and butterflies.

The house was let to Mrs Adelaide Wordsworth and, for over twelve years, the Boyles lived in rented lodgings in London. During his London exile, Boyle continued to send plants to Kew and even wrote to them from an address in Notting Hill.

The Boyles returned to Eller How sometime in 1894. Their son Harry – who grew up wild and was never given a formal education – had already been working for some ten years in the consular service in the Bosphorus. He was later to become Oriental Secretary in Egypt, and then British Consul-General at the embassy in Berlin, where he met his future bride, the very much younger Clara Asch, a Polish secretary.

Henry had little more than six years to enjoy his Lakeland home. He died on Christmas morning 1900, just sixty-two, having supposedly contracted pernicious anaemia while

(opposite left) Fiery *Crocosmia* has naturalized around the tower.

(opposite right) Names carved on the tower read like a visitors' book.

(below) During filming, the summer house became our research centre.

working among rotten manure in the fernery. In his very last years, he may well have added the extension to the fernery that was built between the two Ordnance Survey map revisions of 1897 and 1911–12. News of Henry's death in the *Kendal Mercury* of 28 December 1900 explained much about his character and why he left few traces of his life. 'He was of a very retiring disposition,' ran the short report, 'and was not associated with local movements to any extent, with the exception of the Rushbearing, which he liberally supported. A great student of nature, he spent the greater portion of his time in his lovely garden, to which he was devotedly attached, and he was a collector of almost everything of interest.' According to the *Westmorland Gazette* of 29 December 1900, Henry was also 'a gentleman of high attainments, an accomplished linguist and an artist of considerable ability. He took pleasure in the culture of rare and delicate plants and in his grounds with the miniature lake, caves and underground passages, he found convenient nooks for a valuable collection of specimens.'

Nellie survived him by fourteen years, dying in April 1914 just three months after Harry and Clara were married. Her obituary in the *Westmorland Gazette* of 25 April 1914 also referred to Henry's transformation of the gardens and grounds at Eller How, 'into a retreat which became a source of great pleasure to many people who were invited there.'

Eller How's fame as a garden lived on after Boyle's death. In 1911, a photograph of the lily pond appeared in *The Gardens of England in the Northern Counties*, edited by Charles Holme. Virtually all the other gardens belonged to grand houses, castles and halls. Several were by designer Thomas Mawson who was responsible for another of our lost gardens, at Comrie in Perthshire. The text refers to the late Mr Boyle, saying that he laid out the garden according to his own ideas: 'He planted a great variety of trees and

(left) Delicate bellflowers bloom around the fernery rim.

(opposite) The restored fernery at Ascog Hall provided a valuable model.

shrubs, he constructed miniature lakes and pools, and built rustic bridges; and by judiciously planning his winding walks he succeeded in creating an impression that the garden covers a much greater space than it actually occupies. The pools, in which grow many varieties of water lilies, are made quite charming by being set in masses of greenery and surrounded by clumps of fine ferns.'

Harry and Clara moved to Eller How, which remained their home for the rest of their lives. While neither was a gifted gardener, Clara claims in her book to have spent money repairing the underground ferneries, siphoning out the pond and repairing the tower. Harry died in 1937 and Clara in 1966. Like Henry before her, she rented out the main house, living in the self-contained studio that had once been Anne Jemima's schoolroom. An inventory of the contents of Eller How in 1941, kept at Kendal Record Office, shows the property's sad decline as china became chipped, furniture scratched and broken, and paintings sold off. Among the garden implements listed were two lawnmowers (one not working) and one fork (no handle). The garden degenerated into matted rhododendron scrub and Clara sold off the land beyond the tower. It was only reunited by Eller How's current owners, Jim and Frances Philbrook, who moved one step closer to their dream of restoring Boyle's Victorian extravaganza.

Digging in the dark

Of all our lost gardens, Eller How was the one we could least plan in advance because the kind of garden we put back depended crucially on whatever evidence the archaeologists might unearth below ground. It was to be a drama of discoveries.

We were especially interested in three parts of the garden. Most important was the hollow cut into the hillside below the tower, site of the

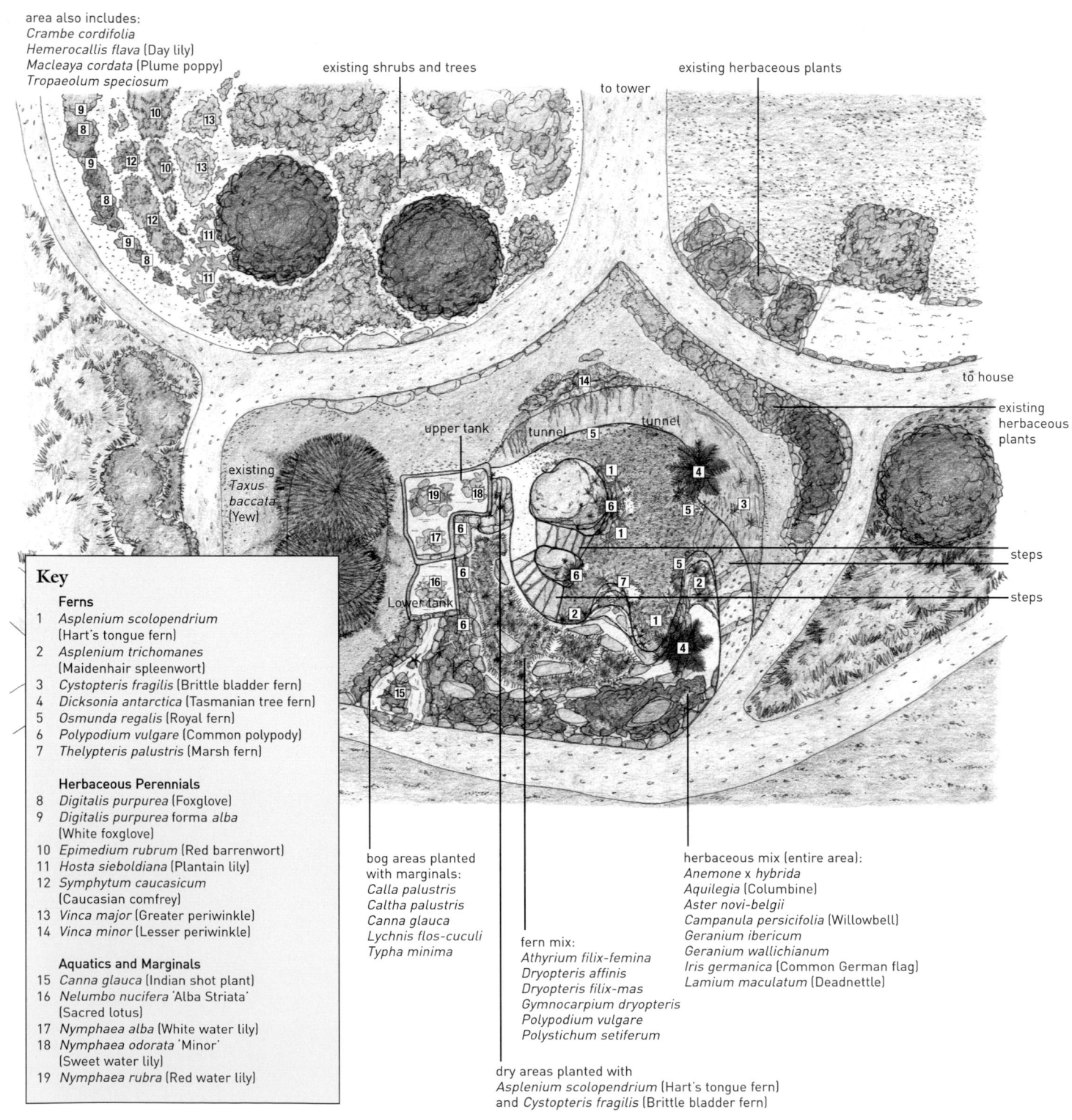

area also includes:
Crambe cordifolia
Hemerocallis flava (Day lily)
Macleaya cordata (Plume poppy)
Tropaeolum speciosum

existing shrubs and trees

to tower

existing herbaceous plants

to house

existing herbaceous plants

upper tank

tunnel   tunnel

existing
*Taxus
baccata*
(Yew)

Lower tank

steps

steps

Key

Ferns
1 *Asplenium scolopendrium*
    (Hart's tongue fern)
2 *Asplenium trichomanes*
    (Maidenhair spleenwort)
3 *Cystopteris fragilis* (Brittle bladder fern)
4 *Dicksonia antarctica* (Tasmanian tree fern)
5 *Osmunda regalis* (Royal fern)
6 *Polypodium vulgare* (Common polypody)
7 *Thelypteris palustris* (Marsh fern)

Herbaceous Perennials
8 *Digitalis purpurea* (Foxglove)
9 *Digitalis purpurea* forma *alba*
    (White foxglove)
10 *Epimedium rubrum* (Red barrenwort)
11 *Hosta sieboldiana* (Plantain lily)
12 *Symphytum caucasicum*
    (Caucasian comfrey)
13 *Vinca major* (Greater periwinkle)
14 *Vinca minor* (Lesser periwinkle)

Aquatics and Marginals
15 *Canna glauca* (Indian shot plant)
16 *Nelumbo nucifera* 'Alba Striata'
    (Sacred lotus)
17 *Nymphaea alba* (White water lily)
18 *Nymphaea odorata* 'Minor'
    (Sweet water lily)
19 *Nymphaea rubra* (Red water lily)

bog areas planted
with marginals:
Calla palustris
Caltha palustris
Canna glauca
Lychnis flos-cuculi
Typha minima

fern mix:
Athyrium filix-femina
Dryopteris affinis
Dryopteris filix-mas
Gymnocarpium dryopteris
Polypodium vulgare
Polystichum setiferum

dry areas planted with
Asplenium scolopendrium (Hart's tongue fern)
and *Cystopteris fragilis* (Brittle bladder fern)

herbaceous mix (entire area):
Anemone x *hybrida*
Aquilegia (Columbine)
Aster novi-belgii
Campanula persicifolia (Willowbell)
Geranium ibericum
Geranium wallichianum
Iris germanica (Common German flag)
Lamium maculatum (Deadnettle)

glasshouse shown on maps from the late 1880s (though built any time after Boyle's purchase of the house and land in 1863). This was where we suspected the underground ferneries might have been. If archaeology backed our hunches, we would then turn to contemporary sources for guidance on reconstruction.

Victorian fern mania gave us plenty of titles to guide our planting plan. The Armitt library in Ambleside (of which son Harry Boyle was a leading member) lent us a number of highly relevant titles, including Mrs Lankester's *British Ferns* and W. J. Linton's *Ferns of the English Lake Country* (1865). We could add these to our library of books lent by the Royal Horticultural Society and the London Library, as well as material gathered for the restoration of the Victorian fernery at Ascog Hall on the Isle of Bute. Particularly useful for thinking about the construction of Victorian ferneries were J. Birkenhead's *Ferns and Fern Culture* (1892) and John

Robinson's *Ferns in Their Homes and Ours* (1875). The restored open fernery at National Trust Cragside in Northumberland also gave us valuable clues.

Adjacent to the probable fernery were the remains of what we suspected was a water feature. Beneath years of garden debris, you could just make out a concrete rim and small stone arch above a dry rocky bed that may once have formed a waterfall. Boyle may well have experimented with his tropical water lilies in or around here. For ideas on replanting we could turn to the lists of seeds and plants sent between Boyle and Kew Gardens, which included a number of aquatics and marginals, some of which were hardy.

On the bank to the west of both hollow and water feature was a patch of woodland which we planned to return to a Robinsonian wild garden, planting a mix of natural and exotic plants that would have been available to Boyle from the mid-1860s. These we would plant informally in drifts, mimicking the way plants naturally reproduce or self-seed. For plant lists, we could turn to the first edition of William Robinson's *The Wild Garden*.

For herbaceous plants and ferns, we could consult contemporary catalogues of firms we knew Boyle had used, including rare plant specialist William Bull and hardy fern supplier H. Stansfield. A previous owner of Eller How had contacted us with scraps of two of Boyle's nursery receipts discovered in Eller How's attic. Based in Sale, Manchester, Stansfield claimed expertise in fern cultivation dating back to the 1840s. William Bull of King's Road, Chelsea, proudly named Her Most Gracious Majesty the Queen among the firm's illustrious patrons, as well as various dukes, dowager duchesses, earls, ladies, lords, barons and 'most members of the Aristocracy in the United Kingdom interested in horti-culture'. Tree ferns were a speciality, ranging in price from 5 guineas in 1869 for a 2-foot 5-inch stem to 40 guineas for a 12-foot 9-inch stem.

The buff-white flowers of *Macleaya cordata* will soon brighten the wild garden.

The drama of recreation

The restoration itself proved even more dramatic than we had anticipated. It started well enough, with the arrival of archaeologist Jamie Quartermaine and his team from Lancaster University's Archaeological Unit. They surveyed the garden and then began to dig, starting with the concrete tanks to the west of the site above the possible cascade. By the end of the first day, these had been completely excavated. There were two squarish tanks, staggered so that water would flow from one into the other. Both were remarkably well preserved and needed little more than reconcreting to make them watertight again. Around the edges were shallow planting ledges, and a deeper planting hole at the centre of the larger tank. Boyle may well have used the tanks to experiment with his water lilies; they could perfectly easily have been heated.

If progress was rapid at the start, however, the sheer scale of the enterprise soon forced the archaeologists to down trowels while we called in the mechanical diggers. Clearing the area of logs and surface debris revealed a tunnel of some kind leading down into the hillside. At some point, the whole of the hollow seemed to have been filled in with topsoil. Eventually, we had three diggers on site – one to dig and two to clear the growing mountain of soil excavated. The archaeologists then concentrated on the more delicate areas, such as the three flights of steps leading down from the water tanks. As the diggers went down, the archaeologists discovered yet more tunnels leading off into the hillside, then stopping abruptly after 8 metres (25 feet).

All the signs confirmed that this area was most probably the site of Henry Boyle's underground fernery and orchid house. The little rockwork that survived included a pillar of stones that may well have clad metal supports for

(top) Monty meets Alice the alligator and his keeper.

(Left) Did Henry Boyle once grow tropical water lilies in these heated tanks?

(top) Candles light the way down into mysterious tunnels.

(right) The glass roof in this photograph of Boyle's fernery proves our hunches were right.

the roof, and we also found some obvious planting pockets and rusting metalwork.

One thing really puzzled us: despite its inclusion on the detailed, large-scale Ordnance Survey maps of 1898 and 1913, the archaeologists found no trace of the glass roof that must once have covered the entire area. Had it simply decayed, the soil would have been full of glass shards, and we would have found evidence of glazing bars as well. We are certain the roof was once there as overlaying the enlarged glass roof of the 1913 map across our site survey produced an exact fit, covering the top tank while leaving the second tank in the open air. We also knew that the structure had vanished by the third edition 25-inch Ordnance Survey map of 1969. Infuriatingly, the smaller-scale 6-inch map of 1956 appeared to show a structure here *without* the cross-hatching indicating a glass roof, but the scale is too small to be certain.

The hardest evidence we found was a rusting metal window-catch of the kind that might have operated a glasshouse ventilation system. We could only assume that at some point the entire structure was removed and quite possibly sold to ease the Boyles' financial pressures (which Clara herself inherited), before the site was filled in with topsoil and garden debris.

By the end of the third day, the archaeologists had finally hit the fernery floor, more than 4 metres (13 feet) down, and the diggers were switched off. The discovery of yet another arch leading out towards the bottom stretch of the garden meant that the tunnels could quite possibly extend towards the garden wall, where the Mackereth boy remembered being held up to view the crocodiles. But any further exploration would have to wait for another time.

The area we had excavated included three flights of steps and two tunnels leading back into the hillside, towards

the tower. There was still much cleaning to be done and drainage was a problem as heavy rains overnight had filled the fernery floor with muddy water. We also needed to construct entrance steps leading down from the bottom path. Excavation had taken much longer than anticipated and we had neither time nor resources to recreate the glass roof. This obviously influenced our choice of plants, as all ferns would have to be hardy, able to survive the Lakeland weather, and we would not be able to add extra shading by installing blinds or coloured glass. This could be a problem as the site faced south and we had felled surrounding weed trees. Now we would need to create extra shade by planting around the outer rim of the hollow, making sure that shade-loving ferns were planted in damper pockets. Rebuilding was limited to naturalistic drystone walling, using slate from nearby Kirkstone Quarries, and creating planting pockets wherever possible with the addition of lime-free mulch to enrich the thin soil.

The rockwork in the cascade needed more attention. Dowsing for underground pipes to feed the cascade suggested that Henry Boyle

(left) Foxgloves in the wild garden mix with more exotic planting.

(opposite) The water feature uses local materials to good effect.

might have brought water across the garden from an upper field. Our solution was to install a pump powered by a windmill, so that water could constantly recirculate. In the little pond at the bottom of the feature and around the sides we planted aquatics and marginals, including some that Henry Boyle had received from Kew: the sacred lotus; water lilies such as *Nymphaea rubra*; *Canna glauca* and the Indian shot plant.

In woodland leading up to the tower we planted the beginnings of a Robinsonian wild garden, first clearing back the brambles and raspberry scrub. Following Robinson's example, we introduced hardy exotics, such as the plume poppy (*Macleaya cordata*) from China and Japan, comfrey and the frothy white-flowered *Crambe cordifolia* from the Caucasus, the violet-blue bearded iris from the Mediterranean (*Iris germanica*) and a plantain lily (*Hosta sieboldiana*) from Japan. We planted in drifts, adding white foxgloves to the existing clumps of common purple, and chose plants that would survive in the shade. The owners hope to extend this planting further up towards the tower.

On the last day of filming, we were visited by Alice the (male) alligator from a reptile centre on the shores of Windermere. He looked quite at home swimming in the restored water tanks where Henry Boyle may once have grown his tropical water lilies. Later, Alice set off just as happily to explore the underground tunnels that ran towards the tower then stopped abruptly.

There were still many questions left unanswered. Had Boyle hoped to tunnel all the way to the foot of the tower, linking his underground world with lofty views of the lake? If so, why did he stop? The greatest puzzle of all was who had sought to obliterate all trace of his achievements – and why?

A new Eden

Eller How's temperate fernery will take some time to establish itself. Its first summer was hot and dry, just the conditions most ferns dislike, and it needed daily watering. But slowly, the plants are adapting to their conditions and beginning to thrive.

Although we were not able to put back the kind of elegant glass roof that must once have shielded the fernery from the harsh, Lakeland elements, we had been able to reveal something of the vision of the garden's extraordinary creator. In out-of-the-way corners of Victorian Britain, there must have been many others in the same mould – passionate, single-minded gardeners whose independence of spirit outstripped their independent means. Restoring at least the spirit of the garden had involved the whole team in an enterprise that mimicked its original creation: dogged, a little frenzied at times, as we dug ever deeper in pursuit of Henry Boyle's long-lost fernery and the garden's history buried underground.

chapter five

shipshape in georgian kent

EVEN ABANDONED GARDENS have a very particular character. The nautical air of number 7 Officers Terrace came from its setting, overlooking Britain's best-preserved Georgian dockyard at Chatham, on the River Medway in Kent.

Completely hidden behind high, whitewashed walls, the block of gardens was separated from the backs of the houses by a narrow carriage road. Doors to one side led to the typically cramped backyards and outhouses of the fine Georgian terrace. On the other side were what looked like storehouses, innocent enough. The door to number 7, as gleaming white as the walls, was studded with thick black bolts. Inside, the air smelt musty, like a cellar. A vaulted passageway and steep stone steps led off to the right then turned a sharp corner. Up a further flight of steps came the first sight of the garden, a tangle of bramble and invasive garden weeds – docks, nettles, thistles, ivy and sycamore scrub.

Out in the light, the full extent of the garden's abandonment became apparent. At the lowest level, cracked concrete and a derelict glasshouse indicated more recent alterations than the garden's enclosing brick walls. Although badly repointed in places, these were of fine, plum-coloured brick, immediately suggesting a pedigree worth investigating. The main part of the garden sloped upwards towards a rubble-strewn top terrace. The grass in early March was brown and matted like clumps of dead hair. You could still make out garden features of indeterminate date – a metal-edged path in the shape of a letter D, a metal arbour cloaked with weeds, a rusty water tank fed by a pipe labelled 'not for drinking'. A few trees survived around the edges – a *Prunus* against the back wall, a holly and a small, mop-headed crab apple just coming into bud.

It was only when you reached the top terrace and turned back towards the houses that the garden's full character revealed itself. The steep steps from the carriage road and the gently rising ground put you level with the rooftops,

(opposite) A rusting water trough signals dereliction.

(below) These vaulted steps lead up to the garden like a secret passageway.

with glimpses of the River Medway beyond. Up here the line of gardens felt moored between river and sky in a panorama of grey pierced with chimney pots and weather vanes. You could almost hear the clink of rigging in a port.

Secret history

This garden would take us in a new direction altogether – into forgotten corners of naval history, for Chatham's garden was secret in a very special way. As part of the naval dockyard, access had long been denied on grounds of national security. Only when the dockyard finally closed in 1984 was the site gradually opened up as a showcase of Britain's fine heritage in industrial shipbuilding.

Unearthing the garden's history was made all the harder by the mountains of naval records held at the National Maritime Museum and the Public Record Office, along with (mostly secondary) sources collected by the Chatham Historic Dockyard library and the Medway Archives and Local Studies Centre. As we couldn't hope to sift through all this evidence ourselves in search of elusive references to private gardens within

the dockyard, we were extremely fortunate in being able to draw on the painstaking research of others. Our guides included Jonathan Coad, respected architectural historian and a leading authority on Chatham; a local Workers' Education Association (WEA) group, led by the late Elisabeth Hall, that had researched the Chatham Dockyard gardens in the 1980s; and landscape historian Todd Longstaffe-Gowan.

As with most of the gardens featured in the series, maps were critical in putting a date on this one's original construction. The terrace was built to rehouse senior dockyard officials on the hillside overlooking the Medway, thereby

freeing the cramped centre of the dockyard for redevelopment. A plan of the dockyard in 1719 shows the area before the terrace was built. Officers were housed in a medley of buildings near the old Commissioner's House, but they enjoyed separate gardens even then. Construction of the new terrace probably began around 1720 and was carried on in stages until 1731, when a final £650 was allocated to finishing the last two houses.

The National Maritime Museum has a number of undated designs for the houses and their floor plans. The closest to when the terrace was actually built shows an elevation plan and section of the twelve houses, 'to be built as the Old decay, in a proper situation for enlarging the Yard'. The most important houses in the terrace are larger and decorated with crenellated parapets: these are the pair in the centre (numbers 6 and our own, 7) and two on either end (1, 2, 11 and 12). As an obvious mark of rank, the grander houses were built for more senior officers whose titles were marked on the plan. At the ends were the storekeeper, clerk of the survey and first and second master attendants. The centre was reserved for the clerk of the cheque at number 6 and the master shipwright at number 7.

The much-raised back gardens were most probably created as the foundations were dug and the sites levelled for each set of houses. Research by the WEA group has unearthed several references to the building of the terrace and some of the hard landscaped features, though sadly nothing about planting or garden design. In August 1720, 'Chalk rubbish' was being dug out of the cellars and carried away by boat. A year later, the master shipwright requested four bricklayers 'for compleating the Bricklayers works of the new houses, Washhouses and

Garden Walls ...'. Prices were then agreed for stonemasonry, and coping stones and chimney pieces arrived in the yard. In July 1722, numbers 1 and 6 were reported to be nearly finished, and a request was sent to the 'Pavier' to lay stones in the storekeeper's yard at number 1.

Two dockyard plans from the mid-eighteenth century show the layout of the terrace and gardens. 'A Geometrical Plan and North West Elevation of His Majesty's Dock-yard, at Chatham', dated 1755, gives a fine view of the dockyard from the harbour. The officers' terrace with its crenellated roofline is clearly visible overlooking the dockyard; the gardens are hidden from view behind the houses. The plan below the elevation includes a crude layout for each of the gardens, merely indicating that they were divided into regular panels surrounded by paths around the edges. Gardens to the larger houses in the terrace (including our own) had a central path as well. In the following year (1756), a plan of the entrenchment surrounding the dockyard also shows

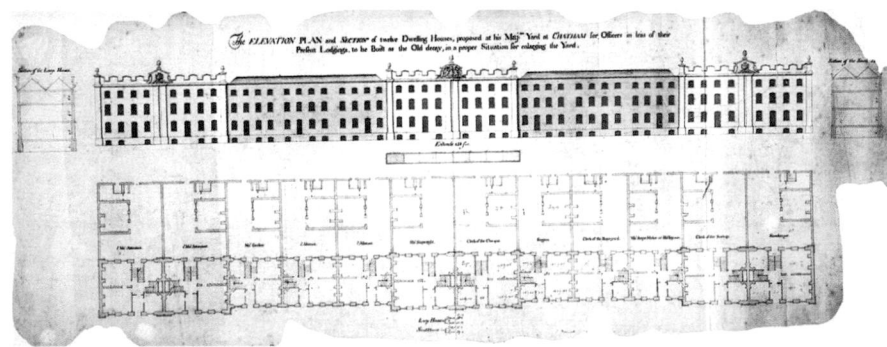

(top left) One of the central pair, number 7 Officers Terrace declares its status with a crenellated roof.

(left) A narrow carriage road separates the terrace from its hanging gardens.

(opposite) This coloured plan accompanies an exquisitely detailed model of 1774.

the neat terrace with its strips of garden abutting the outer wall. The gardens appeared in even more standardized form in this plan.

But the real excitement of discovery lay in examining a timber model (scale 40 feet: 1 inch) of the whole dockyard, housed in a storehouse of the National Maritime Museum, Greenwich. Commissioned in 1771 and finished by 1774, the model of Chatham and other dockyards was designed to show King George III the extent of his naval arsenal at a time dominated by Britain's wars with France. The models aimed for complete accuracy, intended for 'His Majestie's use shewing all Buildings, Docks, Ships etc in their due proportions, and each distinguished whether of brick stone or timber ...'. They came with detailed plans that were to 'agree with the Models of the Yards'.

Great care had been taken to find skilled craftsmen capable of undertaking the commission. A naval order of 13 August 1771 recorded that 'the Officers of the several Yards be directed to look out among their artificers for proper persons ... that are able to make models ... and in the meantime to prepare & send us plans by a scale of 40 ft to every inch ...'

As a guide to the layout and landscaping of the gardens, Chatham's dockyard model and its accompanying plan provide

outstanding detail. By 1774, fifty years or so after the houses were built, each garden had evolved its own design. All were regular in outline and generally consisted of paired flower beds surrounded by gravel paths, with an axial path leading up the centre. Against the walls were trained fruit trees. The entrance steps from the lane were covered by an open-sided structure much like a ship's cabin, with a partially glazed garden room at the back. To accommodate the slope, most gardens were levelled into terraces supported by low brick walls, while a seat at the far end gave a fine nautical view back across the rooftops. The seat in our garden curved into a canopy; next-door-but-one had a wooden gazebo.

According to the model, the most elaborate garden of all was at number 6, which had an oval parterre towards the centre. Our garden was plainer, with three separate terraces joined by simple stone steps. There were two paired flower beds in each of the two top terraces, and four beds in the bottom terrace near the cabin. In the

lane between gardens 6 and 7 was a small building, identified as a pump house. The two centre gardens also had additional garden structures against the lane wall. Those at number 7 are generally assumed to be aviaries.

Colours used in the plan that accompanied the model were carefully graded to show the variations in materials and even planting. Todd Longstaffe-Gowan has counted more than half a dozen different greens and ochres used to distinguish one garden from the next. The plan confirms the relatively simple garden layouts of formal flower borders and gravel. Turf was used sparingly in just a few gardens, either as areas of grass (plats) or paths.

The officers' gardens have remained remarkably untouched for almost three centuries, buried under later Victorian overlays. By the mid-nineteenth century, they were extended backwards and a new garden door added to the wall giving on to the upper road. A map of 1842 shows that our garden at number 7 had changed to a D-shaped parterre in the middle terrace. This was edged with wrought iron, still discernible when we first visited the site. The pump house was taken down and the stairs to our garden realigned so that they now enter the garden in the bottom right-hand corner. A number of the gardens acquired glasshouses and features such as arbours. But the main change was a slow and steady decay so that, by the 1980s, when the dockyard finally closed and the terrace was designated for private sale, all twelve gardens were virtually derelict.

Unearthing history

What happened next was to kick-start the process of recovery. When the dockyard was decommissioned in 1984, the whole precinct was scheduled as an ancient monument and Officers Terrace was ranked as one of the site's thirty-one outstanding historic attractions. Despite this, a renovation scheme was approved that involved demolishing parts of the gardens to make way for garages. A condition of the consent was that garden archaeology and recording would be undertaken first.

Lesley Howes was commissioned to do this work. An acclaimed garden archaeologist (other sites she has worked on include Painshill Park, Osborne House and Ham House), she began excavation in January 1990. The dig confirmed the model's startling accuracy and helped to fill in the gardens' later history. Gravel paths were found to have survived under later layers of Portland stone. Grass plats and cultivated borders could still be separately detected and identified. A small oval basin in one of the larger gardens was dug out from under three layers of silty soil, suggesting it had been filled in deliberately rather than simply abandoned. Tests on the wrought-iron edging in our garden dated it as a nineteenth-century addition. Later gardeners also added heating systems and greenhouses as their interests changed from simple recreation to propagation and horticulture. Lesley Howes' archaeology proved that small town gardens like these may still survive under the weight of later developments, like a time capsule waiting to reveal its secrets.

Grape hyacinth survives as a memory of earlier gardens.

We were impatient to get started. What made Chatham special was the survival of so much evidence (from maps, plans, naval records and the model) for a relatively small, everyday garden rather than for its grander neighbours. First, though, we wanted to find out more about the people who lived in the terrace and about life in the dockyard so that we could imagine how our garden was tended and used.

An officer's retreat

Dockyard records reveal that the tenants of Officers Terrace were either bureaucrats, like the clerk of the cheque, clerk of the survey, boatswain and naval storekeeper; or leading craftsmen, such as the master shipwright and his assistants and the master caulker. These were essentially company houses, tenanted by middle-ranking officers who were moved around at the Navy's whim. Todd Longstaffe-Gowan has calculated that average tenancies here varied according to rank: from as little as three and a half years for second assistant master shipwrights, up to sixteen years for clerks of the cheque and clerks of the survey.

When first built, our house (number 7) was reserved for the master shipwright, Benjamin Rosewell. By the time of the 1774 plan, however, the tenant was the clerk of the cheque, William Campbell. Both men were key figures in the dockyard hierarchy. The master shipwright's role was really that of naval architect, leading a team of several hundred shipwrights who implemented his designs. He would usually have spent his entire career within the royal dockyards, starting off as a lowly apprentice and learning his trade over many years. He would almost certainly have been the architect of the terrace itself.

As his title suggests, the clerk of the cheque controlled dockyard finances – another position of great responsibility. Some of his duties would have overlapped those of the clerk of the survey and the storekeeper (also housed in the terrace), to make sure they kept a check on each other.

This is how Todd Longstaffe-Gowan described the officers' tenancy:

> As officials of HM Navy each officer was assigned furnished lodgings and offices in one of the houses which formed Officers Terrace. The lodgings were spacious and austere, supplied with commodious and substantial fitments, and equipped with a sprinkling of essential furnishings and household accoutrements. By contemporary standards the living space was very generous, as the officers, their families, and their servants, which often totalled as many as sixteen inmates, occupied over four floors in the main house and additional accommodation in the outbuildings. The dockyard officers were men of the 'middling station', professional artificers and bureaucrats, all of whom had risen to their respective positions through rigorous and protracted apprenticeships. Unlike many men of their rank and income, however, they were by virtue of residing within the walls of the dockyard unable to escape the burdens of their wide-ranging responsibilities. As a consequence they had limited time, but sufficient means, to indulge in leisure pursuits, among them gardening.

An open doorway invites exploration.

It may seem surprising that busy officers like these were provided with such generous gardens on company land. But gardens were indeed a dockyard tradition. Portsmouth, Plymouth and Sheerness all had similar terraces for their officers. At Chatham, the dockyard commissioner had enjoyed a fine Italianate garden since the mid-seventeenth century, when it was admired by both Samuel Pepys and John Evelyn. Evelyn recorded his impressions in his diary after visiting Commissioner Pett in August 1663: 'He has a pretty garden and banqueting house, potts, statues, cypresses, resembling some villa about Rome.' The commissioner's garden pots were soon to become a bone of contention with the Navy, however for, in 1667 Pett was imprisoned in the Tower of London after a devastating raid by the Dutch fleet. Pett's crime was to have saved Chatham's collection of models rather than the dockyard itself. Humiliated, he wrote to Samuel Pepys complaining that his personal garden effects had been confiscated, including 'my great dial, garden pots and figures, and marble table and two brewing vessels, which are as much my own as the coat on my back'.

The gardens of Officers Terrace would have lacked Commissioner Pett's flourishes, though one at least (at number 12) had an oval pool and officers may have introduced statuary and garden ornaments that they could take with them to their next navy quarters.

With their limited time and demanding schedules, the occupants of number 7 would almost certainly have employed jobbing gardeners. As it would have been a private arrangement, paid for out of their own salaries, no documents have yet been found to confirm this. But officers were ordered 'not on any account [to] employ any workmen or labourers that belong either to the Yard or Ordinary on your private affairs, either in your Gardens, Stables, Houses, or on any other account than his Majesties service'.

It is probable, too, that the occupants of Officers Terrace were far too busy to become seriously involved in matters of garden design, especially as they would not have expected to stay in the properties for more than a decade

or two at most. Each man, his family and dependants would have brought to the terrace their own particular enjoyment, however, and all would surely have valued their gardens as a quiet haven where they could escape the pressures and close proximity of the 'bustling, noisy, smelly, company town'.

Life in the Georgian dockyard

Chatham in the eighteenth century was one of the country's principal royal dockyards. It was an enormous enterprise by the standards of the day, employing thousands of men at a time when Britain's industry was largely rural and very small scale.

In the 1770s, shipbuilding and repair were the yard's main functions – a lengthy and complicated procedure demanding the expertise of a whole range of skilled craftsmen. Chatham's most famous legacy was HMS *Victory*, Nelson's flagship at the Battle of Trafalgar and one of more than a hundred ships constructed by the dockyard between 1700 and 1815.

The Seven Years War (1757–63) was a time of particularly intense activity when Chatham produced sixteen warships and carried out hundreds of repairs. This war ranged Britain, Prussia and Hanover against Austria, France, Russia, Saxony, Sweden and Spain. A central issue concerned naval power and the struggle between Britain and France for supremacy overseas.

In fact, Chatham's heyday as a *fleet base* for the Navy lay back in the 1600s during Britain's successive wars with the Dutch. According to Jonathan Coad, 'As long as the Dutch were the chief maritime enemy, Chatham, with its sheltered and safe anchorage, remained pre-eminent among English naval bases.' But the growing power of France and attempts by English merchants to break Spains monopoly of trade with her colonies shifted the advantage to Britain's south-coast dockyards with their easier access to the Atlantic.

The once-frenetic dockyard spreads out below the neat line of Officers Terrace.

Another factor in Chatham's decline as a fleet base was its location on the narrow, winding River Medway that had been slowly silting up since at least the 1660s. Attempts to dredge the river in subsequent decades failed and were eventually abandoned. In the meantime, the development of ever-larger ships also created problems for Chatham as these could reach the yard only during the few days of the spring tides – and then only with favourable winds.

In 1773, the Earl of Sandwich (then head of the Admiralty Board) confirmed Chatham's emerging status as a building yard:

> I am now more and more convinced that if it is kept singly to its proper use as a Building Yard, possibly more useful service may be obtained from it than from any other dockyard in His Majesty's Dominions; the great extent of the yard which faces the River, and the great length of the harbour which has room to moor half the fleet of England of a moderate draught of water, are conveniences that are not to be found elsewhere … The best use to be made of this port now, is to build or repair ships sent from Portsmouth and Plymouth; therefore all improvements at this yard should be for that end, in preference to any other consideration.

So Chatham in 1774 (the year of the model) would have been a hive of activity. Though peace might be expected to bring respite to some of the dockyards, Chatham was busier than ever repairing the damage inflicted on the British fleet and building new ships. Facilities included four dry docks for cleaning and repairing ships, three building slips, forty saw pits (where timber was prepared), mast houses, boathouses, a forge, a ropery, sail yard and various storehouses.

An account of 14 January 1774 listed 2,131 officers, clerks, artificers and workmen. Nearly one-third of these were shipwrights. In addition to the skilled workers, such as caulkers (who made the ships watertight), sailmakers, ropemakers and sawyers (who prepared the timber), the yard employed a large number of unskilled labourers, such as scavelmen who cleaned out the mud from the docks. Salary books show that all members of staff were paid quarterly, so many would have had to resort to credit with local businesses to survive. The typical working day started at 6am. Hours were long and arduous and conditions often difficult, with the result that industrial relations were frequently strained. We can only imagine how much the officers whose job it was to make the dockyard run smoothly would have needed the respite their gardens provided.

The rise of city gardening

If the 1774 dockyard model and plan gave us a very clear design for the garden, we now wanted to know how this formal arrangement of terraces, beds and gravel walks fitted with changing tastes in garden design.

Eighteenth-century Britain heralded one of the great revolutions in gardening tastes that was to spread like a contagion through the grander estates of Europe and America. Before the Hanoverian George I came to the throne in 1714, formality was all the rage, with grand avenues, rigid parterres and clipped shrubs in the French and Dutch manner. As the century progressed, lines were softened and curved according to new ideas of 'Nature' and out of this transformation the landscape garden was born.

But for most of the century, these new ideas made few inroads into the city. Indeed, before about 1720, ordinary city-dwellers had very little garden space at all – just a cramped backyard housing an outdoor privy. Then, slowly, gardens like those at Chatham began to appear behind terraced houses. By the time of Rhodes' map of Kensington in 1766, many houses had small front gardens as well. In all these early city maps gardens, both front and back, were universally shown as formal in layout with paths and geometrical beds. While map makers undoubtedly employed stock conventions to represent gardens and did not attempt to survey each one individually, their designs were almost certainly taken from life. Other rare survivals of early town gardens – such as the buried Georgian garden of number 4, The Circus, Bath – confirm that they remained remarkably formal until at least the last quarter of the eighteenth century.

For an idea of how city folk viewed their gardens, we turned to the very first English book written specifically for town gardeners and amateurs – Thomas Fairchild's *The City Gardener* of 1722. A nurseryman from Hoxton, on the outskirts of London, Fairchild was a noted grower of exotics and one of the first to begin experiments in hybridization. This also gave him an uneasy conscience. To appease the wrath of his Creator for meddling with His creation, he left money in his will for the preaching of an annual sermon in praise of God's wonderful works.

Fairchild's book is a delightful celebration of the joys of gardening against the odds, which in London

included sea-coal smog; gardening in dank, dark spaces; and ignorant gardeners. The frontispiece shows two well-dressed gentlemen strolling up a broad garden walk between four tubs apparently containing an agave, a banana, a dwarf palm and a cactus. Though he gives little advice on designing individual gardens – presumably because few townsfolk had space worthy of the term – he devotes a chapter to the design of London squares provided for the enjoyment of (and paid for by) those living around the perimeter. And he admirably conveys the passion with which Londoners of all walks of life crammed every available corner and windowsill with living, growing plants:

> One may guess at the general Love my Fellow-Citizens have for Gardening, in
> the midst of their Toil and Labour, by observing how much Use they make of
> every favourable Glance of the Sun to come abroad, and of their furnishing
> their Rooms or Chambers with Basons of Flowers and Bough-pots, rather than
> not have something of a Garden before them.

The City Gardener is invaluable for its descriptions of plants able to survive the capital's sea-coal smokes. Evergreens included box, holly, privet, ivy, evergreen oak and bay. To soften the effect, he recommended flowering shrubs. Lilac, laburnum, broom, jasmine and Russian honeysuckle were all said to flower well in London, along with passion trees, apples and pears. His many suggestions for smaller perennials included thrift, white lilies, sunflowers, sweet William, campanula, everlasting sweet peas, the double rose and large numbers of annuals.

Fairchild devoted a whole chapter to plants suitable for courtyards and 'close Places in the City'. He particularly liked pots of apple trees grafted on to Paradise stocks, and miniature water gardens for city balconies with fountains, flowing streams and imported rockwork, 'or if such a Figure should not be agreeable, a Model might be made from some of the Waterworks in *Versailles* Gardens, to be fixed at Pleasure to the Water-Pipe, and changed for others if we saw convenient'.

Fairchild gave his readers sound horticultural advice: avoid buying plants forced into flower at market, but rather buy bare-rooted stock and plant out in the autumn; talk to experienced gardeners (such as the nurserymen of Hoxton) about the plants most likely to survive in the city; employ good gardeners accustomed to town rather than country conditions. Fairchild's warning against cheats and scoundrels strikes a chord today: 'There are many ignorant Pretenders, who call at Houses where they know there is any Ground, let it be in Season or out of Season, and tell the Owners it is a good Time to dress and make up their Gardens; and often impose on them that employ them, by telling them every Thing will do, when perhaps it is a wrong Season.'

Other eighteenth-century writers also gave us insights into how people cared for their gardens. Particularly useful was Philip Miller, curator of the Society of Apothecaries' physic

(above) Diagonals of lavender and santolina add a relaxed formality.

(opposite) An illustration from Thomas Fairchild's *The City Gardener* of 1722 which launched the fashion for books aimed at urban gardeners.

garden at Chelsea, who became one of the most celebrated gardeners of the century. His *Gardeners Dictionary*, first published in 1731, went through eight editions before his death in 1771, letting us track changes in taste and gardening practice between the construction of our garden and the year of the dockyard model.

For walks, Miller recommended gravel laid over a good layer of lime rubbish to destroy worms (an alternative was to water the walks with an infusion of walnut leaves). The best gravel came from Blackheath, he said, 'consisting of smooth even pebbles, which, when mixed with a due quantity of loam, will bind exceeding close, and look very beautiful'. Very white gravel could be troubling to the eyes. He advised laying the walks in March and rolling after rains and frost, to help kill weeds and moss. A 5-foot walk should rise at least an inch at the crown, to aid drainage.

For edging gravel walks, he recommended dwarf box. Although box had gone out of fashion as an edging for central flower beds and fruit borders, it was still considered necessary to keep gravel walks clean 'by keeping the earth of the borders from washing down into the walks in hard rains'.

The 1768 edition of his dictionary included a long entry on walls that stressed their value in helping to ripen delicate fruits. 'Of all material proper for building Walls for fruit trees, brick is the best,' he advised firmly. Miller also provided instructions on training fruit trees with wooden lattices of ash or fir:

> Where persons are very curious to have good fruit, they erect a trellis against their Walls, which projects about two inches from them, to which they fasten their trees; which is an excellent method, because the fruit will be at a proper distance from the Walls, so as not to be injured by them, and will have all the advantage of their heat; and by this method the Walls will not be injured by driving nails into their joints.

Another good, practical author – and one of the century's most successful – was John Abercrombie who wrote at least fifteen books on horticulture between 1767 and 1789. New editions of his most popular books continued to appear more than fifty years after his death. *Every Man His Own Gardener* was first published in 1767 (though most of the quotations here are taken from the 1782 edition), apparently written by Mr Mawe, gardener to the Duke of Leeds, 'and other gardeners'. This was simply a ruse to increase sales. Mawe's name had been added to lend greater credibility (he was indeed the Duke of Leeds' gardener). The pair later became friends and 'collaborated' on other books, to which Mawe continued to contribute little more than his name.

Written as a month-by-month calendar of gardening tasks, *Every Man His Own Gardener* constantly stressed the values of neatness and order in the garden. Digging, raking

(left) Annual planting included the brightly coloured *Clarkia*.

(opposite) Edging the formal beds were 1,500 bare-rooted plants of dwarf box.

and weeding were to be regular tasks from early spring onwards: 'Let the surface of the beds and borders be lightly and carefully loosened with a hoe, in a dry day, and let them be neatly raked, which will give an air of liveliness to the surface, and the whole will appear neat and very pleasing to the eye, and will be well worth the labour.' The sight of neat, bare earth was a source of pleasure: 'Nothing looks better in a garden, than to see the ground neat and fresh between flowering-shrubs and evergreens.' Gravel walks could happily be rolled two or three times a week – but never less than once.

Herbaceous planting, he wrote, should follow a strict hierarchy of height: 'The rule is, the taller the plant, the more backward in the border or clump it must be placed, and the shortest plant should be placed nearest the front, so as the whole may stand in a kind of theatrical order.' Perennials should be staked when necessary, for 'nothing looks better than to see all the plants standing firmly in their places, and neatly trained with straight and upright stems'. Straggling side-shoots were to be shortened, to let each plant stand on its own, for 'Flowers always appear best when they stand clear of one another'.

Symmetry and regularity were equally important for shrubs, which should be planted so that 'every plant

can be regularly viewed with distinction from the walks'. The recommended planting distance between shrubs was a generous 5 to 6 feet, and low plants 'should not be planted promiscuously among tall growing plants'. Constant training and pruning once a year were recommended so that shrubs were 'always kept somewhat regular and within due bounds'. Where shrubs were to be wall-trained, 'They must be planted close to the wall, and their branches must be regularly spread and trained to the wall in the manner of a wall-tree; they will shoot in a quick but regular manner, and their beautiful green leaves will effactually hide the most deformed or ill-looking wall.'

For box edging, Abercrombie recommended short bushy box with the long sticky roots cut off and the tops trimmed. To plant the box, he advised stretching a line along the edge, treading the soil and then digging a neat trench 6 or 8 inches deep. 'The box is to be planted in this trench close against the upright side next the line, placing the plants so near together as to form immediately a close compact edging without being too thick and clumsey, and with the top of the plants as even as possible.' After treading in the plants, 'let any unequalities of the top be cut as even and neat as possible with a pair of shears.'

(left) A splendid bouquet of June flowers from Robert Furber's nursery catalogue of the 1730s.

(opposite) *Viola tricolor*, also known as Love-in-idleness and Heartsease.

gardeners of the day used their own tools and sometimes supplied their own plants or seeds from their own gardens. Or their masters could order from the thriving nurseries that had turned London into the centre of the nursery trade: Christopher Gray at Fulham; the Brompton Park nursery near Kensington; James Gordon at Mile End; the Vineyard Nursery at Hammersmith; Loddiges of Mare Street, Hackney – all these and many more are listed in John Abercrombie's *The Gardener's Daily Assistant* of 1786. And with the dockyard's seaborne connections, is it fanciful to suppose that the garden may have found a home for some of the plants then beginning to flood in from North America?

A model of formality

Having gathered together all available evidence about our garden and horticultural practices of the time, we were now ready to plan its restoration. Although house and garden were first constructed in the 1720s, the dockyard model and plan gave us the best evidence about the garden's design and materials used. We decided, therefore, to take 1774 as the date for our restoration, which aimed to put back as accurately as possible the garden shown in the model. This would involve reinstating the three terraced levels shown in the model, with gravel paths, formal flower beds and espaliered fruit trees against the wall.

Two major changes had occurred in our garden since the model was built. First, the whole terrace had been extended backwards, adding an extra section of garden at the top. We would deal with this by erecting a trellis screen to mark the garden's original end. The second change was harder to accommodate as it concerned the steps up into the garden, which had been moved from the centre to the side.

Later editions of *Every Man His Own Gardener* listed shrubs, trees and other plants 'cultivated in most of the common nurseries in England'. These would prove invaluable for our planting plan, together with the old nursery catalogues collected by the RHS Lindley Library. A really special leather-bound catalogue of 1778 survives as *The Beauties of Flora Display'd* by Brentford gardener and seedsman Nathaniel Swinden. As well as listing the available seeds, this mapped out circles, spirals and other plans showing how the plants might be displayed to their best advantage.

We can only hope that in 1774 clerk of the cheque William Campbell (then resident at number 7) had taken all this advice to heart and made sure that his garden was kept as shipshape as the dockyard model suggests. Jobbing

To emphasize the symmetry of the Georgian garden, we decided to erect a cabin-like pergola where the original steps had been. It would need to reflect the spirit of the original without being an exact copy, as it was no longer performing the same function.

One of our main tasks would be to remove the later (largely Victorian) garden. This had added the now-derelict glasshouse and metal arbour and a Victorian rockery close to the bottom wall. The later garden had also changed the layout of paths and beds and extended the middle terrace down towards the bottom level.

As a Scheduled Ancient Monument, the dockyard enjoys special protection, which meant we had to proceed very cautiously. To undertake any work in the garden, we needed consent from the Secretary of State for Culture, Media and Sport, advised by English Heritage. As part of the consent, we were pleased to give archaeologist Lesley Howes a watching brief to inspect the site at all times and record findings of archaeological or historic interest. As well as supervising any work that involved ground disturbance, Lesley was specifically asked to oversee the dismantling of the terrace walls and any paved or hard surfaces and later garden features, such as the Victorian rockery, derelict glasshouse and metal arbour close to the entrance steps.

The need to preserve any buried archaeology naturally affected the way we approached the whole restoration. Generally the aim was to avoid disturbance wherever possible and build up rather than down. The two trees we removed (the small crab apple and the holly) were cut off at ground level and the roots left to decay in situ. English Heritage would allow no new tree planting in the garden, but we were able to plant espaliered fruit against the walls.

An initial geophysical survey had suggested that the original paths might be lying some 1.5 metres (5 feet) below

(top) The recreated pergola uses trellis to suggest a back room.

(right) Bay laurel and wall fruit await planting.

Key

Espaliers and fans
1 Apple – espalier
2 Apple – fan
3 Cherry Lapins – fan
4 Apricots – fan
5 Damsons – fan

Shrubs
6 *Vinca minor* (Lesser periwinkle)
7 *Arbutus unedo* (Strawberry tree)
8 *Buxus sempervirens* (Box)
9 *Cistus albidus/salviifolius*
10 *Cotinus coggygria* (Coconut palm)
11 *Cydonia oblonga* (Quince)
12 *Daphne mezereum*
13 *Ficus carica*
14 *Hibiscus syriacus* 'Pink Giant'
15 *Laurus nobilis* (Bay)
16 *Myrtus communis tarentium* (Common myrtle)
17 *Phlomis fruticosa* (Jerusalum sage)
18 *Prunus laurocerasus* (Cherry laurel)
19 *Prunus lusitanica*
20 *Rosa centifolia*
21 *Rosa moschata* (Common moss)
22 *Rosa eglanteria* (Sweet briar)
23 Rosa Mundi
24 *Rosa* 'Dupontii' (Snowbush rose)
25 *Rosmarinus officinale* (Rosemary)
26 *Viburnum nudum*
27 *Viburnum opulus* 'Rosea'
28 *Viburnum tinus*

Climbers
29 *Campsis radicans* (Trumpet vine)
30 *Clematis recta*
31 *Parthenocissus quinquefolia* (Virginia creeper)
32 *Passiflora caerulea* (Passion flower)
33 *Vitis vinifera* (Grape vine)

All beds bordered with
Buxus sempervirens 'Suffruticosa'

Annuals

Antirrhinum majus
Calendula officinalis
Lobelia erinus
Matthiola incana
Tagetes patula
Viola (mixed cultivars)
Zinnia elegans (mixed cultivars)

Herbaceous Mix

Acanthus mollis (Bear's Breeches)
Alcea rosea (Hollyhock)
Anemone blanda
Aquilegia vulgaris
Aster novi-belgii
Campanula persicifolia
Campanula pyramidalis
Coreopsis verticillata (Tickseed)
Delphinium grandiflorum
Digitalis purpurea (Foxglove)
Dodecatheon media
Echinacea purpurea
Eryngium plenum
Geranium maculatum
Hemerocallis flava (Daylily)
Liatris spicata (Gay feather)
Lychnis chalcedonicum
Paeonia officinale
Primula (auriculas)
Salvia officinalis
Thalictrum aquilegifolium
Thalictrum parthenium
Verbascum phoeniceum
Veronica spicata
Viola odorata (Sweet violet)

Garden plan labels: seat, steps, trellis (*Clematis integrifolia* and *Clematis viticella* 'Mary Rose' trained against trellis), herbaceous mix (see list), rose beds, terracotta pot with annuals (see list), *Lavandula angustifolia* (Old English lavender) and *Santolina chamaecyparissus* (Cotton lavender), lead-roofed pergola, terracotta pot with annuals (see list)

the surface. So our first main task was to see what Lesley might uncover, as number 7 had not been one of the gardens investigated as part of the earlier excavation.

The results were very encouraging. Lesley found remains of the original planting beds and the Georgian gravel paths mixed with clay, consistent with the descriptions of Blackheath gravel recommended by Philip Miller in his *Gardeners Dictionary* of 1731. One of her most engaging finds was a clay pipe, Georgian in origin, which brought the archaeology sharply to life. One small surprise: the terraced walls were not uncovered precisely where we expected them to be, leading us to question the scale used in the dockyard model. They were eventually discovered about a metre away, completely buried under the later garden. And the excavations uncovered stone steps that were not part of the original Georgian garden. These were recorded then removed.

Carefully watched by Lesley, the next stage was to strip off the turf and begin to remove the existing Victorian garden. This meant breaking up the low wall around the bottom terrace so that we could take the terrace back to its original position. In all, we removed more than 300 tons of spoil using a makeshift system of dumper trucks and conveyor belts to get this mass of material over the high wall at the back of the garden. We were hoping to uncover enough stone to rebuild the original steps; and we decided to salvage as many of the metal border edges as we could for reuse in the new garden. Although these were part of the Victorian garden, they may well have survived from an earlier time. In a dockyard metal would have been readily to hand and it is quite possible that metal finishings were used here before they became commonplace elsewhere.

Finding the original terrace walls was very exciting and gave us precise positions for the new ones. These we built several centimetres above the originals to help in their long-term preservation. English Heritage helped to choose the bricks for the new walls, which were to match the colour of the original outer ones. In the end, they selected a new brick (Capel Dark Multi) from the dozen or so examples we provided of both new and reclaimed bricks. Although its colour looked startlingly bright when first built, it can be softened with soot to bring it closer to the garden's existing ones. English Heritage also supervised construction techniques and the mortar used – a weak mix of soft and sharp sand, cement and lime mortar. It looks whiter than the outer walls, which had clearly been repointed in the Victorian era and ash added to the mix. Ours is closer to the Georgian original, however.

For the steps, we found enough Portland stone buried in the garden to rebuild the lower flight. For the second flight, we used the same bricks as the wall.

Next came the pergola for the bottom terrace to mark the site of the original entrance steps. The model shows a structure with a brick base and open sides. A small garden room at the back could be reached only from the sides. We couldn't use brick for the new structure, however, as the footings might disturb buried archaeology, and our structure was no longer needed to protect the steps. Our design solution was to create a wooden structure roofed in lead that would give the 'feel' of the original, with archways to indicate the garden room at the back. The structure's open latticework is Georgian rather than Victorian; an alternative would have been to use the 'Chinese Chippendale' style often favoured for garden furniture and bridgework of the time.

Once the terraces were laid out, we were able to mark out the planting beds, basing their geometry exactly on the model. Although we had expected some of the beds to be simple grass plats, a close inspection of the model proved that all were gaily planted, probably with a fairly formal mix of perennials, shrubs and annuals. Plenty of bare earth was left between the specimen plants, as recommended by Mawe and Abercrombie. The borders were edged with low plants – almost certainly the dwarf box proposed by Miller to separate borders from gravel walks.

The plants we used would all have been available to the tenants of number 7 Officers Terrace, and we excluded modern cultivars wherever possible. Round all the beds went a total of more than 1,500 dwarf box, *Buxus sempervirens* 'Suffruticosa'. Planting in the borders varied in each of the terraces. The most formal came at the bottom, with a lavender bed mixed with cotton lavender and a pair of rose beds full of lovely old varieties such as 'Rosa Mundi', the common moss rose, sweetbriar and the vigorous *Rosa* × *centifolia*. In the centre of the beds were formal box cones. A trumpet creeper (*Campsis radicans*) was planted to cover the pergola's latticework.

The middle terrace had two box-edged beds reserved largely for herbaceous perennials, planted in carefully graded heights to give the theatrical effect recommended by Mawe and Abercrombie. At the centre were standards of *Cotinus coggygria* and sun roses (*Cistus* spp.). In the top terrace, Portugal laurels (*Prunus lusitanica*) formed the centrepiece.

In the perimeter beds around the whole garden went a mixture of espaliered fruit, such as apple, damson, cherry, apricot; a grape vine; climbers including *Parthenocissus quinquefolia*; and favourite shrubs such as *Daphne mezereum* and the common myrtle. At the top went old clematis varieties supplied by clematis expert Robin Savill, including the 'rediscovered' *Clematis viticella* 'Mary Rose'. Annuals were planted later in all the beds, in small uniform clumps to fill the spaces, while still leaving sight of bare earth.

Before we could begin actual planting, we needed to lay the paths. For the base we used clay hoggin, which we overlaid with gravel. Although Blackheath gravel is no longer extracted, we managed to locate a similar seam further up the Thames. The walks were then compacted and rolled.

The final touch was a seat for the top of the garden, where William Campbell might have come to enjoy a quiet smoke at the end of a bustling day. In the model, seats are shown in this position for nine of the twelve gardens. A tenth has a covered arbour, leaving just two gardens without a feature at the end of the central path. Our new seat was made by a carpenter from the dockyard, its curved top constructed from overlapping planks, like a boat's hull.

(this page) The flaking pink, white and red strips of Rosa Mundi first mutated in sixteenth-century Norfolk.

(opposite top to bottom) Advised by English Heritage, materials were chosen to blend with the originals.

Return to order

Of all the gardens featured in the series, the transformation at Chatham was one of the most radical – from urban wasteland into the neatly regimented pattern-book garden of a naval officer, in the years before the Napoleonic Wars ushered in a new age and a new spirit. Town gardens after this would begin to lose their rigid lines, with winding paths and flower beds scattered like baskets of posies about the lawn. But Chatham's bones were laid in an earlier age that favoured the naval virtues of neatness, order, regularity. Whatever individuality the gardens possessed would have come from the officers and their families, who may well have grown their favourite plants in pots, much as Thomas Fairchild proposed when the gardens were first laid out. His favourites included French honeysuckle, pinks, daisies, double stocks, wallflowers or breeding tulips, which flowered much better, he said, than the striped tulip varieties.

Despite the absence of lawn, the garden would have needed constant attention to keep it within bounds – all the monthly tasks of clipping, rolling, weeding, pruning, as recommended by Mawe and Abercrombie. Modern tastes favour a more relaxed planting and it would be unrealistic to expect the owners of number 7 Officers Terrace to keep twenty-first century habits at bay. Gardens are living spaces, after all, not museums, but we hope today's owners will gain the same quiet enjoyment as the master shipwright and the clerk of the cheque before them. The dockyard itself may have closed but its memories live on.

(above) Order returns with neat gravel, regimented box and symmetrical planting.

(opposite top) Annuals in pots echo Thomas Fairchild's advice to early city gardeners.

(opposite left) Clerk of the cheque William Campbell may once have enjoyed his garden from an identical seat.

(opposite right) The fragrant *Rosa* 'Dupontii'.

chapter six

canalside
coventry

CLOSE TO THE MOTORWAY near Coventry lies a forgotten patch of Britain's industrial past. Now marooned among housing estates, the road to Hawkesbury Junction takes you over a humpback bridge then along a canalside lane to a pretty group of cottages and the Greyhound Inn. The area is known as Sutton Stop. The lock-keeper's cottage stands alone at the end, narrowly Victorian, beside the lock gates and a graceful horse-and-foot bridge over the canal.

In the curved brick wall beyond the house, a wooden doorway leads directly into the garden. When we first visited the site early in February, there wasn't much to see: just a rectangle of unkempt grass sloping towards a tumbledown fence and a rusting gate that opened on to rubbished land, overgrown with elder, blackberry, dead bracken and willow. The garden lay in a scooped-out hollow: to one side a brick wall that hid the embanked canal, to the other a hawthorn hedge gone wild. Up near the house were two brick outhouses that mimicked the gaunt outline of the cottage, extended with ugly sheds. Only a brick path at the top end of the garden and scattered remnants of planting (cherry, overgrown roses, forsythia, privet and a large yew stump) gave any hint that the land had once been gardened.

Canal fever

Investigating the story of the lock-keeper's cottage at Hawkesbury Junction soon took us back to the Industrial Revolution, and the great flurry of canal-building that began when the Duke of Bridgewater opened the first fully fledged canal in 1761. Local industrialists such as the Warwickshire coal barons poured money into this brand-new technology, which would solve their transport difficulties and bring them added profits at the same time. Among early investors was Richard Parrott, owner of the surrounding Hawkesbury coal mines, who had already experimented with his own small waterways at least two decades before Bridgewater.

Hawkesbury benefited from not one, but two, canals that ran side by side for several years without joining, so intense was the competition between canal-builders. First came the Coventry Canal Company, with a proposed 32-mile canal joining Coventry to the Trent and Mersey rivers. Engineering it was the famous James Brindley, engineer to the Duke of Bridgewater. Within a year, the Oxford Canal Company proposed an even more ambitious

(above) The lock at Sutton Stop, Hawkesbury Junction.

(opposite) A canal map of *c*.1790 first records both house and garden.

route of 91 miles linking Oxford to Coventry – also to be engineered by James Brindley.

Construction of the two canals began around 1770 and took twenty years. By 1777, the two had met at Hawkesbury, although (by oversight or design?), the Oxford Canal was 6 inches higher than the Coventry Canal. A lock would be needed to mark the boundary between the two companies and stop water passing from one canal to the other. As neither company was willing to forgo profits from this valuable stretch of waterway, the two canals were not finally joined for another eight years.

Canal maps give us our first sight of the lock-keeper's cottage. The earliest is an engineer's plan showing the two canals after they had reached Hawkesbury in about 1777 but before the junction was created in 1785. A toll office is marked on the Oxford Canal side – most probably the original building on our site, provided for a solitary toll clerk. No indication is given of any garden or adjoining land. The next map of *c*.1790 shows the two canals joined at Hawkesbury Junction. The office has been extended with outhouses, and a long stretch of garden land added alongside the canal. There are no other buildings close by. The embankment from the garden up to the canal is clearly shown, and the canal company is marked as owner of the horseshoe of land bordering the southern edge of the canal.

Together these two maps suggest that the extended cottage and its garden date from the 1780s, built to coincide either with the opening of Hawkesbury Junction or the final completion of both canals in 1790. Certainly from 1790, traffic increased considerably – so much so that Hawkesbury's toll collector was provided with firearms to defend himself.

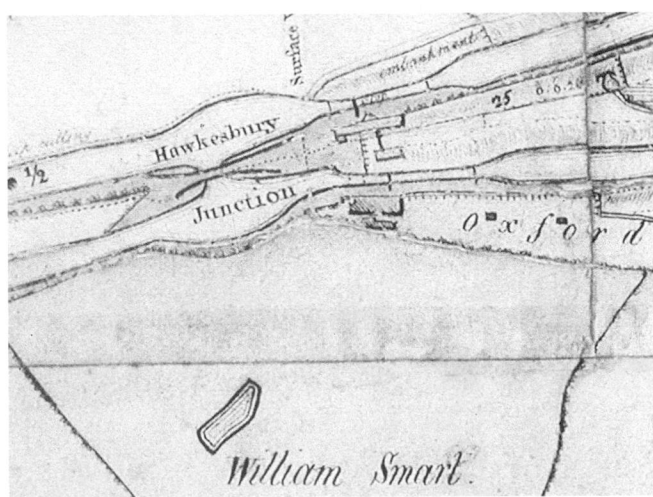

The story of the cottage and garden is taken up in ledgers of the Oxford Canal Company lodged at the Public Record Office at Kew. From April 1791 at least, John Brown was employed as Hawkesbury's lock-keeper, remaining in his post for sixteen years until Richard Sutton moved into the cottage with his wife Ann and small son Henry, sometime between October and December 1807. Sutton had been an employee of the company for ten years or so, the previous seven as stop-keeper at Stretton Wharf further along the canal.

Sutton's official title at Hawkesbury was wharfinger, and he was responsible for operating the lock and administering the company's toll charges. It was an important position and one of the few to bridge the two worlds of water and land, as it involved lending money, support and advice to the itinerant boat people as well as representing the canal company. Tolls were charged on tonnage and boatmasters were required to carry papers showing the goods they carried, their destination and the distance they were covering. Certain goods, such as those transported to help the poor, were carried free.

Despite his position of responsibility, Sutton's pay would have been low. From an employment contract of 1821, with another local canal company, we know that a lock-keeper's weekly wage amounted to some 15 shillings. A wharfinger's wages would have been only slightly higher and rent would have been charged for the cottage and garden. In 1830, rents varied from about £6 a year (for a house and quarter of an acre of land) up to £10 (for a house with half an acre). To help the family finances, cottagers grew much of their own produce and kept livestock such as pigs, hens and possibly a cow Many lock-keepers were also able to sell produce to the boat people passing through, and may have been involved in stabling the horses that were required to pull the boats.

From plans drawn up later in the century, showing the cottage before it was 'modernized', we gain a glimpse of the Suttons' way of life. The cottage served as home and office, a tradition that survives in lock-keepers' cottages today. On the

A pot of lavender adds its cottage-garden scents.

ground floor, looking out towards the canal, was a small parlour with a bay window, and a sitting room, nursery and office. Running along the back were the serving rooms: bakehouse, cellar, back kitchen, pantry and two smaller offices marked 'office sundries' and 'private office'. Stairs led up from the sitting room to one large main bedroom and two smaller ones. Outside was a good-sized stable abutting the back of the house, and a privy in its own outhouse.

Sadly none of the early maps contains any precise information about the layout of the garden, although it was clearly extensive and contained culverts and watercourses at the far end, as well as outbuildings closer to the house. Nigel Crowe in his *Book of Canals* describes the yards and outbuildings that were typically part of a lock-keeper's domain, with a wash house, vegetable store, coal store, pigsty, wooden pigeon box and hen runs. He also paints a charming picture of the gardens themselves:

> Cottage gardens had their own peculiar
> sweetness. There was no lawn, and flowers and
> vegetables were mixed together; roses and sweet
> peas grew alongside onions and cabbages. Broad
> beans, runners, caulis, kale, peas and radishes
> were cultivated. By the late nineteenth century
> everyone grew potatoes: the popular Midland
> variety was White Elephant. Apple, plum and pear
> trees were common – their gnarled remains still
> haunt derelict canalside gardens. Herbs like
> thyme, parsley, peppermint, balm and rue were in
> daily use. When time and inclination allowed, old-
> fashioned flowers such as hollyhock, love-in-the-
> mist, rosemary, sweet briar, Michaelmas daisies
> and lupins were grown.

All the while, Hawkesbury Junction was growing at a steady rate. By the mid-1830s, a rather grand establishment called 'Worthys' had turned itself from a farm into a licensed house. It would later become the Greyhound Inn. A larger toll office

had been built on the Coventry Canal, along with an engine-house to keep the correct water levels in the two canals. The Oxford Canal Company proposed a number of improvements, few of which were carried out due to lack of funds, except for replacing the wooden bridge with an elegant iron one in 1837.

Changes were also taking place within the Sutton household. The first national census was carried out in 1841. Then living in the lock-keeper's cottage were Richard Sutton, his wife Ann, son Henry (aged about thirty-six) and a girl of fifteen, Mary Smith, most probably a servant. Their neighbours included a clerk, engineer, builder, watchmaker, butcher, blacksmith and farmer – a whole community that had grown up to serve the floating population of boat people. By the time of the next census in 1851, Richard and Ann had both died (Richard in 1846, aged seventy-nine). Living at 'Canal Stop' were Henry Sutton and his wife Barbara, with four children aged five and under (Frederick, Eliza Ann, Emily and Barbara) and a servant girl of seventeen, Emma Devonport.

Henry had, in fact, been working on the canals for several decades, appointed first as assistant wharfinger to his father in 1819, aged just fourteen, and then as full wharfinger in 1842, when he worked alongside his father for another two years until Richard retired in 1844. From Henry comes much of our detailed information about the Sutton family, for he kept a petty accounts book between 1831 and 1884 – a small, battered, leather-bound notebook now in the archives of British Waterways. In it he meticulously recorded his expenses, allowing a privileged insight into the family's way of life.

Henry spent a lot of time and money buying (and presumably selling) horses, ponies and mules, which must have included working barge ponies. Expenditure is also recorded on shoeing, bridles, saddles and nosebags of hay for feeding. Spending on clothes indicates fairly refined tastes, with entries for hats, silk handkerchiefs, waistcoats, tanned breeches, shoes, boots and a gentleman's watch. Music was also important – Henry bought violin bridges and bows, as well as a keyed bugle. Other domestic items included guns and dog collars, suggesting that dogs may have been kept for hunting. Little expenditure is recorded on food, except for occasional gallons of gin and rum and some sacks of potatoes. All this supports the conclusion that the family was largely self-sufficient, growing the produce it needed and raising livestock for the table.

By the time Henry took over as wharfinger from his father in the 1840s, canals were no longer technological innovators. Their monopoly had lasted more than sixty years but now the railways offered investors a cheaper, faster method of transport. Coventry's industrial boom during the 1850s at least spared the two local canals. Hawkesbury Junction would still have been busy, though Henry Sutton would have seen a different kind of traffic from his father.

In 1862, modernization came to Hawkesbury Junction in an effort to enhance the image of canals. Many of the buildings around the junction were rebuilt or modernized, including Sutton's cottage. The disruption must have been enormous for, as working plans show, the old cottage was chopped in half (perhaps to leave the Sutton family somewhere to live during building). A new, taller, redbrick Victorian house was built on the old foundations, facing down the garden rather than out towards the canal. The resulting T-shaped house-and-cottage is shown in a charming amateur oil painting on cardboard by local boatman Arthur Atkins, donated to the British Waterways' archives. Already ivy is creeping up the new facade, while trees burst out behind the garden wall. The roof of a garden structure (possibly a glasshouse) can also be seen behind the canal wall. It was still there on the first edition 25-inch Ordnance Survey map of 1888, which also indicated the presence of trees or large shrubs in the lower garden.

Henry remained as wharfinger until he retired at the age of seventy-one. Besides his canal duties and his interest in horses, he was listed in a local trade directory for 1874 (with his son Frederick) as a coal, blue brick and tile merchant operating out of nearby Stretton Wharf. Henry noted in his petty accounts book, 'left company service 1876 after serving 57 years of service that will be 8 years ago the 1st of October next.' As the cottage went with the job, he would have left the only home he had ever known, bringing almost seventy years of continuous occupation by his family to an end. All that remained was the name, 'Sutton Stop', and the boatmen's stories about Sutton himself that we would hear from an unexpected source when filming was almost over.

Although by the 1880s most canals had been forced into steady decline by the faster, more efficient, railways both the Oxford and Coventry canals maintained a respectable trade due to the continuing vigour of Coventry's industry. The lock-keeper's cottage remained home to the Oxford Canal Company's wharfinger, its extensive garden clearly maintained, as shown in a hand-coloured map of 1904 in Warwick Record Office. For the first time, this map gave details of pathways and a square garden area close to the house.

During the 1920s and 1930s, many of Hawkesbury's collieries closed, further denting the use and revenue of the area's canals. The growth in motor transport dealt the final death blow to the waterways as a commercial carrier. After the Second World War, the canals were nationalized and individual canal companies absorbed into British Waterways. The lock-keeper's cottage remained in use as a tied cottage for waterways staff but, in the mid-1950s, the old Georgian cottage was pulled down, leaving the Victorian house as a lone reminder of busier days. In 1963, the British Waterways Board introduced a new system of annual licences, ending the wharfinger's role as a collector of tolls.

From the 1970s, the use of canals for leisure has brought a steady turnaround in their fortunes. The new lock-keeper is Steve Faulkner, who came to Sutton Stop in 1999 with his wife Darinda, a clutch of ferrets, three lurchers and dreams of self-sufficiency. As lock-keeper, he has 19 kilometres (12 miles) of canal to maintain and, like the Suttons before him, acts as the point of contact between the boaters and the people on land. Though new to gardening, the couple were keen right from the start to bring the garden back to its working origins.

(left) The original Georgian cottage and Victorian addition as painted by local boatman Arthur Atkins.

(below) Today, only the Victorian house remains.

Digging for history

The next stage in recreating the Suttons' garden was to investigate the site more thoroughly with a geophysical survey. For this, we called in Stratascan, a company that had already helped us to uncover the early Tudor garden at Shelley Hall in Suffolk. Coventry was to prove a much more difficult site. The area beyond the temporary fence was so densely covered with scrub and trees that Stratascan could survey only the area of rough grass closest to the house (about half the garden). They suggested, too, that dredgings from the canal had been dumped in the part of the garden beyond the fence – as we would ourselves discover later.

In conducting the geophysical survey, Stratascan used two complementary techniques. First the team conducted a resistivity survey, which relies on the relative inability of soils (and objects within soil) to conduct an electrical current passed through them. The degree of resistance is related to moisture content, so hard, dense features like buried walls or rock give a relatively high resistivity response. Features that retain moisture, such as ditches or back-filled ponds, give a relatively low response. The second technique used was ground-probing radar, in which a short pulse of energy is emitted into the ground and echoes return from different objects or material in the soil. This provides valuable information about depth, even in cluttered environments that normally defeat other geophysical techniques.

The initial results were encouraging, although not as conclusive as those at Shelley Hall. Both techniques picked up a strip of hard, dense material (a terrace wall or path, perhaps?) running across the garden in roughly the same place as shown on the 1904 map, and a further strip running up past the outbuildings – probably a continuation of the brick path in front of the house. Ground-probing radar (but not resistivity) had recorded a third strip running at right angles from the house, parallel with the canal. There were also two areas of debris – one running along the temporary fence and another in the upper garden. Below the cross-path

or wall there appeared to be little of interest. Resistivity alone had picked up an area of high resistance close to the canal wall (roughly the place of the garden structure shown in the 1888 Ordnance Survey map), and another down near the temporary fence.

To throw more light on what this meant for the garden, we called in independent archaeological consultant Nick Russell, who carried out a trial excavation and maintained a watching brief during filming. Instead of confirming the geophysical findings, Nick found the ground too disturbed to produce any useful evidence. The site had been repeatedly built up with building rubble and layers of ash, he said, which made the results unreliable.

Nick's first trench, dug across the apparent path or wall, revealed finds from the late eighteenth century to the mid-twentieth century, including an infilled ditch, a shallow pit containing lime mortar, a clay edging tile with the rope design popular in Victorian times, and improved soil, indicating a garden bed. But there was nothing to confirm either a path or a wall. Nick dug a further four trenches: one (unpleasantly) uncovered a sewage drain that may have

The Suttons' garden held its secrets almost till the end.

dated from the original house, while another found unbonded bricks (most probably from the twentieth century) laid as a pathway and wall. This last feature was one that had shown up on the resistivity survey. Liz Pearson of Worcester County Archaeology Service sampled deposits within one of the uncovered drains and found common garden and meadow plants and tomato seeds, most probably from the nineteenth century. Overall, the archaeologists concluded that evidence from the site gave general credence to the story revealed by documentary records, but little specific information. The site contained elements relating to successive building stages and had been used as a garden for at least some of its history – possibly more so since the later nineteenth century.

Of all the gardens examined in the series, only the lock-keeper's cottage at Coventry had by this stage thrown up no real evidence about its design or planting. Although we were confident that a garden had existed here for much of the nineteenth century and well into the twentieth, we could neither state definitely how it looked nor pinpoint its date with any certainty. We took this as a challenge, for at least it freed our hands to recreate the *idea* of a canalside garden as faithfully as we could, using documentary sources from the time and expert knowledge of historical fruit and vegetable growing.

First, we needed to choose the period of our reconstruction. Although our best information related to Henry Sutton, we decided to concentrate on his father's time at Sutton Stop – from 1807, when the family first came to the house, to Richard's death in 1846.

As the first really long-term occupant of the house, Richard Sutton would inevitably have shaped its design. His occupation of the cottage coincided, too, with the great heyday of the canals, before the railways sapped their vitality. And it covered a key transitional time in the history of gardens – through the Regency years of 1811 to 1820, the reigns of George IV and of his brother William IV ('Silly Billy'), into the dawning of the Victorian age. What made the project really exciting, for us, was its focus on the humble and everyday – the garden of a working lock-keeper, at a time when gardening writers were beginning to address the needs of simple cottagers.

From a practical point of view, Sutton would have kept a typical canalside productive garden, with livestock, fruit, vegetables and basic herbs. But the family's taste for finery would surely have added the flowers (both annuals and perennials) that made cottage gardens such a joy. Illustrations of gardens like these (not necessarily attached to canals) cropped up in the small books and pamphlets that appeared with increasing frequency throughout the nineteenth century. Even earlier was Thomas Bernard's account of a cottage and garden near Tadcaster in Yorkshire, published in 1797. The author's aim was to encourage the provision of cottages with small pieces of land to aid the labouring poor. An illustration shows a neatly thatched cottage surrounded with trees, a few bushes, rows of vegetables, beehives and a trim, quickthorn hedge. On just a quarter-acre plot, the garden was described as having 'fifteen apple-trees, one green gage, and three wine-sour plum-trees, two apricot-trees, several gooseberry and currant bushes, abundance of common vegetables, and three hives of bees; being all the apparent wealth of the possessor.'

A similar plan appeared in James Rennie's tiny manual of 1834, *The Hand-Book of Gardening in Principle and Practice*, intended as a guide for self-instruction rather than a polemic. This time the thatched cottage had simple oval flower beds in the front garden; climbing roses and honeysuckles above the front door; outhouses that included a pigsty, privy and coal- or woodshed; beehives; and an immaculate back garden for fruit and vegetables in which the crop beds were edged with flower borders and reached by simple gravel walks. These were just the kind of models we needed.

An early nineteenth-century writer who gave us even more detail was the hugely prolific John Claudius Loudon, who dashed off some sixty million words on gardening, horticulture, architecture, agriculture, cemeteries and a lot more besides, before his early death in 1843. As well as writing books, encyclopaedias, magazines and instruction manuals of all kinds, he designed parks and gardens. For our reconstruction, he was particularly fascinating because of the interest he took in small, cottage gardens and the reforming zeal with which he promoted gardening as a moral and physical force for bettering the conditions of the labouring classes.

Loudon's fat and comprehensive *Encyclopaedia of Gardening* (first edition 1822) contained a masterly summary of gardening throughout the British Isles, which he considered rather patriotically to be 'naturally and politically, more favourable to the practice of horticulture in all its branches than any other country'. About gardens in Warwickshire he noted, 'There are many neat cottage gardens in the county, especially near Coventry. The principal nursery is at Birmingham, and there are several market gardens for the commoner culinary crops near that place.'

Of Loudon's many publications, the one of greatest practical use for our reconstruction was a pamphlet he published in 1830 with extracts from his own *Gardener's Magazine*. Called *A Manual of Cottage Gardening, Husbandry, and Architecture*, it set out the cottage system and gave instructions for cultivating all the crops necessary to self-sufficiency: vegetables, salads and herbs; hops, tobacco, opium; fruit trees, shrubs and flowers; corn plants and timber trees. Several pages were devoted to manure, a subject of endless debate throughout the century. The manual also covered the rearing of livestock (cows, pigs, sheep, goats, rabbits, poultry, pigeons, bees), and described the lifestyle of cottagers, with tasks for the housewife and children. 'Where there are children,' said Loudon, 'the task of catering for firewood is generally committed to them. The mother sends them out, as soon as they can walk, to bring in sticks.' Apart from all the house wifely duties, such as making bread, brewing beer and turning mangold wurzel into sugar, wife (and children) were to be kept busy weeding: 'Hoeing, weeding, and gathering the Vegetables must be done by the wife and children; for which I shall not account, as every hour that is to spare may be devoted to some useful purpose in the garden.'

All these very practical directions were set within a moral framework: that raising vegetables, pigs, poultry and fuel should be considered the cottager's recreation, for, 'Recreation is not idleness, but a change in the kind and degree of labour or occupation'. The sense of property and comfort would in turn increase the cottager's enjoyment, 'and in every way render him a better member of society'. Politically, too, society would benefit, by attaching the cottager to his home and his country, and by keeping the household out of the workhouse

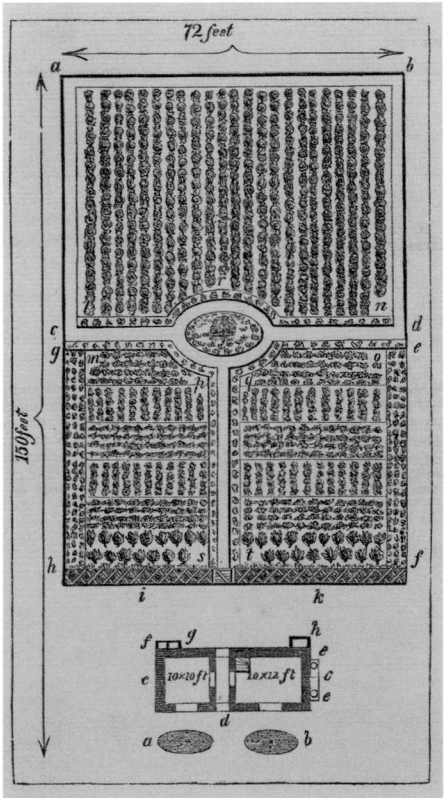

(opposite) Poppies and cornflowers in the newly seeded meadow.

(left) Vegetable-growing in the 1830s, from James Rennie's tiny handbook.

where they would be a charge to the whole community.

A working garden

We were now ready to plot our eventual design. The first decision, made as late as lunchtime on the second day of filming, was to create an upper terrace, building a low, L-shaped retaining brick wall below the top third of the garden, roughly along the line revealed by the geophysical surveys and 1904 map. There were two main paths: a brick and then grass path leading down past the outhouses, and a slightly off-centre brick path parallel to the canal, cut with brick steps where the level changed. Taking our cue from Nigel Crowe's description of canalside cottage gardens in the *Book of Canals*, there would be no lawn. Sutton would surely have been too busy to include purely ornamental grass in his working garden, and lawnmowers were not in common use until much later in the century. (Edwin Budding's patented machine went on sale in 1830. It needed two men to operate it and, despite praise from Loudon, it was not an immediate success.) Instead of a lawn, the garden would have vegetables and old-fashioned flowers, with herbs and fruit.

Flowers were almost always planted close to the house. Loudon's manual of cottage gardening

recommended 1-foot beds around the house for wall trees and flowers such as 'carnations, picotees, pinks, Brompton and ten-week stocks'. Oval beds were also popular. We chose instead to plant a mix of herbaceous and annual plants in the top two squarish beds of the terrace, giving Steve and Darinda a charming view from their cottage windows and heady scents in summer. Our choice of plants reflected favourites of the time: florists' flowers such as tulips, anemones, carnations, pinks and polyanthus; and old cottage faithfuls such as early pansies and heartsease, forget-me-nots, hollyhocks, delphiniums, campanalus, wallflowers and London pride. More herbaceous plants went in as an edging border by the vegetables and lots of annuals everywhere. Along the canal wall we planted the flowering climbers – many of them scented – so often seen in engravings of the time. Among those Loudon specifically recommended for cottages were jasmine, roses and honeysuckle; we also planted a blue passion flower and a fig tree.

We had plenty of contemporary source material to help us plan our vegetable garden. The vegetables recommended by Loudon for cottagers were potatoes, radishes, peas and beans, early Barnes cabbage,

The wild-flower meadow in the orchard bursts into colour.

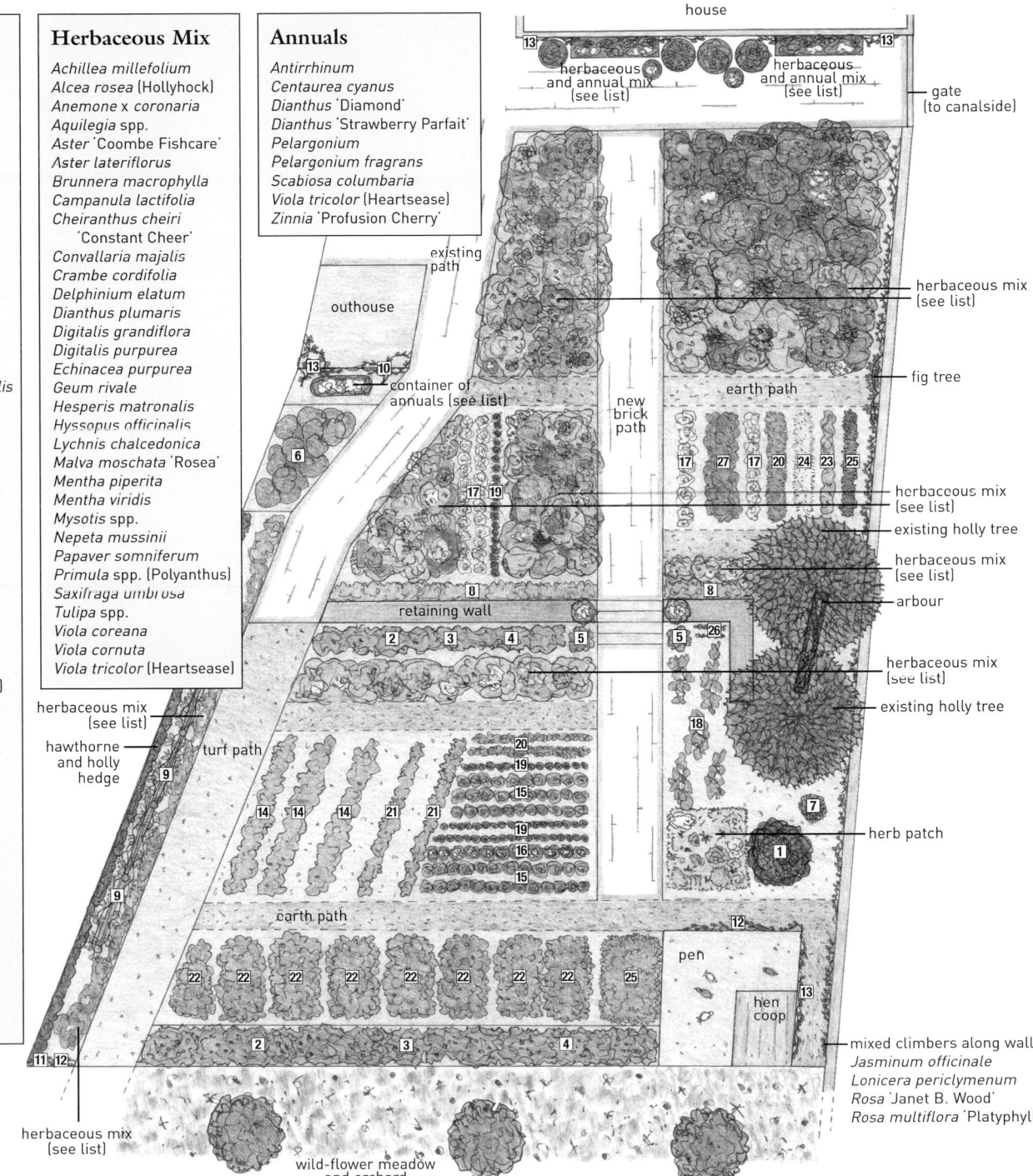

Key

Trees
1 *Mespilus germanica* (Medlar)

Fruit bushes
2 Whitecurrants
3 Red currant
4 Gooseberry

Perennials
5 *Acanthus mollis* (Bear's breeches)
6 Rhubarb 'Timperley Early'

Shrubs
7 *Laurus nobilis* (Bay)
8 *Rosmarinus officinalis* – rosemary hedge

Climbers
9 *Humulus lupulus* (Hop)
10 *Jasminum officinale*
11 *Lathyrus latifolius* (Everlasting pea)
12 *Lonicera periclymenum* (Honeysuckle)
13 *Passiflora caerulea* (Passion flower)

Vegetables
14 Broad Beans (Seeds)
15 Cabbage
16 Cauliflower
17 Lettuce
18 Marrow
19 Onion
20 Parsley
21 Peas
22 Potatoes
23 Ruby chard

Herbs
24 Fennel
25 Mint
26 Rocket

Annuals
27 *Zinnia* 'Profusion Cherry'

Herbaceous Mix

Achillea millefolium
Alcea rosea (Hollyhock)
Anemone x *coronaria*
Aquilegia spp.
Aster 'Coombe Fishcare'
Aster lateriflorus
Brunnera macrophylla
Campanula lactifolia
Cheiranthus cheiri 'Constant Cheer'
Convallaria majalis
Crambe cordifolia
Delphinium elatum
Dianthus plumaris
Digitalis grandiflora
Digitalis purpurea
Echinacea purpurea
Geum rivale
Hesperis matronalis
Hyssopus officinalis
Lychnis chalcedonica
Malva moschata 'Rosea'
Mentha piperita
Mentha viridis
Mysotis spp.
Nepeta mussinii
Papaver somniferum
Primula spp. (Polyanthus)
Saxifraga umbrosa
Tulipa spp.
Viola coreana
Viola cornuta
Viola tricolor (Heartsease)

Annuals

Antirrhinum
Centaurea cyanus
Dianthus 'Diamond'
Dianthus 'Strawberry Parfait'
Pelargonium
Pelargonium fragrans
Scabiosa columbaria
Viola tricolor (Heartsease)
Zinnia 'Profusion Cherry'

house

herbaceous and annual mix (see list)

herbaceous and annual mix (see list)

gate (to canalside)

existing path

outhouse

container of annuals (see list)

herbaceous mix (see list)

fig tree

earth path

new brick path

herbaceous mix (see list)

existing holly tree

herbaceous mix (see list)

arbour

herbaceous mix (see list)

existing holly tree

retaining wall

herbaceous mix (see list)

hawthorne and holly hedge

turf path

herb patch

earth path

pen

hen coop

herbaceous mix (see list)

wild-flower meadow and orchard

mixed climbers along wall
Jasminum officinale
Lonicera periclymenum
Rosa 'Janet B. Wood'
Rosa multiflora 'Platyphylla'

dwarf marrow peas, Windsor beans, onions, spinach, early turnip, lettuce, scarlet runners, parsnips, carrots, barley, sugarloaf cabbage, Savoy cabbage, green curled borecole, cucumbers, leeks, herbs and mercury. We planted a good number of these in neat rows – including Carlin peas which had been specifically mentioned in Sutton's petty accounts book – as well as chard, fennel, rocket, marrow and cauliflower.

Helping us find the closest matches to early vegetable varieties was Bob Sherman, head of horticulture at HDRA – the organic organization. He was able to provide some seeds from the heritage seed library. Plant breeding and selection really started in the Victorian age and it is hard to find older vegetable varieties. Nurserymen and breeders often used synonyms while the more disreputable simply borrowed names for their stock. HDRA's catalogue ('The Organic Gardening Catalogue') contains introduction dates where known, but few go back to the 1820s, so we had to take the closest we could.

Cottagers in Sutton's time were not expected to grow many pot herbs. Loudon's encyclopaedia of 1822 listed parsley, marigold (*Calendula officinalis*) and nasturtium (*Tropaeolum majus*) as the only herbs commonly found in the cottager's garden. Nasturtium leaves and flowers were frequently eaten in salads: 'they have a warm taste, like the common cress.' Once added to broths and soups, marigold flowers had long been considered 'comforters of the heart', and though little used in cooking, they kept their place in most cottage gardens. Common sweet herbs in cottage gardens were thyme, mint, sage and tansy, grown as single plants. Rhubarb was especially recommended for tarts, with or without gooseberries, and for medicinal use. Camomile was another recommended medicinal plant – and opium. 'Opium is a most important medicine as a general alleviator of pain,' said Loudon's manual of cottage gardening, 'and every cottager may produce it either from the common lettuce or the garden poppy.'

Along poles down the far side of the garden, we planted a row of hops, *Humulus lupulus*, following the advice of Loudon's manual: 'Nothing can be easier than for every cottager to grow his own hops. He may either plant a single hill, as the term is, of four plants on a surface of a square yard, to run up four poles 12 or 15ft. high; or he may plant five or six roots round an arbour; or, if his cottage has a rustic veranda, a plant may run up each column.' (Our own hops, sadly, were stunted by a cold, wet spring.) Brewing the actual beer would have been Mrs Sutton's responsibility. The instructions in Loudon's manual involved mashing malt and hot water in a washtub, boiling it with hops then fermenting with a small teacup of yeast for two or three days before storing in jars – the aim was to prove that beer could happily be made with everyday utensils. Three pints a day were

(above) Double-flowered cultivars of *Anemone coronaria* from Jane Loudon.

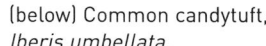

(below) Common candytuft, *Iberis umbellata*.

proposed, infinitely preferable to the 'pernicious, and expensive use of tea.'

Along the bottom of the vegetable garden, we planned a productive hedge of white and red currants and gooseberries, which fruited well in their first year. Loudon had a slightly different model for a fruiting hedge that involved grafting apples, pears, plums and cherries on to wild stock: 'The principle is to form the hedge of a double row of wildings; and when it is grown 5 or 6 years, to cut down the inner row, and graft it with the cultivated varieties of the species; apples on a crab hedge, on hawthorns, or quinces; pears on wild pears, on hawthorns, mountain ash, or service; plums on sloes, and cherries on bird cherries or geans.' If there was already a good whitethorn hedge, he recommended cutting down every third or fourth plant and grafting the rootstock with pears, apples, quinces and medlars, all

of which grow happily on the common thorn, 'the medlar more especially'. In fact we chose to plant a medlar tree in the main part of the garden, close to a patch of wild cornflower and scabious.

The lower garden we planned as an orchard, with space for twenty-one trees in three rows: a cherry, another medlar, apples and pears. Help in choosing the varieties came from several contemporary sources, including *A Guide to the Orchard and Kitchen Garden* by George Lindley (1831) and William Forsyth's *A Treatise on the Culture and Management of Fruit Trees* (seventh edition, 1824). It is extraordinary just how many different varieties of fruits were available: Lindley listed 1,400

(right, top to bottom) Adding a retaining wall involved serious digging and clearance.

(below) Poppy seed heads hold their attractions long after the flowers have gone.

varieties of apples grown in the garden of the Horticultural Society of London.

Many of these fruits had very individual histories that were still remembered and passed on. Of the apple trees we planted in Richard Sutton's garden at Coventry, we learned from Lindley that the Blenheim Pippin had been raised in a garden belonging to a baker at Old Woodstock; the Claygate Pearmain originated in a hedgerow near Thames Ditton; the Lamb Abbey Pearmain came from a kernel of the Newtown Pippin raised by Mrs Malcolm of Lamb Abbey in Kent; while the Ribston Pippin was reputedly raised from some pips brought over from Rouen in about 1688 and planted at Ribston Hall in Yorkshire. Most local of all to our garden was the Wyken Pippen. George Lindley recorded that the original tree – by then very old – was still growing in May 1827 at its native Wyken, two miles from Coventry. 'The seed, it is said, was planted by a Lord Craven, who brought it from a

fruit he had eaten on his travels from France to Holland. All the cottagers round Wyken have from two to twelve trees each of this apple in their gardens, and it is a great favourite throughout the whole county of Warwick.'

We planted several pear trees as well: 'William's Bonchrêtien' and 'Glout Morceau' were both described in admirable detail by Lindley. The latter, for instance, had skin that was 'pale dull olive green, a little inclining to yellow, and covered with numerous grey russetty specks, with russetty blotches round the stalk. *Flesh* whitish, firm, very juicy, but a little gritty at the core.' First sent to the Horticultural Society by M. Parmentier of Enghien in 1820, it was judged very beautiful and best grown against an east or south-east wall.

Our two medlar trees were of the Nottingham variety. Medlars have long been cultivated in Britain, appearing in some of the very earliest plant lists and are much valued for making preserves. Unlike apples and pears, the number of varieties available has always been small. Lindley listed just five: Blake's Large, Dutch (producing the largest fruit), Nottingham (the best quality), Stoneless ('of little merit') and Wild ('dry and worthless').

It is much easier to find old varieties of fruit trees than old varieties of vegetables. Anyone needing help or advice can turn to the Brogdale Horticultural Trust in Kent, which cares for the National Fruit Collections on behalf of the Ministry of Agriculture, Fisheries and Food. The collections include nearly 5,000 varieties of fruit and an astonishing 2,300 varieties of apples. A commercial arm has a wide range for sale; its catalogue includes introduction dates where known. Amazingly, Brogdale even managed to find for us two very rare Wyken Pippens, grown on graftwood from the national collections.

(left) Flowers and fruit of the very local Wyken Pippen apple.

(opposite) A new brick path leads past the ornamental garden towards the lower vegetables.

137

Animal farm

Next we had to think about livestock. The Suttons would almost certainly have kept a pig and some hens, possibly also a cow. In his *Book of Canals*, Nigel Crowe notes that:

> One or two pigs were kept and fed on scraps, swill and grain. Occasionally a canal worker owned a cow which was allowed to graze along the water's edge. A wooden pigeon box might be attached to a gable or convenient piece of wall. Hen runs were more temporary affairs, although canal men often took a pride in their birds: Rhode Island Reds and Light Sussex were reliable favourites. Smart-looking Leghorns, White Wyandottes (which laid pink eggs) and bow-legged, heavy-chested Indian Game were exotic extras.

For our reconstruction, we would be restricted to a dozen hens. Steve didn't want a pig, and a cow was out of the question. Loudon's manual of cottage husbandry gave valuable hints:

> Every man who keeps a pig should keep fowls. Three or four hens and a cock will prove no small addition to a poor man's stock; and a few potatoes and peelings, with the *run* of the pig's trough, which they will always keep clean, will be all they require in the summer; but to make them lay eggs, when eggs are valuable, they must be well fed with oats, barley-meal, or Indian corn; have a dry place to roost in, to shelter them from the wet weather; and be kept quite clean.

Steve's hens were given a house and a chicken run at the bottom of the productive garden, close to the canal wall. As Richard Sutton doubtless sold surplus eggs to the boat people, he would have kept many more birds than the three or four suggested by Loudon.

The loss of a pig would have been unthinkable in the nineteenth century and not just because of the pork and bacon forgone. Pigs produced that most valuable commodity for the garden – plentiful manure – and Loudon devoted several pages to its management. Cottagers were advised to construct a channel from the pigsty running into two cisterns or cesspools, to catch every last drop of manure, 'liquid as well as otherwise'. Liquid manure was especially recommended for watering early cabbages. Solid forms of manure, including rabbit-hutch cleanings, garden litter, dead leaves and animal droppings scavenged from roads and commons, were also to be collected into a pit and layered with earth to prevent the escape of gas.

There were other sources, too, of this gardener's gold. Loudon recommended separate water closets for male and female members of the household, connected by earthen pipes to the cesspools. 'The liquid manure thus gained will be of so much value to the garden, as alone, independently of cleanliness and decency, to justify the expense of two closets, and both of these *water*-closets.' An early issue of the *Cottage Gardener* gave an enterprising coachman's account of his home-made watering device: a carriage on wheels on to which he hoisted tubs sunk into his cesspools that took the drainings from his house, pigsties and cow stalls. 'I wish I could show you the fine brocoli and Brussels sprouts I am now selling to those who have gardens of their own, and are getting nothing out of them,' the coachman said proudly. 'I have made £18 in the last twelve months of its produce, besides what we have ourselves consumed.' Is this how the Suttons supplemented their income from the canals?

Making the garden

Making the lock-keeper's garden at Sutton Stop was, in many ways, more straightforward than planning it, despite the slow start while we waited for the (inconclusive) results of the site investigations.

As soon as we could get to work, the first task was a massive clearance operation – in the orchard especially, where we removed the dense scrub and a wide earth ramp leading up to a gate in the canalside wall. British Waterways staff coppiced the ragged hawthorn hedge down to the ground to help it regenerate; behind it we planted a mix of hawthorn and holly. Specialist operators were also needed to demolish and remove asbestos from the extension to the outbuildings.

Although archaeology had not confirmed the existence of terrace walling, we did find some lime mortar along the line indicated by the geophysical survey. Here we laid the footings for a new terrace wall that would divide the upper garden in two, concentrating the ornamental beds close to the house. Close to the canal wall went a rustic arbour, sheltered by the existing holly and planted with roses and jasmine. We could imagine Richard and Ann Sutton sitting here on a summer's evening – if their many labours (and all Loudon's

(opposite) Clearly happy with their surroundings, Steve's hens have quickly multiplied.

(below) Volunteers help with the massive clearance.

instructions) gave them a moment's peace. To cope with the sloping terrain, the terrace wall ended in an L-shape that sheltered a marrow bed planted also with rocket; while two statuesque *Acanthus mollis* flanked the adjacent steps.

The main paths – one slightly off centre, the other continuing past the outhouses – were surfaced with reclaimed engineering brick to match the pathway directly in front of the house. Cross-paths into the vegetable beds were made of soil, while turf was used for the far path into the orchard. Behind the productive hedge of gooseberries and currants went a simple picket fence, of the kind seen in early nineteenth-century engravings, while the gate into the orchard was planted with old-fashioned everlasting peas (*Lathyrus latifolius*).

Once the orchard was cleared, we added soil and turf removed from the top garden and brought in a horse-drawn plough. The area was then seeded to create a wild-flower meadow. Planting the fruit trees was one of the very last tasks, together with filling the troughs near the house with climbers and later annuals for a summer display. The troughs and pots had been painted specially for us by canal artist Ron Hough in the traditional 'roses and castle' style that dates from the mid-nineteenth century at least. Several authors have drawn parallels with the painted art of the Balkans and Romany art generally, although there is no evidence that Romanies took to the canals in any large numbers. Whatever the case, the boat people certainly formed a community apart.

A surprise in store

Once we had finished recreating the lock-keeper's garden, we had simply to sit back and wait for it to grow. There the story might have ended, but for a completely unexpected letter from someone who had grown up in the house and knew the garden well: Phillip Prior-Pitt, a graphic designer with a security company, now living in Nuneaton. Phillip's father had come to Sutton Stop as lock-keeper in the mid-1930s (some sixty years after Henry Sutton left) and stayed until he retired in 1962.

Here, suddenly, was our link with the past for, just like Sutton, Phillip's father (Gilbert Wallace James Prior-Pitt) bridged the two communities. He even wrote love letters for the travelling boat people. And just like Sutton, the Prior-Pitts grew vegetables, soft fruits, pears and apples – and sold them from their canalside house. In Phillip's childhood, stories still circulated about Sutton and his famous produce, and the stable he kept with the Greyhound Inn, looking after the horses that pulled the canal boats.

We learned, too, why we had been unable to uncover real evidence of Sutton's garden. Early on in the

Second World War, when Gilbert Prior-Pitt was the local ARP warden, a German bomb aimed at the power station that supplied Coventry's armaments factories breached the canal wall and 16 miles of water crashed into the lock-keeper's garden. Prior-Pitt Senior was catapulted through the open door of his house and landed with such force at the far side of the hall that his wife thought a second bomb had exploded. While the upper garden survived, there was little left of the rest.

After the Prior-Pitt family left in 1962, the garden suffered a second devastation as, from then onwards, it was used as a dumping ground for canal dredgings, completely changing its topography.

Born towards the end of the war, Phillip could remember with startling clarity the rural cottage garden of his childhood, recreated after the bomb had fallen. He even drew us a map from memory, plotting his way down the garden by reference to the trees. Though the layout was not the same as ours, there were many similarities in the planting schemes.

The garden Phillip described had a top lawn stretching right to the bridge, broken up with beds for cottage-garden flowers and a privet hedge. Trees and shrubs grew along the canalside wall, including a few that survived into the new century: forsythia, holly, lilac and an old pear tree. Just where Nick Russell had uncovered unbonded twentieth-century brick was a low brick wall, forming a terrace of sorts. Vegetables and many fruits grew in the lower garden, and wild flowers along the steep banks on either side – foxgloves, primroses, daffodils, bluebells.

Our orchard struck a particular chord. One of Phillip's strongest memories was of sitting up in the fruit trees, especially an apple tree at the end of the upper garden. It was a very old tree with forked branches

(above) The cottage garden runs riot with colour and smells in its first year.

(opposite left) Snapdragons take to their makeshift planting tub.

(opposite centre) Rose campion (*Lychnis coronaria*) adds bright stabs of colour.

and had obviously been grafted as it bore two kinds of fruit: sweet, juicy eating apples and the sourest kind of cooking ones. Was this the work of Richard Sutton or his son Henry, wharfingers of Hawkesbury Junction?

Now Steve and Darinda are carrying on the same traditions. Their summer diet consists of salads, rocket, spinach and eggs. In just a few short months, the twelve chickens have multiplied to thirty-four. The top garden is alive with the scent of honeysuckle, jasmine, lavender. Meadow grass in the orchard is more than 1 metre (3 feet) high. The informal bartering of home-grown produce may once again return to Sutton Stop.

chapter seven

tree ferns
in a hidden
cornish valley

EVEN IN MIDWINTER, the Cornish valley garden of Penjerrick, near Falmouth, was lush like Eden. Up by the rambling slate-hung house, camellias were flowering in late January. The view down across the mossy lawn embraced cordylines and spiky phormiums from New Zealand, monkey puzzles from Chile, giant-leaved rhododendrons from the Himalayas, a massive redwood from West Coast USA and in the distance, a snatch of Cornish sea.

It was the lower garden we had come to investigate, reached by a wooden footbridge over a sunken road. The way here was wilder, more unkempt, but still with a magic of its own. Up near the top of this wilderness garden was the first of a series of pools, ringed with tree ferns. Wisps of early morning mist rose from its still, black waters, which mirrored the fronds and trunks of the surrounding vegetation, upside down. The valley dripped with moisture as the sun dispersed the last traces of an unexpected frost.

(opposite) Penjerrick's springs reputedly never run dry.

(below) Constant downpours during filming turned the garden into a temperate rainforest.

The path skirted thick clumps of bamboo then dropped through twisted, moss-covered rhododendrons. Buried among the undergrowth and almost smothered by trees were the crowns of giant tree ferns, *Dicksonia antarctica*, that appeared to march down the valley towards a towering Lawson cypress. Close by was a large area of bog, and the dry bed of a stream. More pools followed, clumped with the dead winter leaves of giant gunnera and joined by a stream that fell eventually into a small cascade.

By the bottom pool, the path gave up at a wall of rhododendron scrub and circled back on the far bank, only to stall among fallen trees. On both sides of the valley, trees thrust upwards to reach the light: a mix of conifers, deciduous natives and yet more tree ferns. Closer to knee level were fleshy clumps of ginger and arum lilies (*Hedychium* and *Zantedeschia* spp.), still green despite the season.

So this was Penjerrick's wilderness garden – a wild place with a spirit all its own. Attempting a conventional restoration was out of the question – this was not a garden to tame and manicure. Yet nature over the years had blurred the edges of its design and threatened to engulf its hidden treasures. Was there a corner we could patiently reveal, unearthing its story hidden under the weight of years?

The tree ferns up by the magic pool looked promising. Though cosseted under glass in most of Britain, here they survived and multiplied out of doors. Even buried in the scrub, these ones looked massive, twisting towards the light. Had they been planted deliberately to flank the path into the wilder heart of the garden, like some exotic avenue? If so, when and by whom? There was much to discover, as well as to restore.

Peeling back time

The transformation of Penjerrick into one of Cornwall's most spectacular valley gardens can be dated from maps, starting with the detailed tithe map of 1840. This shows the house of Penjerrick set above grounds stretching down to

the sunken road. The grounds were plainly wooded, with no drives or paths marked. The area beyond the sunken road was also wooded. A path or track snaked down the valley towards the nearby farm at Tregedna. Up by the road was a single leg-of-mutton pond.

By the first 25-inch Ordnance Survey map of 1880, the house had been extended with two long glass corridors and a square glasshouse attached to the south-western end. The upper grounds were planted with a mix of conifers and deciduous trees edged with a circular walk, and the footbridge was already in place across the sunken road. But the greatest transformation had taken place in the lower valley garden that ran south-east towards the sea. The single pool had now multiplied into five: four joined by a stream along the valley bottom and a fifth lying just beyond the top pool. Two path circuits met the sunken road but did not join. One hugged the western slope of the valley, weaving among the top three ponds like an ornamental walk designed to take in the beauties of the valley. The second route (shown as wider on the map) kept to the top of the eastern slope and returned to the road along the edge of a bare field – its purpose looked practical rather than ornamental. The whole lower garden was thickly planted with a mix of deciduous trees, conifers and

bushes; and several garden structures had appeared in both the upper and lower gardens.

The garden changed little in the twenty-five years or so until the second edition 25-inch Ordnance Survey map of 1907, though most of the garden structures had gone and the path network had been simplified. This process of simplification clearly continued in the decades that followed for, by 1970, the two lower pools had disappeared completely (one has since been reclaimed), as had the eastern path circuit. The house itself had been rebuilt, with a single glasshouse detached from the house. But if the detail has gone, the bones of the ornamental landscape remain intact from its maturity in the 1880s,

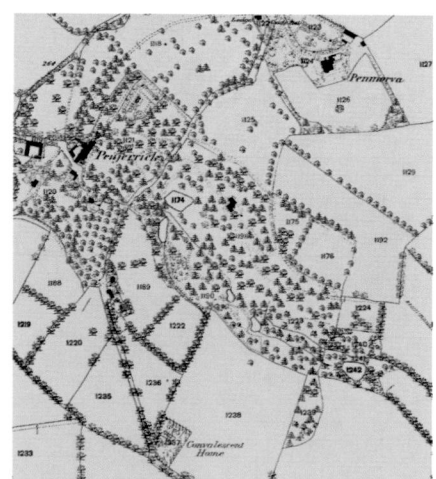

(above) An Ordnance Survey map of 1880 shows the valley garden in its prime.

(opposite) The Indian shot plant (*Canna indica*) introduces the flaming reds of subtropical South America.

and many fine trees survive from the original planting.

A Quaker family

Parish records tie the Penjerrick estate to the renowned Fox family of Falmouth – leading ship agents, Quakers and entrepreneurs. Originally from Wiltshire, the first Foxes settled in Cornwall in the mid-seventeenth century. They became Quakers soon after, when founder George Fox (no relation) came to preach in the county. As nonconformists, Quakers were persecuted in the early years and barred from universities until the 1850s. Many turned to commerce and industry as a result, driven by the moral virtues of integrity and hard work.

The Fox family's fortunes flowed initially from their ship agency business, G. C. Fox & Co., set up in Falmouth by George Croker Fox in 1762. The family's prestige grew as the company moved into mining machinery, tin mines, commercial pilchard fishing and the timber trade. Falmouth at this time was a busy, thriving port, chosen because of its deep natural harbour as the headquarters for the Royal Mail packet service that carried mail throughout the world. During the Napoleonic Wars especially, many ships docked at Falmouth rather than risk venturing further up the Channel, and brought more business to the town and the Fox ship agency. The firm's local importance meant that, for many generations, its partners were appointed consuls for overseas nations, including the newly independent America. This contact with the New World and overseas markets in turn reinforced the firm's success.

As the family businesses prospered, the Foxes started to acquire country retreats as well as their Falmouth town houses. According to Cornish garden historian the Reverend Dr Douglas Pett, at least fifteen of their gardens became famous in the last century, against which 'the reputation of others pales into insignificance'. Other Fox family gardens that are still visited today include nearby Glendurgan (now owned by the National Trust), the fine Cornish valley garden of Trebah and a delightful subtropical park in Falmouth since renamed the Fox Rosehill Garden.

From the 1770s at least, Foxes rented part of the Penjerrick estate, gradually acquiring more so that by the 1840s they owned a substantial portion of the land and properties about the main house. Three Foxes from two generations played leading roles in the transformation of Penjerrick's garden into the earliest, and quite possibly the best, of Cornwall's valley gardens: Robert Were Fox II (1789–1877); his son

Barclay Fox who died tragically young in 1855; and Barclay's elder sister, Anna Maria Fox, who outlived them all. A second sister, Caroline, also spent much of her time at Penjerrick (she died of bronchitis in 1871).

Establishing precise ownership of Penjerrick is complicated as family members owned, occupied or rented various properties on the estate. The tithe apportionment of 1844 shows Robert Were Fox and his cousin George Croker Fox III as the main landowners, both jointly and separately, with Robert's son Barclay installed at one of the farms. Robert Were's main residence at the time was in fact Rosehill in Falmouth, but he also occupied Penjerrick's main mansion and there is little doubt that the estate became the family's favoured home where they spent much of their time.

Fox family journals take up the story of the garden's early development. Keeping a journal was a good, Quaker tradition and Robert Were Fox offered all his children a guinea if they would keep one regularly. Extracts from the journals of Caroline and Barclay have since been published, but there are tantalizing gaps. Caroline's original diaries were burnt on the terrace at Penjerrick, according to instructions left in her will, and any diaries her elder sister may have kept are assumed to have suffered the same fate.

Barclay Fox

Excitingly for our story, Barclay's journal allows us to put a precise date on the garden's earliest beginnings. On Sunday 19 March 1837, he revealed his father's plan to put him in charge of the Penjerrick estate at Michaelmas. Already getting involved in the family business, he would have been just twenty years old. He wrote in his diary:

> Walked two miles before breakfast & to Pennance Point before dinner & to Penjerrick before tea. On my return from the latter my father made me the following proposition, which of course I jumped at like gold, viz. Penjerrick estate (which is now let to Uncle G. C. [George Croker Fox] at £20) together with the cottage & four fields adjacent … To come into hand at Michaelmas. This is an object which would suit me best of any I could name. The loveliness and interest attached to the spot from old associations, invest it with a charm to my mind far beyond any pecuniary advantages I can hope to reap from it.

On 29 September 1837 (Michaelmas Day) Barclay recorded his new status: 'I come today into possession of Penjerrick. Though somewhat abused it is a hopeful material to work on.' He was not to move in for another two years. Throughout the winter of 1837–38, his Penjerrick concerns centred on the farm: replacing an unsatisfactory tenant and ploughing a field for potatoes. Then, on 23 March 1838, he recorded his pleasure at spending a night there:

> By way of a change I lodged at Penjerrick, carrying with me my dinner & night shirt & mould candle. Worked hard all the afternoon. Chalked out forty-six trees for the slaughter & cut down several. Made a choice of the best saplings in the orchard of various sorts to supply their places. Worked as long as daylight lasted. Spent a truly enjoyable evening in solitary sway with books and paper beside a glorious wood fire in the inner parlour & turned into bed with a keen relish.

1839 was another key year. Barclay set up bachelor quarters at Penjerrick, cultivating the estate and engaging in small-scale farming. He received a stream of visitors. In the autumn, the house was enlarged to provide a second home for his parents and two sisters. And from June onwards, his diary charts the progress made on the valley landscape. On 24 June he records:

> A day of grand havoc at Penjerrick. The new owners, Uncle G. C. & my father, made a day of it, slashing the big trees right & left. We had 7 men with hatchets, ropes, & saws, & by evening the lawn looked like a battle field – heaped with prostrate corpses of trees. The ladies joined us … & we dined & tead on the walk in front of the house.

Tree ferns ring the mysterious waters of the upper pool.

Barclay's journals naturally embrace all facets of his life – notably his encounters, opinions, visits and travels – so we can pick up only occasional hints about Penjerrick's progress. Nevertheless the picture emerges of an estate and valley garden *consciously* planned rather than one that emerged haphazardly. 1839, for instance, was a year of tree-felling and the creation of vistas – a key feature of landscape design that added interest through manipulated views and prospects. Here is Barclay's journal entry for 5 July 1839: 'Drove my father to Penjerrick after breakfast where Uncle G. joined us & we made much progress amongst the trees in the higher "Tub Field", opening new vistas before unknown, until the womenfolk arrived with dinner.'

Then again, on 28 September: 'Penjerrick. Fresh changes & improvements have opened a beautiful vista of the meadows below. With their fringe of fine trees they are a vast additional beauty.'

The next year (1840), Barclay was busy making a 'beautiful entrance' to the property and claimed astonishing progress, having 'laid out a new entrance drive before breakfast'. The year also saw the creation of the pond – presumably the leg-of-mutton pond shown on the tithe map of the same year. On 7 December, Barclay wrote: 'Rode to Penjerrick with my father. The new pond has reached the hobbledehoy stage & is really a great set-off to the place.' They were there again on Christmas Eve: 'Met my father at Penjerrick, where the pond-scenery lit by a bright sun looked surpassingly lovely. Where the old muddy lane was, is now a beautiful glade (the hedges being thrown down) sloping to the pond, from whence 3 or 4 elms, a towering poplar, and a noble ash start up in the foreground in fine bold drawings, beyond the pond which mirrors back the tall trees bending over it.'

Attention moved on immediately to creating a rockery (Douglas Pett interprets this as rockwork around the pool) aided by deep snow, which allowed Barclay and his father to slide the rocks into place. In April 1841 came the planting of wild flowers: 'Our Grandparent & Aunt C. gave us their company at Penjerrick. We regaled on

stew & spent the afternoon in planting wild flowers. Spring is calling them forth in myriads, spangling the old borders & long-walk-hedge with a prodigality of beauty.'

But soon, Penjerrick begins to fade from the published parts of Barclay's journal as other concerns come to the fore: a failed courtship, worsening family fortunes, a tour of Italy and eventual marriage in 1844 to Jane Backhouse from a Darlington Quaker family. Journal entries become more infrequent. Ten years of happy married life followed, producing four sons and a daughter. But then Barclay's health began to fail and in 1855 he travelled to Egypt in a vain attempt to regain his strength. He died at Giza, Cairo, at the tragically early age of thirty-seven and was buried under a slab of Cornish granite sent out to mark his grave.

Robert Were Fox

If Barclay Fox can claim the designer's vision for Penjerrick, credit for much of its exotic planting must go to his father, Robert Were Fox, who occupied the mansion as his country retreat and retired there in 1872, selling Rosehill to a nephew. Already

(left) Robert Were Fox applied his science to horticulture, rearing tender exotics outdoors.

(opposite) *Canna iridiflora* was among the exotics brought back to the wilderness garden.

familiar to us from Barclay's journals, Robert Were was the most famous Fox of his generation. A distinguished scientist and Fellow of the Royal Society, he was especially renowned for his invention of the dipping needle compass, a navigational instrument that played its part in the discovery of the South Pole.

Robert Were's fame, aided by the family's shipping links and Falmouth's status as a port, meant that his household attracted many of the century's most eminent thinkers, scientists, geologists, writers, poets and philanthropists. 'Captain Fitz-Roy came to tea,' noted Caroline in her journal for 3 October 1836. 'He returned yesterday from a five years' voyage, in H.M.S. *Beagle*, of scientific research round the world, and is going to write a book. He came to see papa's dipping needle deflector, with which he was highly delighted.' Charles Darwin was one of the scientists on board and Caroline duly recorded his new theories about coral in her diary though, sadly, Darwin himself never appears.

Robert Were Fox also applied scientific experimental principles to horticulture, taking a special interest in exotics and the outdoor culture of plants considered tender in the rest of Britain. A foreign visitor to Rosehill in 1865 marvelled at his success in encouraging orange, date and lemon trees to overwinter and fruit outdoors:

Mr Fox has naturalised more than 300 exotic species; he has thus brought together the plants of Australia and New Zealand, the trees of cold countries and those of hot countries, loaded all year round with flowers and fruit; large aloes, not imprisoned in a box or under glass houses, but planted freely in the ground ... they grow as if they were at home.

The visitor was equally impressed with Mr Fox's country house at Penjerrick:

whose situation is really admirable ... In front of the house stretches out a vast lawn terminating in a clump of tall trees, cut through about the centre to offer a prospect of the distant sea. Forests of rhododendrons and camellias grow with wild profusion in the beds, from which also rise the unctuous and thorny plants of the torrid zones.

More articles in praise of Penjerrick followed in the national gardening press, presenting the garden as a kind of heaven on earth. The *Gardeners' Chronicle* was particularly seduced. In 1871 came its first report by 'HM' (identified by Douglas Pett as Henry Mills, head gardener at Enys). 'Although small in extent,' he wrote, 'it is one of those lovely spots which Nature seems to have dressed herself, to give to the beholder feelings something akin to those which man must have felt when he gazed on her loveliness in primeval days.'

The report shows how great a transformation Penjerrick had undergone since Barclay Fox, his father and Uncle George Croker had slashed the first vistas through the woods. Adjoining the house was a cave-like passage leading to an underground grotto lit by a skylight, dedicated to the culture of filmy ferns and moss. Another unheated glasshouse (presumably to the west of the house, as shown on the Ordnance Survey map) was devoted to tree ferns, some with magnificent fronds 10 feet long. Out in the grounds were choice rhododendrons (including *Rhododendron falconeri* and *R. thomsonii*); bamboos; a grand Chilean fire bush – *Embothrium coccineum* – with flowers like flaming honeysuckle (a fine example still flowers at Fox Rosehill); oleanders; an olive tree; a Japanese umbrella pine; magnolias; camellias; a beautiful Madeira fern (*Woodwardia radicans*) with fronds 8 feet long; an extraordinary collection of conifers; and many choice plants from Australia and New Zealand. Penjerrick's owner displayed all the passion of a true plantsman: 'Mr Fox receives seeds from all quarters,' the writer explained, 'and buys anything which he thinks will grow at Pengerrick [sic].'

Already the wilderness area of the lower garden had been developed as a water garden with a fine late-spring show of rhododendrons, azaleas and roses: 'Passing over a rustic bridge covered with variegated Ivy, the visitor comes amongst water-ponds, fountains, grottoes, and their accompaniments, Water Lilies, grasses, Ferns, &c., which luxuriate.' Spring began in earnest with snowdrops, then forget-me-nots. The gardener, Mr Evans, was praised for the delight he took in shrubs and ferns, along with his employer, 'and in keeping up the characteristics of the place, so as to show forth the beauties of Nature'.

Some two and a half years later, on 7 March 1874, the *Gardeners' Chronicle* ran an even more fulsome report on Robert Were Fox's Cornish retreat. Gaining entry posed the first problem, as the house crouched behind a dense shrubbery of fuchsias, lilacs and laurels that hid a small glass door. Once inside, the writer was whisked round the house by Robert Were's surviving daughter, Anna Maria, followed by a pet marmoset. The whistle-stop tour took them along a glazed passage 'brilliant with blossoming plants, Japanese porcelain vases, and the plumage of a superb peacock'. Next came the drawing room of a natural scientist, 'full of books, photographs, water-colours, microscopes &c.; and last, not least, its green, live, tree-frogs', then they came into a warm, fern-filled grotto and out into the Madagascan heat of a tropical fernery. The dining room and study were likewise full of exotic fauna – weaver birds, monkeys, green parrots and a huge white cockatoo – while another conservatory boasted fine Norfolk Island tree ferns.

But Penjerrick's real magic lay in its grounds and the report came close to defining their unique spirit – a combination of place, 'the spot is naturally lovely, but not exceptionally so'; climate; 'exquisitely cultivated taste' in landscape design; and a very Quaker stillness: 'even above all this there is a delicious mysterious genius presiding over this small paradise – a sweet influence of peace and quiet rest, perhaps the consequence of the unpretentious humility everywhere manifest, which conquers one's inmost heart.'

Just two weeks later, the *Gardeners' Chronicle* published more details about the gardens and their horticultural gems. In the upper gardens were several winding shady paths, bordered near the house with roses, geraniums, verbenas and pampas grass. The trees mixed glorious natives with hardy palms, Australian blue gum, Spanish chestnut and Californian sequoia, underplanted with camellias, veronicas, azaleas, rhododendrons and foreign ferns. A full column was devoted to Penjerrick's magnificent conifers, including the mammoth Wellingtonia, introduced in quantity to Britain by Cornish plant hunter, William Lobb (he named the tree after the 'Wellington' mine, not the Iron Duke).

The wilderness garden across the bridge was also visited:

and here we follow the course of a limpid brook, which, by skilful direction, meanders through the grounds, taking its rise from a romantic pool, bordered with thickets of Osmunda regalis and Hydrangeas, whose brilliant blossoms of pink and azure are doubled by reflection. A few yards lower down are more basins, with artificial fountains and various kinds of Water Lily, whilst from the lower of these reservoirs the stream dashes in a tiny cascade close by a miniature Swiss chalet. Near to this is a perfect collection of all the Cornish Heaths, including the beautiful

Erica vagans, and an open air fernery, including not only every known English Fern, but many acclimatised species from Madeira, France, and Italy, but all growing in unrestrained luxuriance, as though in their native country.

Robert Were Fox died on 25 July 1877. Obituaries made much of his scientific achievements, Christian character and philanthropy but found space, too, to comment on the 'vista of lovely exotic vegetation' he had created at Penjerrick, with its views down to the sea where his grandfather had seen the massed invasion fleets of France and Spain. 'Few places come nearer to the ideal of a terrestrial paradise,' noted one obituary, '… the plants and shrubs and many exotics, each with its own particular history – the luxuriousness of the vegetation – all in such poetic harmony and repose.'

Anna Maria and after

Penjerrick then passed to Robert's surving daughter Anna Maria and, after her death (in 1897), to Barclay's eldest son, Robert. As singular as the rest of her clan, Anna Maria shared her father's taste for science and philanthropy and (aged just seventeen) co-founded the Cornwall Polytechnic Society (it soon added 'Royal' to its title) to help promote education, art, science, commerce and manufacturing among the underprivileged. The society held annual exhibitions and awarded prizes for essays and new inventions; its artistic ambitions were attributed to Anna Maria, an 'Artist of no mean order'.

She inherited the family passion for horticulture in equal measure. In her hands, Penjerrick's fine gardens entered the third phase of their development. Samuel Smith was appointed head gardener and began planting and hybridizing rhododendrons, for which Penjerrick later acquired fame.

Anna Maria's tastes in gardening tended towards the wild and the natural. She filled the gardens with monkeys and cockatoos and believed (like her father) that art in gardening should never disfigure nature with shams. Two articles published a year or so after her death recorded her achievements. In the *Garden* of 21 January 1899, F. W. Meyer praised her love of simplicity. The house itself was almost hidden by flowering climbers that included *Solanum jasminoides*, Banksian roses, jasmine and *Clematis montana*. From the windows of the house stretched an apparently unbroken lawn – it is, in fact, traversed by a public road – with charming vistas to the sea. Planting in the upper grounds included a fine *Magnolia grandiflora*, a copper beech and rare Himalayan rhododendrons, among them *Rhododendron roylei*. 'Four ponds and delightful woods studded with Daffodils and a profusion of wild flowers still further enhance these charming grounds, which are undoubtedly among the fairest spots in the naturally attractive county of Cornwall.'

In the same year, the *Cornish Magazine* likened Penjerrick to three other iconic gardens created by writer-poets and lovers of nature: American Henry David Thoreau's Walden, Gilbert

(above) Even after rain, Penjerrick casts its spell.

(top) Scarlet-flowered *Mitraria coccinea* came to Britain from Chile and Argentina.

(opposite) The sea can still be glimpsed today from Penjerrick's top lawn, seen here in the *Gardeners' Chronicle* of 1874.

White's garden at Selborne and William Wordsworth's at Rydal Mount in the Lake District. The attraction was the same: 'Nature enriched and beautified by association with the pure and the beautiful in the human soul.'

Writer Fred Hamilton Davey drew attention to the garden's constant surprises that came from varied planting and paths that twisted and turned 'like true Cornish lanes'. Aisles flanked by dense cypresses and formal monkey puzzles alternated with Chinese palms and gorgeously scented shrubs. 'Plants which are the glory of the equatorial belt here attain the status of giants; others which obstinately refuse to lay on colour in neighbouring gardens become in their season rich sheets and cascades of bloom.'

Like her father, Anna Maria loved conifers, which thrived in the valley's microclimate. And she dearly loved the lower wilderness garden where:

> the wizardry and abandon of Nature are felt to
> their full. What you see is a wild woodland
> garden of a kind enchantingly and indescribably
> romantic. Cunningly imitated fragments of
> primeval forests alternate with leafy corridors and
> hedgerows; great billows of rhododendrons,
> laurels, and bamboos sweep away on all sides,
> and afford ample shelter to less hardy plants …

Penjerrick's story in the twentieth century echoes that of many other great Cornish gardens. The century began promisingly enough. Barclay's son, Robert Barclay II, was a passionate grower of rhododendrons and the gardener (still Samuel Smith) continued to raise several new varieties. Indeed, during the First World War, rhododendron fanatic J. G. Millais singled out Penjerrick as England's rhododendron garden par excellence, commending its perfect soil,

(left) Giant buds of *Gunnera manicata* begin to unfurl.

(opposite) Penjerrick once boasted fronds of *Woodwardia radicans* 2.5 metres (8 feet) in length.

shaded position and ever-present moisture. But then rising labour costs and storm damage took their toll.

In the 1930s, the estate passed to the father of the present owner, Rachel Morin. The original house was rebuilt and is now divided into flats. Following the great Fox family tradition, the gardens are open to the public on three afternoons a week from spring through to autumn and, though the garden has lost much of its definition, the old spirit survives. Visitors still come for the trees. The *Cornish Garden* of 1982 quoted comments from tree expert Alan Mitchell to the owner:

> *Podocarpus salignus* biggest tree known of its kind; *Thuja plicata* probably from original seed brought by William Lobb to Penjerrick in 1853; *Thujopsis dolabrata*, tallest ever recorded; *Fagus sylvatica* 'Pendula' – easily the tallest, biggest and finest of its kind in Britain. No other specimen is comparable.

Penjerrick's special spell

Even making allowances for the florid style of much nineteenth-century gardening writing, Penjerrick in its prime exerted very strong magic indeed. The character and passions of the Fox family undoubtedly contributed to the garden's rare spirit. Artistic vision plus a passion for the *science* of gardening meant that they pushed against the boundaries of what was possible, extending the range of plants grown without sacrificing the garden's overall design. As Davey commented in his elegiac appreciation of Anna Maria's contribution, 'Ideas rather than objects have been planted at Penjerrick, and as a result the place is nowhere marred by tame uniformity.'

The family's Quaker values were also much in evidence, celebrating the wonders of God's creation from the simplest wild flower to the most flamboyant species from the furthest corners of the world. Gardening and especially the introduction of new plant species had long been Quaker tradi-

tions. More than a century before Robert Were Fox, the North American trade in seeds and plants was conducted largely by Quakers such as Peter Collinson, English cloth merchant and naturalist, and his North American agent, Pennsylvanian farmer John Bartram.

Climate and topography played a part, too, as Penjerrick enjoys all the natural advantages of a Cornish valley garden. These gardens are mostly found on Cornwall's favoured southern coast between the Helford Estuary and Fowey. A combination of acid loam, high rainfall and a relatively equable climate have turned them into havens for temperate plants from around the world, much favoured for experiments in growing exotics outdoors. Spring starts early and winters late in Cornwall and while summer temperatures are not especially hot, the growing season is long and light levels high for Britain. The valleys are not frost-free, however, and Cornish gales demand the creation of shelter belts around their sides.

Plant hunters at Penjerrick

Penjerrick's role in the history of plant introductions gave added excitement to our planned restoration. The mid- to late nineteenth-century years saw the great expansion of plant-collecting, as the Victorians raided the globe for bigger, better, brighter specimens. Fanning the enthusiasm were displays and celebrations like the Great Exhibition of

1851, where Robert Were Fox exhibited his dipping needle compass and lofty glasshouses were transformed into exotic landscapes.

Private enterprise had a part to play, too, especially the famous West Country Veitch nursery at Killerton and then Exeter (the Chelsea branch came later). The history of this great dynasty of nurserymen is told in the privately printed *Hortus Veitchii* by James H. Veitch (1906), illustrated with photogravure plates of the nursery's finest plants and trees.

From its earliest days, the nursery had sent out plant hunters charged with introducing new plants directly to the Exeter nursery. Two Cornish brothers – William and Thomas Lobb – were among the most successful. Thomas had worked in the nursery from a young age, but brother William was the first to travel, sailing from Falmouth to Rio de Janeiro in 1840. He travelled extensively throughout South America on two collecting tours, visiting Argentina, Brazil, Chile, Peru, Ecuador and southern Columbia. He later travelled to California and is credited with introducing the giant Wellingtonia (*Sequoiadendron giganteum*) to Britain in commercial quantities. Many of his introductions found their way to Penjerrick, including the Chilean fire bush (*Embothrium coccineum*); *Fitzroya patagonica* (now *F. cupressoides*); and the lantern tree from Chile, now known as *Crinodendron hookerianum*.

Brother Thomas was equally successful, travelling extensively in South-East Asia. His finds included pitcher plants, tropical rhododendrons, orchids, many hothouse plants and the giant lily from the borders of Nepal, *Cardiocrinum giganteum*.

Another plant collector whose travels had an influence on Penjerrick was botanist Sir Joseph Hooker, who was appointed Director of the Royal Botanic Gardens, Kew, in 1865, succeeding his father, Sir William Jackson Hooker. The younger Hooker had sailed to the Antarctic with explorer Sir James Clark Ross (who used Robert Were Fox's dipping needle compass in his search for the South Pole). In 1847, he set off for the Himalayas, returning several years

Brought back from the Himalayas by Sir Joseph Hooker, *Rhododendron wallichii* will once again flower at Penjerrick.

later with nearly 7,000 plant specimens. Hooker senior had already begun to publish some of his drawings and plant descriptions. Especially influential in Britain was the massive folio volume, *The Rhododendrons of Sikkim-Himalaya* (1849–51). Again, many of Hooker's introductions found their way to Penjerrick. As J. G. Millais confirms, 'Penjerrick was one of the first places to receive the seeds and young plants of Himalayan Rhododendrons, and all the first species sent home by Sir Joseph Hooker are represented by huge bushes or small trees.'

We know that Robert Were Fox was in touch with Sir William Hooker. In 1856, after a visit to Kew, he wrote to him suggesting that many of Kew's hardier plants grown under glass 'might live in the open air in my garden near Falmouth, which is very sheltered', and he respectfully requested some cuttings with which to experiment. Sadly the archives at Kew contain no letter in response, nor any list of cuttings sent.

The tree fern puzzle

We had one final mystery to solve: who planted the tree ferns that drew our attention when we first visited the wilderness garden? On closer inspection, they did indeed appear to form a rudimentary avenue, though depleted and twisted out of shape as individual specimens struggled against competing vegetation. Their size suggested to botanist Dr Chris Page that they might be among the oldest tree ferns growing out of doors in Britain – an intriguing possibility.

The species of tree fern was confirmed as *Dicksonia antarctica*, a genus named after British botanist James Dickson. The RHS *Dictionary of Gardening* (1956) dates its introduction into Britain as 1786, some fifty years before it was introduced into the glasshouses of the Royal Botanic Gardens at Kew.

The popularity of tree ferns grew with the Victorian fern craze and, by the 1850s and 1860s, specialist nurseries, such as Veitch's in Chelsea and William Bull's on the King's Road,

The tree fern avenue begins to emerge from the dense undergrowth.

were offering specimens for sale as greenhouse plants. E. J. Lowe's eight-volume *British and Exotic Ferns* (1856–60) reported particularly fine specimens of *Dicksonia antarctica* at Chatsworth, Wentworth, Kew and Crystal Palace. One fern at Wentworth had fifty-six fronds up to 3.5 metres (11 feet) in length. Although classifying virtually all *Dicksonias* as greenhouse or stove plants, Lowe hinted that *D. antarctica* 'might live in the open air in the west of England'. Did this perhaps encourage keen gardeners in Cornwall to bring their tree ferns out of their conservatories?

The 1871 *Gardeners' Chronicle* article about Penjerrick suggests that Robert Were Fox had indeed experimented with growing tree ferns outdoors but had not initially been successful. Although magnificent tree ferns from Australia and New Zealand were admired in an unheated glasshouse, there were none in the grounds. 'Mr Fox plants many things that any one situated a few miles distant would not think of doing,' explained the author. 'The severe winter of 1860–1, and those since that date, have, however, made sad havoc amongst the Palms and Tree Ferns, &c., which might previously have been seen. Of Palms, Chamaerops excelsa is still there, apparently not at all hurt.'

A scientific paper of 1863 listing tender plants growing outdoors at Penjerrick and two other gardens (Grove Hill and Tresco, on the Scilly Isles) made no mention of *Dicksonias*. Nor did the 1874 article on Penjerrick in the *Gardeners' Chronicle*, although Norfolk Island tree ferns were growing well in a conservatory. Down in the wilderness garden, an open-air fernery was planted with ferns from Madeira, France and Italy, 'all growing in unrestrained luxuriance'. At least one *Dicksonia* – *D. culcita* – did come from Madeira, but the author would surely have used the Latin name, as he did for other special trees and shrubs. As late as 1871, in his book *The Subtropical Garden,* garden writer William Robinson assumed that tree ferns such as *Dicksonia antarctica* might be placed outdoors from the middle of May to the beginning of October – and then only in the sheltered shady dells of warmer and milder districts.

The first definite sighting of an outdoor *Dicksonia* in Cornwall came in December 1889 in another *Gardeners' Chronicle* article, entitled 'Cornish Gardens and their lessons'. This airily claimed that *Dicksonias* flourished exceedingly well in Cornwall's mild climate, and that 'D. antarctica has grown for twenty years out of doors', taking us back to a date of *c*.1870 and Robert Were's time at Penjerrick. *Where* in Cornwall the *Dicksonias* flourished is not specified, although Penjerrick is a strong contender as it is one of the gardens most frequently quoted in the article.

At least we can be certain that by the turn of the century *Dicksonias* were well established at Penjerrick. In 1897, an investigation by Fred Hamilton Davey into the acclimatization of exotics reported that Penjerrick was one of four Cornish gardens happily growing *D. antarctica* in all conditions (the others were Trelissick, Menabilly and Heligan). At Rosehill they survived the severest winters with slight protection, so even in Cornwall they stood on the margins of hardiness. Penjerrick's success was confirmed the following year, again by the *Gardeners' Chronicle*: 'In shady nooks were big Dicksonias,' ran a report of 3 December, 'and forming a turf about them, Selaginella Kraussiana (denticulata) was as happy as a Hypnum.'

It seems most likely that the tree fern avenue in the wilderness garden was planted in the late 1870s or 1880s, most probably by Anna Maria as her father was eighty-nine when he died in 1877 and suffered failing health in his final years. The tree ferns themselves could be older than this, having started life under glass.

Where the Foxes obtained their tree ferns is a matter for speculation. The Cornish nursery firm of Treseder has been suggested as one possibility (one of the family went out to live in New Zealand at the end of the nineteenth century). Or might the Fox's shipping connections have given them access to tree-fern trunks transported cheaply as ballast during the dormant season, when they would need no attention?

Taming the jungle

We were now ready to plan our restoration. As we had expected, we decided to concentrate on the area of lost tree ferns that stretched from the black waters of the magic pool down to the Lawson cypress, and behind to the dry stream. Our aim was to strip the area back to reveal the tree ferns in their original state and replant with woodland plants and exotics available before 1880, when the original tree ferns may have been planted here.

Guiding our restoration was a diocesan map in the owner's possession. Although undated, it was the only one we had seen that showed the two streams running in parallel. It also revealed an island in the upper pond that had since disappeared under the weight of tree ferns and encroaching undergrowth. Investigating the island, and getting the dry stream to flow with water again, became part of the plan.

(opposite top) *Trachycarpus fortunei.*

(opposite bottom) *Dicksonia antarctica.*

(below) Cleared vegetation is chipped and used as mulch.

TREE FERNS IN A HIDDEN CORNISH VALLEY

159

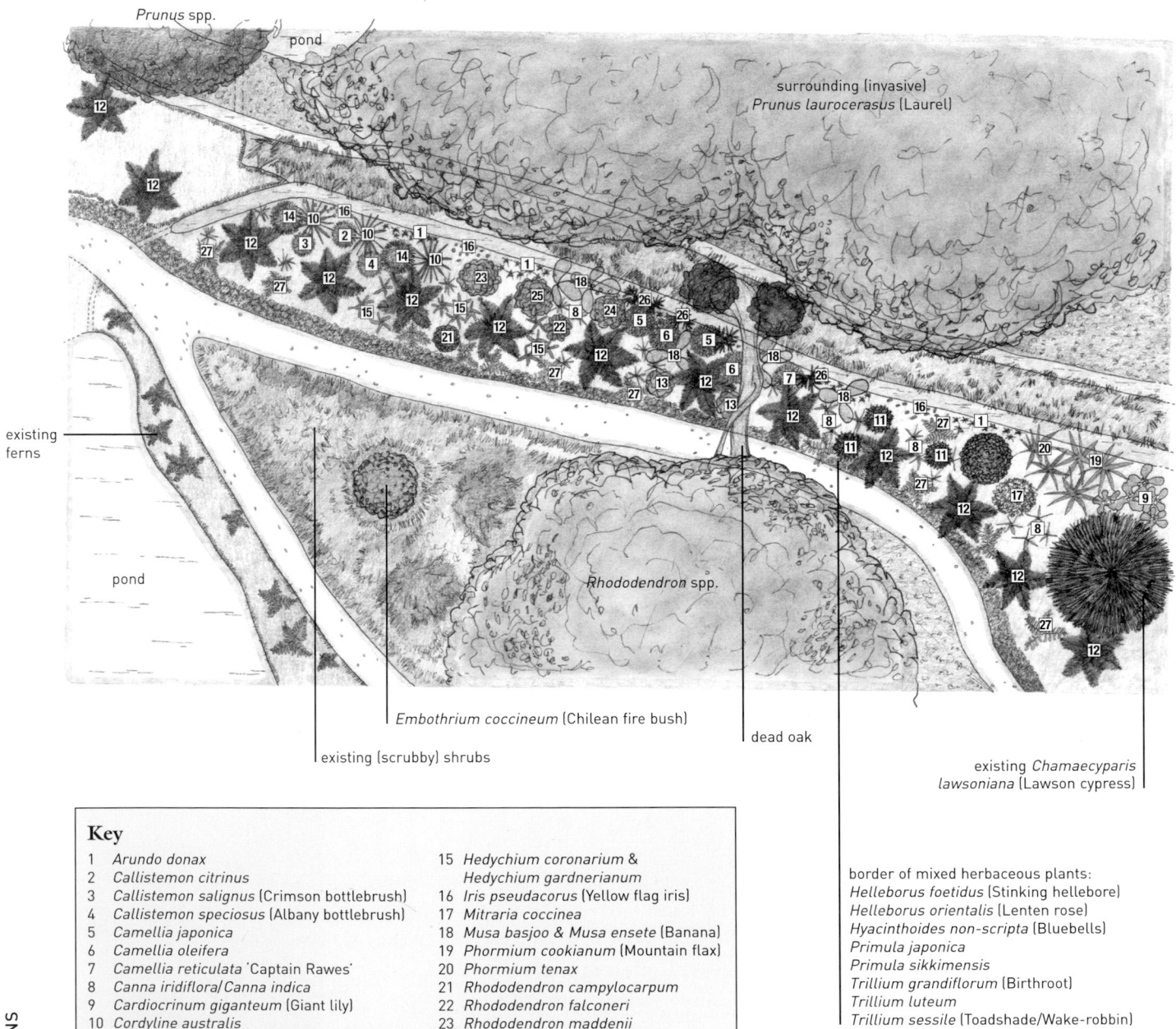

Prunus spp.

pond

surrounding (invasive)
Prunus laurocerasus (Laurel)

existing
ferns

pond

Rhododendron spp.

Embothrium coccineum (Chilean fire bush)

dead oak

existing (scrubby) shrubs

existing *Chamaecyparis
lawsoniana* (Lawson cypress)

Key

1   *Arundo donax*
2   *Callistemon citrinus*
3   *Callistemon salignus* (Crimson bottlebrush)
4   *Callistemon speciosus* (Albany bottlebrush)
5   *Camellia japonica*
6   *Camellia oleifera*
7   *Camellia reticulata* 'Captain Rawes'
8   *Canna iridiflora/Canna indica*
9   *Cardiocrinum giganteum* (Giant lily)
10 *Cordyline australis*
    (New Zealand cabbage palm)
11 *Desfontaina spinosa*
12 *Dicksonia antarctica* (Tree fern)
13 *Eriobotrya japonica* (Loquat)
14 *Grevillea rosmarinifolia*

15 *Hedychium coronarium* &
    Hedychium gardnerianum
16 *Iris pseudacorus* (Yellow flag iris)
17 *Mitraria coccinea*
18 *Musa basjoo* & *Musa ensete* (Banana)
19 *Phormium cookianum* (Mountain flax)
20 *Phormium tenax*
21 *Rhododendron campylocarpum*
22 *Rhododendron falconeri*
23 *Rhododendron maddenii*
24 *Rhododendron thomsonii*
25 *Rhododendron wallichii*
26 *Trachycarpus fortunei*
    (Chusan palm)
27 *Woodwardia radicans* (Chain fern)

border of mixed herbaceous plants:
Helleborus foetidus (Stinking hellebore)
Helleborus orientalis (Lenten rose)
Hyacinthoides non-scripta (Bluebells)
Primula japonica
Primula sikkimensis
Trillium grandiflorum (Birthroot)
Trillium luteum
Trillium sessile (Toadshade/Wake-robbin)

In a fairly straightforward restoration, the toughest job by far was clearing away the rhododendrons that had crept over the stream, along with thoroughly invasive bamboo. This we strimmed then grubbed out using hand tools only: rotivating the soil would simply have spread the problem further. All material removed was chipped and laid on paths elsewhere in the garden. Clearance work like this can look brutal at first, but is necessary for a garden's long-term survival. The real problem for us during the week was the weather: endless rain that turned the site into a bog.

As we stripped away all the undergrowth, the tree ferns began to emerge in a formal line flanking the path. A little bowed by the vegetation that had crowded about them, they were majestic specimens none the less and their impressive height of some 4.5 to 6 metres (15 to 20 feet) confirmed their age. But two of the original thirteen tree ferns were missing and one was dead, smothered by a nearby *Prunus*. As part of the clearance, we felled two ash trees and lifted the crown of the *Prunus* to let in more light. We also gained consent to the felling of the Lawson cypress, which would not have been part of the original plan but the owner decided in the end that she wanted to keep the tree and we naturally respected her wishes.

Cutting back the ivy from the surviving tree ferns was a delicate operation that had to be done by hand. For some trees we used ladders and for others, massively heavy 'cherry-picker' machinery that needed fifteen pairs of hands to remove it again from the garden when we had finished with it.

We replaced the two missing tree ferns with specimens of a similar size to the surviving ones. For the dead tree fern, our landscaper experimented with grafting a younger head on to the old trunk. Tree ferns don't root like other plants: their roots are packed around the trunk, which contains a central core of leaf bases and a vascular stem. If the old trunk

(left) Many choice rhododendrons survive in Penjerrick's wilderness.

(right) The landscape team prepares to reveal the tree fern island.

could be kept damp, then a living crown had a chance to survive.

To create the graft, we first removed the dead trunk from the ground, cutting off the top to make it level. It was then soaked for several hours in the pool to draw in as much water as possible and reinstated in its original position. Using a wooden dowel and metal pins we then grafted the new, younger tree fern on top. To keep the trunk as moist as possible we joined the base to a system of French drains we were creating for the path. These drains were made from landscape fabric stretched across the path then wound around a strip of granite chippings laid in a trench to one side. By running a lateral drain to the base of the grafted tree fern, we hoped to keep the trunk perpetually damp. Fed by springs, the pools at

Penjerrick are said never to run dry so we could only hope for plenty of rainfall until the graft was successful.

For the surface of the path, we used a tiny white shingle extracted under licence from nearby Gunwalloe Beach. Only small amounts of the shingle are taken each year, to aid its preservation. Its whiteness was startling in the primeval shade of the wilderness garden.

Coaxing water to flow down the dry stream was another exhilarating moment in the process of renovation and renewal. While clearing the stream we removed mountains of peaty debris and heaped them on the banks where they would eventually form valuable mulch. We also uncovered the original clay pipe that had fed the stream from the upper pool. Once unblocked and cleaned, it proved to be in good working order.

Clearing away the undergrowth from the tree-fern island in the pool was a much tougher task. As the bamboo growing on the bank was virtually impenetrable, we reached the island by wading across the pool and clearing away the undergrowth with hand tools. With more light, the understorey has a better chance of survival.

The rain continued all week, drowning the site so that wherever we walked our boot marks filled with water. Planting was out of the question – we would have to wait until the soil had dried out more. Although frustrating for the team, the garden's long-term regeneration was more important. Students from the Duchy College would return with members of the landscape team when conditions allowed. So when we left the site at the end of the week, it was with the feeling of a job only half-completed.

Paradise found

Revisiting one of our lost gardens after an interval of weeks or months is always a shock but here the transformation was subtly reversed. Instead of turning brambly jungle into pattern-book Arcadia, we had tried at Penjerrick to breathe new life back into the original jungle.

Ultimately our aim was to echo the glorious descriptions of the garden in the 1870s and 1880s: Robert Were Fox's collection of fine exotics mixed with Anna Maria's wild woodland garden and fragments of primeval forest. Inevitably it will take a season

(top) *Phormium cookianum* was introduced to Britain from New Zealand.

(left) From Australia came the crimson bottlebrush, *Callistemon citrinus*.

(opposite) A path of local white pebbles leads down past the majestic avenue of tree ferns.

or more for nature to soften and reclaim the new garden's rawness, but Penjerrick's remarkable spirit lives on.

The new planting in the strip between the path and the stream forms an understorey beneath the canopy of fern fronds. It offers an eclectic mix of woodland and herbaceous plants; bulbs; unusual shrubs introduced by plant hunters such as William Lobb, Sir Joseph Hooker and Sir Joseph Banks (who travelled around the world with Cook in the *Endeavour*); and other exotics featured in contemporary articles about Penjerrick.

At the back, closest to the stream, are several rhododendrons brought back by Hooker from the Himalayas, including *Rhododendron falconeri* with its huge creamy yellow bell-shaped flowers, the lilac-flowered *R. wallichii* and the blood-red *R. thomsonii*. Lobb is represented by the holly-like *Desfontainea spinosa* and *Mitraria coccinea* from his Chilean travels. Introductions by Sir Joseph Banks come in from Australia and New Zealand: the spiky bottlebrush, *Callistemon salignus* and *C. citrinus*; and striking clumps of New Zealand flax, *Phormium tenax*. Other exotics and plants known to have flourished at Penjerrick or in Fox family gardens include bananas from Japan and Ethiopia (*Musa basjoo, M. ensete*), *Camellia japonica, Cordyline australis, Grevillea rosmarinifolia*, and the architectural *Eriobotrya japonica* from China and Japan.

Spring will see the flowering of the many woodland species planted as the bottom layer in the planting scheme: hellebores, bluebells, primulas and the wood lilies from North America, including *Trillium grandiflorum* and *T. luteum*. Summer brings into flower the lily, *Cardiocrinum giganteum*, the tender ginger lilies (*Hedychium* spp) that thrive in Penjerrick's extraordinary microclimate), and scarlet bursts of the Indian shot plant, *Canna iridiflora*.

All you need is a little imagination to add Anna Maria's weaver birds, monkeys, parrots and her huge white cockatoo.

chapter eight

scottish arts and crafts

HE FIRST SIGHT of Dunira was both awe-inspiring and undeniably sad. Just past the village of Comrie, on the main road west from Perth, an avenue of trees led up to the main house tucked in below the hill. The track then skirted the cluster of farm buildings and estate cottages before swinging round at a clump of rhododendrons. Here the ground opened out before the ruins of an earlier mansion. One small wing looked inhabited. The rest was reduced to a roofless ruin, its great blank windows revealing glimpses of bare hillside and darkening sky.

The old house had been built on a levelled bluff looking south and west along the valley. At the south front, the ground dropped to a ragged, rectangular terrace that ended in a balustraded wall with a view down across wildly overgrown yews and conifers. The ground to the west of the house looked more promising: a series of terraces sliced into the bluff, all held together with steps and retaining walls of black stone, much degraded. The terraces overlooked a large sunken garden, the size of three tennis courts at least, pointing up the valley. Jagged hills on either side framed the view perfectly, holding the sky in an open 'V'. But now the space was choked with cornus, brambles, sycamore, reeds and the papery dead heads of *Ligularia dentata*. Most poignant of all were the remnants of water features – a half-moon wall fountain with a semicircular pool cut into the bottom terrace; a reed-choked channel that ran down the centre like a misshapen spine; and a circular depression (presumably a pond) before the wild stream at the end.

Abandoned *wild* gardens simply melt back into wildness, like waves on sand. But the buried stones of a formal garden provide haunting reminders of pleasures long since gone. Nowhere was the pull of ruins stronger than at Dunira, where its vanished pleasure gardens were fast returning to a Scottish glen.

Alone of all the sites in the series, we had relatively little searching to do to discover the garden that still lay just beneath the surface. Edwardian landscape architect Thomas Hayton Mawson included the making of this garden in the fifth edition of his huge folio manual, *The Art and Craft of Garden Making*, published in 1926. There was even a detailed plan.

(opposite top) Dunira's fabled rose garden lies forgotten under the scrub.

(opposite right) Despite Mawson's grand plan, the western half of the rose garden was never built.

(below) Crumbling stone steps lead down to buried water features.

For this garden at least, we would not need to rummage in obscure archives to discover pieces of the puzzle. But there was still much to explore before we could properly imagine it in its prime. Most intriguingly of all, what drove a Scottish landowner to create so extravagant a garden at such a late date? The Great War of 1914–18 had supposedly brought country-house-building to a virtual halt, taking away the armies of men needed to keep the gardens in immaculate condition. Yet here was a garden created in the 1920s as if the war had never happened.

Singular beauty

The estate's name is commonly thought to have derived from the Celtic 'Dun-iar-a', which means the fort at the west water. In her guide to the beauties of Scotland (1799–1803), Sarah Murray called Dunira 'the most singular spot, I believe, in the world; singular to a degree, by nature, and made beautiful by a little assistance from art'. It was then owned by Henry Dundas, who became one of Scotland's most powerful men. Solicitor General, Lord Advocate, Secretary of State for the Home Department during the French Revolution, MP for Edinburgh, Dundas was later created Viscount Melville and Baron of Dunira but was impeached on charges of corruption. Though acquitted, he never held public office again.

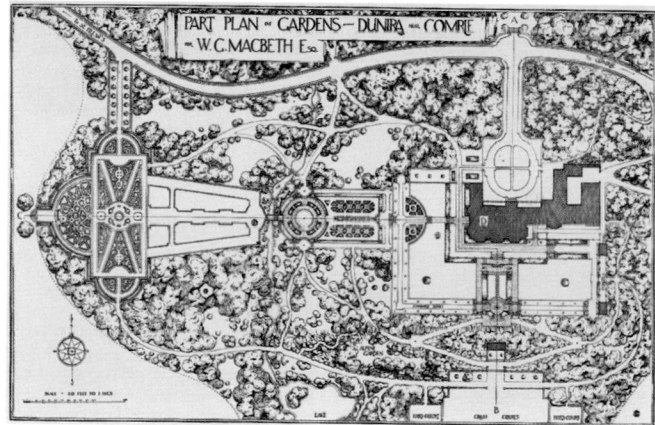

Melville's son sold the estate in 1824 to Sir Robert Dundas of Beechwood, whose son David built the new house on higher ground to escape constant flooding. Constructed of Bannockburn freestone brought in specially by rail and then carted some way from the nearest station, the house was finished in 1852. It was described in suitably glowing terms in Thomas Hunter's *Woods, Forests, and Estates of Perthshire* (1883) as being 'of mixed baronial style' and 'a very beautiful structure, thoroughly in keeping with its magnificent surroundings'.

The new house is shown on the first 25-inch Ordnance Survey map of 1866, sitting in a series of plain terraces that had literally been carved out of the hillside. Thomas Hunter described the labour that went into their creation: 'The lawn

surrounding the mansion is laid out in four fine terraces, the making of which involved a great deal of excavating and carting, the ground having originally been bare rock and heather. The main entrance, beautifully ornamented with heather and shrubbery, was excavated out of solid rock for about 15 or 20 feet, with a breadth of 25 feet.' There was also a Swiss-style wash house, built of quartz, hill stones and hot lime, and some fine trees in the surrounding park and woods. These included a weeping birch (moved to make way for the house at the immense cost of £50), purple beech, *Abies menziesii*, *Cedrus deodara* and a *Sequioadendron giganteum*.

For Dunira, we were lucky to find a series of Victorian photographs still owned by the Dundas family that brought these descriptions vividly to life. The terraces on the western front were monumentally plain. Steps provided the only ornament: two flights leading from the west door, then two further flights at either end of the lower terraces. A pair of urns stood at the top of each flight, displaying fairly standard bedding plants. The terraces looked down on a typically Victorian arrangement of flower beds at the bottom, with mounded beds cut in circles and

The burnt-out shell of the great house looms above the bare terrace.

simple geometric shapes, filled with broadly massed bedding plants, edged with a strip in paler colours. Clothes worn by the carefully posed figures on the terrace (presumably members of the Dundas family or their guests) suggested a late Victorian date.

By 1919, however, the estate was beginning to look tired and old-fashioned. Having suffered heavy personal losses in the First World War, Sir George W. M. Dundas Bart sold the house by private bargain to a wealthy Glasgow shipowner, George Alexander Macbeth, who very soon afterwards gifted the estate to his son, William Gilchrist, then aged thirty-seven. This was the new laird of Dunira, who brought to the estate what it needed most – money, and lots of it. Not surprisingly, there was great local interest in the village of Comrie about the kind of man he was and the changes he might bring.

Singular wealth

Macbeth senior had come to Glasgow as a young man from his native Sutherland on Scotland's most northerly coast and started business as Macbeth & Gray, shipowners and chandlers. By 1905, 'Gray' had disappeared from its name and the firm's fortunes had risen to a peak ownership of nine steamers. This would decline back down to two, without any diminution of

wealth. With the outbreak of war in 1914, there was plenty of money to be made from the sale of serviceable ships.

Son William enjoyed a privileged upbringing. Educated at Fettes College, he played little part in business, concentrating instead on activities he enjoyed such as golf, winning competitions at St Andrews in his youth. Although attached to a Scottish regiment during the First World War, William never saw active service, spending time instead with his increasingly sick father who was then resident at the Strathearn Hydropathic in Crieff – a clinic-cum-hotel that still exists today as the Crieff Hydro. In 1918, William married the eighteen-year-old Miss Winifred Maurice. She was already engaged to a Glasgow doctor, but Winifred's family decided William would make a better match and the wedding took place at the Hydropathic.

Macbeth senior bought Dunira for his son as a wedding present. The gift was clearly substantial. A newspaper report of the day listed ten arable and sheep farms, a large range of hill ground with grouse shooting and low-ground game, fishing on the River Earn, the 'charmingly-situated mansion-house' erected in the 1850s and a large fruit and vegetable garden. In all, the estate extended to several thousand acres.

William Gilchrist Macbeth and Winifred on their wedding day.

Sadly, the father did not long outlive his gift. On 28 July 1919, the *Strathearn Herald* reported his death at the age of seventy-six, describing him as 'among the last of the older generation of Glasgow shipowners'. He was remembered as a sympathetic supporter of local charities and one of the founders of the Irvine Golf. When the will was confirmed in February 1920, the value of Macbeth's estate was put at £880,333 16s 9d – more than £20,740,000 in today's money. Apart from some £15,000 left to various charities, George's son William was the main beneficiary.

So William was not just in possession of a grand estate, he also had the money to 'improve' it to his heart's content. Immediately he set about modernizing the Victorian mansion, bringing in Glasgow architects Clifford & Lunan to remodel the existing block, adding a new billiard room, kitchen wing and a spacious *porte-cochère* to create a fitting entrance.

As the improvements would take two years to complete, William and Winifred moved into nearby Auchtertyre House in 1920, under the curious eyes of Comrie village. 'Mr Macbeth, the new laird of Dunira, made his first appearance in the village,' ran a report in the *Strathearn Herald* on 17 April 1920. 'He proved himself an ideal Chairman, and is a distinct asset to the public life of the village.' Macbeth's largesse was noted from the start and especially his employment of men disabled during the Great War:

> His vast improvements at his newly acquired residence – Dunira – has given employment to all the surplus labour of the village, and that at a figure which has staggered the local landlords and employers of labour. Remembering those who were maimed in the great war, a job was found for them also, no deduction being made because of their Army pensions.

'Capability Brown of Empire'

At the same time as he was remodelling the house, Macbeth had grandiose plans for his garden and, on the suggestion of his Glasgow architects, hired noted landscape architect Thomas Mawson. It seems unlikely that Macbeth and Mawson knew each other before the commission, although Macbeth would certainly have been aware of his landscaper's impressive reputation. Mawson had risen through his chosen career to become the most prolific

A feature of many grand Edwardian gardens, the wall fountain here lies abandoned.

English garden designer of his day, with many wealthy private clients, especially in the northern counties and Scotland. He would go on to become president of the Town Planning Institute, a founding member of the Royal Fine Art Commission and first president of the Institute of Landscape Architects. Known as the Capability Brown of Empire from his grand schemes overseas, he was in many ways an obvious choice for a man used to buying the best.

Mawson's beginnings were very different from his client's, however. The son of a Lancashire cotton-worker, he went to work (aged just twelve) as office boy to his builder uncle in Lancaster, where he also learnt drawing and horticulture. After his father's early death, he decided on landscape gardening as a career and joined the London firm of Wills & Seger, floral decorators and landscape gardeners. When Wills went bankrupt, Mawson broadened his experience with other nurseries before joining Thomas Ware of Hale Farm Nurseries, Tottenham – noted grower of hardy plants and bulbs. Amos Perry, a world authority on irises, worked there for a time as a bulb specialist.

Mawson was soon put in charge of the firm's correspondence, which brought him into contact with many of the leading gardening figures of the day. 'There was Miss Jekyll writing about daffodils,' he later noted in his autobiography, his only mention of the grande dame of Edwardian gardening. (As rival designers, their relations were notoriously prickly.) William Robinson was another famous correspondent of the nursery, although his and Mawson's temperaments were poles apart. The champion of wild gardening, Robinson dismissed Mawson's later adoption of the title 'landscape architect' as 'a stupid term of French origin implying the union of two absolutely distinct studies'.

Mawson's own success was firmly grounded in the nursery business he set up in 1884 with his brothers and other members of his family, Lakeland Nurseries of Windermere. By the end of the decade, he had established a separate landscape gardening business as well, and commissions slowly came his way. One of his favourite gardens – which can still be seen today – was Graythwaite Hall on the western shores of Lake Windermere for Colonel T. M. Sandys, MP. Graythwaite has all the hallmarks of a Mawson garden: respect for the natural beauties of the site combined with a strong architectural anchoring of the house in its surroundings. Throughout this time he continued to teach himself the principles of design, studying the works of John Ruskin, J. C. Loudon, Humphry Repton and Edward Kemp, whose influential *How to Lay out a Small Garden* (1864, third edition) he particularly admired.

Mawson's practice really took off in 1900 when he published the first edition of his hugely influential design manual, *The Art and Craft of Garden Making*, dedicated to his client Colonel Sandys of Graythwaite Hall. With some qualms, he decided to illustrate the work almost exclusively with his own designs, as Kemp and others had done before him. The enterprise could have brought disaster: he paid the publishers, Batsford, to issue 1,000 copies, distributed by *Country Life*. In fact the first edition sold out within three months, at one guinea a copy, and Mawson received many requests for more articles and lectures. The manual went through five editions in his lifetime, each expanded with new Mawson designs.

His wider fame had begun to spread so he was able to support his growing family. With four sons and four daughters, all musical, he needed space to house a small orchestra. His clients included successful businessmen such as soap manufacturer Lord Leverhulme, store owner Gordon Selfridge and Samuel Waring (later Lord Waring) of the furniture firm Waring & Gillow. Waring recommended him to HM Queen Alexandra, for whom he designed a delightful rose garden at her beloved summer retreat at Hvidöre, near Copenhagen. His practice soon extended into public work, with parks, town planning (notably in Greece and Canada) and civic landscaping. After losing his much-loved third son (also a gifted architect and horticulturalist) in the war, he devoted considerable energies to planning industrial villages for disabled ex-servicemen – a cause he shared with his future client, W. G. Macbeth.

By the time Macbeth approached him to design the gardens at Dunira, Mawson had reached the apex of his career. A few of his wealthier clients were again requiring his services; and he would gain new ones, such as the Maharajah of Baroda for whom he remodelled Tennyson's old home in Surrey. He was still much involved with replanning the northern Greek city of Salonika, destroyed by fire in 1917, and other projects in Greece. He was so busy, in fact, that Dunira was finished under the direction of his son, E. Prentice Mawson, who had trained in the formal French style at the Ecole des Beaux-Arts in Paris and who helped his father on the fifth and final edition of *The Art and Craft of Garden Making*.

Mawson senior immediately fell under the spell of Dunira's magnificent setting, which he described as 'one of the most beautiful estates it has ever been my pleasure to study'. It reminded him of his native Lake District, with rocky outcrops rising from the Scottish valley floor like islands in Lake Windermere. The encircling hills, too, were like Grasmere seen from Dunmail Raise. The view from Dunira's rose garden has strong echoes of an earlier garden Mawson had created close to Grasmere at Rydal Hall, just below Wordsworth's last home at Rydal Mount.

But Mawson had few kind words for the mansion house or its 'vapid' gardens. Though large and well placed, he considered the house was 'not built in a fortunate period of architectural taste', needing the combined efforts of the architects and 'a generous client' to bring it into harmony with Scottish traditions. The grounds fared even worse. 'Originally what passed for the gardens,' he wrote waspishly in his autobiography, 'was a number of uninteresting grass slopes, unrelieved by flower bed or shrub, to all appearances arranged by a waterworks engineer with railway experience.' A steep bank in front of the house had been left unfinished then 'roughly planted with yew, hollies and timber trees, making a ragged outline across the southern view'.

Mawson was given a virtually free hand to replan the gardens as he wanted, without any apparent restrictions on his budget. His design solution was typically (if anachronistically) Edwardian, with strong axial lines; hard, architectural features (walls, paths, water features) softened by planting; and separate areas devoted to different activities. It was also typical Mawson: monumental and Italianate with strongly traditional bones.

He retained the fairly plain levels around the house, adding a balustraded wall to anchor it into the landscape (as he had done at Graythwaite and Rydal Hall). To the south front, he created a crazy-paved sundial terrace blocked with more balustrades, giving fine views over the tennis courts (four grass, two hard) that formed such a vital part of leisured

(opposite) A climbing hydrangea smothers a mossy remnant of Mawson's stone balustrade.

(below) In the 1930s, winged beasts guarded the steps to the rose garden.

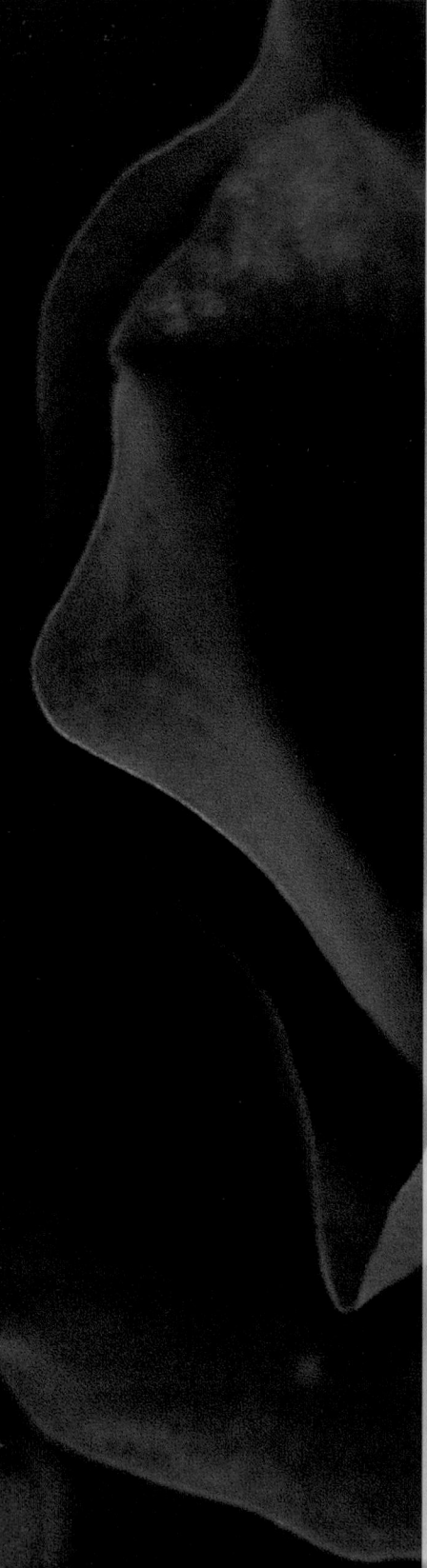

country-house living. Into the rocky bluff overlooking the courts he cut diagonal and curving walks leading down to the lower level and built a sturdy tea house where the paths met.

The garden's real splendour lay to the west, with a sunken rose garden of panelled beds stretching into the park like a fantastically elaborate paper doily. All the hard work of terracing and digging and levelling had, in fact, already been done for him when the new house was built in the 1850s. Mawson simply took the plain grass slopes and replaced them with retaining walls built of local black whinstone without mortar. For decoration he added coping coins and pilasters in yellow sandstone or grit stone, 'to give it strength and stability'. In the crevices of the walls he planted alpines and rock plants in the fashion of wall-gardening made popular by Gertrude Jekyll (her *Wall and Water Gardens* had first appeared in 1901). The top retaining wall he built as a semicircle, giving a pleasing symmetry to the half- and full-circles repeated throughout the design. To create the sunken effect he simply built viewing ramps along each side, reducing the four terraces to three with masterly economy. Even the steps remained more or less in their original positions.

For the spine of his rose garden, he created the typically Edwardian water features that gave the garden such pathos in its ruined state. Against the retaining wall he built a half-moon wall fountain fed by a piped water supply through the mouth of a mythical Edwardian lion. An overflow from the fountain's pool then fed a planted iris rill running up the centre of the garden. Underground pipes took the water into a circular lily pond at the far end, graced with a simple jet fountain. Surrounding the pool was a bracelet of flower beds cut in a circle of smooth crazy paving.

In Mawson's plan (but never implemented) the western garden then continued with an apron of lawn leading the eye on towards his final flourish – more panelled rose beds set within semicircular bastions, the whole effect scrolled and patterned like a mini-Versailles. Everything suggests the beaux-arts training of Mawson's son, with its emphasis on strong axial planning and logic. In *The Art and Craft of Garden Making* Mawson lamented the loss of this and hoped (vainly) that 'this much needed terminal will be carried through'.

While Mawson was proudest of the rose garden, Macbeth's favourite area was the wild garden around the stream that ran southwards beyond the lily pond into a man-made lake. Although Mawson had constructed similar gardens for clients such as the Marquess of Bute, the making of Dunira's rock and water garden was entrusted to Mr James Pulham of Hertfordshire – premier rock builders for three generations. (The firm had earlier been involved at Sir Jeremiah Colman's Gatton Park, also one of our lost gardens.) Macbeth clearly felt able to call on the top man for everything.

A Scottish laird

Entries in Mawson's ledger book show that his firm continued to work on Dunira's gardens for at least two years from 1920. At the same time, work continued on the house itself and by the end of 1922 William and Winifred were ready to move into their vastly improved new home. Looking after house and grounds was a staff of more than fifty, many housed on the estate.

There are people still living in the neighbourhood who remember the Macbeths' arrival. David MacFarlane, a gardener at Dunira during the 1930s, was born on the estate in 1912. Just eight when work started there, he can recall the sense of local excitement that so much money was being spent on improving the house and grounds. Trainloads of men arrived each day to labour on the estate – returned soldiers especially and unemployed Glasgow shipworkers. Macbeth had his own railway siding and station built at Dunira to bring in his labourers and materials.

As a boy, David MacFarlane used to work as a beater on grouse and pheasant shoots. William Macbeth remained an enthusiastic participant until the late 1930s, when ill heath forced him to ride ponies instead of walking.

In 1928, when he was sixteen, MacFarlane was taken on as apprentice gardener under the then head gardener, Mr Robert White. He was put to work in all areas of the estate – the formal gardens, the vast glasshouses and the tennis lawns. Everyone had his own task, with one man for the west lawn, another for the rose beds and so on. MacFarlane has clear memories of the sunken rose garden where the water features were a source of great pride, with goldfish in the iris rill and lilies in the pond. Work in the garden entailed endless mowing, raking and pruning, all to a very high standard. Every day, Mr White would patrol the grounds, checking the work of his twenty-two under-gardeners.

Social life at Dunira was good, remembers MacFarlane – it was like a small village, all sharing a common purpose. There were certainly enough workers on the estate, with more than twenty indoor staff (who wore different uniforms, morning and afternoon) in addition to the ranks of gardeners. As a young man, he was involved with the estate cricket team, captained by Macbeth and coached by a professional who had played for England. At one of the dances in the recreational hall, to the music of Macbeth's

(top left) Macbeth's rose garden was always immaculate.

(top right) The rill is just visible, leading away from the dried-up fountain.

(opposite) One of the first roses to flower in the restored garden.

of his class. Winifred Macbeth was remembered less fondly, however. The gardeners were instructed to vanish whenever they saw her, which was not always easy. Extremely particular about everything, she had a special fondness for roses and would search for any leaf or bud out of place. Joanna Goddard, the Macbeths' granddaughter, believes that Winifred was simply overwhelmed by the size and grandeur of Dunira and not comfortable in her new life. Never one for socializing, she much preferred walking the Perthshire hills with her husband. And her character was shaped by a misfortune that blighted her enjoyment of the estate for ever.

A family tragedy

As the only son of an only son, William Macbeth had dreams of founding a dynasty of his own to inherit Dunira. Within the first year of their marriage, Winifred gave birth to a baby girl called Mary but she died when only a few months old. The first surviving child, Pamela, was born in 1922 followed by Fiona in 1926. With few friends of their own age, Pamela and Fiona were brought up on the estate with a governess and numerous nannies. There were orders that they should lack for nothing and the men who worked in the garden were instructed to take them fishing or riding, or whatever they wished.

In 1930, Winifred became pregnant for the fourth time. Certain that this child would be a boy, Macbeth had bonfires built around the periphery of the estate, ready to be lit in honour of the birth of his heir. Although a doctor had been resident at the house for several weeks before the due date, when Winifred started haemorrhaging there was nothing anyone could do. Estate workers were lined up outside the house, to be given blood tests in the hope that one would be suitable for transfusion. It was too late. A baby boy was born dead and Winifred herself was declared to be in grave danger.

Distraught, William took his dead son and laid him in the family vaults, then fled the house. He returned a week

own Comrie Pipe Band, MacFarlane met his future wife, who was employed in the house laundry.

Another local man with memories of Dunira from the mid-1920s is Jimmy Mitchell. Born in 1917 in a cottage near the estate he, too, joined children from the estate and surrounding villages to work as a beater during the shooting season. They would be given two weeks off school and paid relatively well, so it was a popular activity with the children.

In the late 1920s Mitchell became an apprentice plumber and was often called up to Dunira. He remembers how it was completely self-sufficient, with its own dam supplying water for the household and the garden features. The custom-built generator supplied hydroelectric power to the whole estate. Mitchell's main memories of the garden are of 'sneaking a look' whenever the family was not in residence – normally no one was allowed to walk in front of the house where they could be seen by them.

Both MacFarlane and Mitchell remember William Macbeth as a generous and benevolent 'laird', a bit of a 'soft touch' to anyone in need, but still maintaining the distance later expecting to find his wife dead, too. Winifred in fact recovered but was so traumatized by her ordeal that she did not speak for almost two years. She became a shadow of her former self and remained a semi-invalid for the rest of her life. William could refuse her nothing and she became very particular about many aspects of life around her, especially the garden. Her sudden changes of mood and petulant desires did little to endear her to those who worked on the estate.

About this time, Macbeth started drinking heavily and was sometimes taken to a hotel by Winifred's nurse to dry out. He might be literally locked in his room for days. By 1937, with both girls away at boarding school, Winifred managed to persuade William to put his beloved estate on the market, hoping perhaps to check the tide of misfortune.

A series of beautiful photographs was taken of the gardens, and a sumptuous sale catalogue was produced listing the fineries inside and out. Included in the sale were seven tenanted farms and four farmed by Macbeth himself; garaging for eight cars; various cottages and village properties; an employees' recreation hall; hard and grass tennis courts; a nine-hole golf course; cricket ground; walled kitchen garden with extensive glasshouses, including a tropical house for

(oppsite) Dry heads of *Ligularia dentata* crowd the fountain.

(below) Mawson's vision returns to this fine Perthshire valley.

bananas and other exotics; more than 1,000 acres of woodland; some of Perthshire's best shooting, with grouse moors, luncheon huts, and an estimated 3,000 pheasants; trout fishing on the rivers Earn, Ruchill and Lednock – in all, nearly 7,000 acres of prime Perthshire land.

But the catalogue's highest praise was reserved for the natural and man-made beauties of the site. Dunira 'is encircled by some of the finest scenery in Perthshire and nothing is more apt than to state that it has one of the most BEAUTIFUL GARDENS imaginable, situate in a fertile valley surrounded by an equally beautiful if more awe inspiring setting of Nature's grandest scenery.' These same gardens were 'Renowned as being amongst the Finest in Scotland. They were designed by the eminent Landscape Gardener, the late Mr. Thomas W. [*sic*] Mawson, being created from what was little more than a grassy hillside, and are an example of Landscape Gardening art in its highest form.'

Already an anachronism when Macbeth poured his money into it in the early 1920s, the estate found no buyer – quite possibly because Macbeth had no real intention of selling. But though it continued to be well maintained, Dunira's best days were over. Gardener David MacFarlane recalls that in 1939, when he was 'headhunted' for the post of head gardener to the Duke and Duchess of Atholl, Mr White recommended he should take the job as Dunira was all but finished.

The Second World War broke out soon afterwards. The Macbeths moved out to Home Farm, turning the mansion over to the armed services for use as a convalescent home for soldiers. Most estate workers left to join the war, leaving just three men to do the work of twenty-three. Head gardener Mr White left in 1943, unable to oversee the slow decline in standards. But the family was happy at Home Farm, it seems, even though William was becoming ill with a weak heart like his father before him.

In 1947, the family was preparing to move back into Dunira. Although a few patients were still in residence, workmen had already begun rewiring and redecorating in preparation for the owners' return. As reported in the local press, fire broke out in the recreation room at the top of the west wing. Fanned by a strong wind, it destroyed the centre and west wings within two hours. The blaze was discovered by two orderlies who attacked it with stirrup pumps and extinguishers, helped by nurses and patients. Estate and farm workers helped members of staff rescue patients' belongings. Winifred and her daughters gave the patients tea at Home Farm while the convalescents waited for ambulances to take them to a local hospital. According to his granddaughter Joanna, Macbeth stood and watched his house burn. He

threw his wine cellar open to anyone who would brave the flames, and many did. If he couldn't enjoy his fine wines, others might. Damage was estimated at £80,000 and most of the house was reduced to a charred ruin.

Less then a year later, William died – aged just sixty-seven, his heart almost certainly strained by the calamity. His obituary remembered his famous herd of Aberdeen Angus cattle, his practical interest in farming and the sporting facilities he generously provided for his staff. 'The late Mr Macbeth was at all times a very liberal supporter of local charities,' said the local paper, 'and, in particular, recreational clubs, such as football and cricket, appealed to his generosity.' He also gave £20,000 to Glasgow's Victoria Infirmary, in memory of his father.

Winifred and her two daughters remained at Home Farm for another two years, finally selling the estate in 1950. With the insurance money from the fire, she was able to buy a large, comfortable house in Dunblane where she lived until the 1970s with her nurse. Joanna would stay with her grandmother every holiday and visit her great aunt (Winifred's sister) who still lived in a small cottage on the estate. Winifred herself never returned to Dunira as its memories were too painful. But her eight grandchildren never tired of stories about the estate in its heyday.

It was broken up and the garden slipped slowly into decay. With the house gone, it had anyway lost its point.

Dunira's passing really did mark the end of country-house living on a grand scale. The immaculate photographs taken for the abortive sale of 1937 are especially sad. As in any sale catalogue, the photographs are empty of people. No one is shown enjoying the beauty of the gardens, just as no gardener is shown keeping that beauty in its pristine state. The lines from poet William Wordsworth with which Mawson ended his biography resonate with special meaning in the face of the Macbeths' evident unhappiness:

A garden … the place
Where good men disappointed in the quest
Of wealth and power and honours, long for rest;
Or having known the splendours of success,
Sigh for the obscurities of happiness.

An Edwardian garden par excellence

One final question remained. Mawson undoubtedly created for his client a sumptuous garden that carried high Edwardian taste and lifestyle into the 1920s and 1930s. But just how original was it as a design, and how did Mawson's work compare with that of his contemporaries?

(opposite) Water flows once more into the iris rill.

(below) The intricately panelled rose beds will require meticulous maintenance.

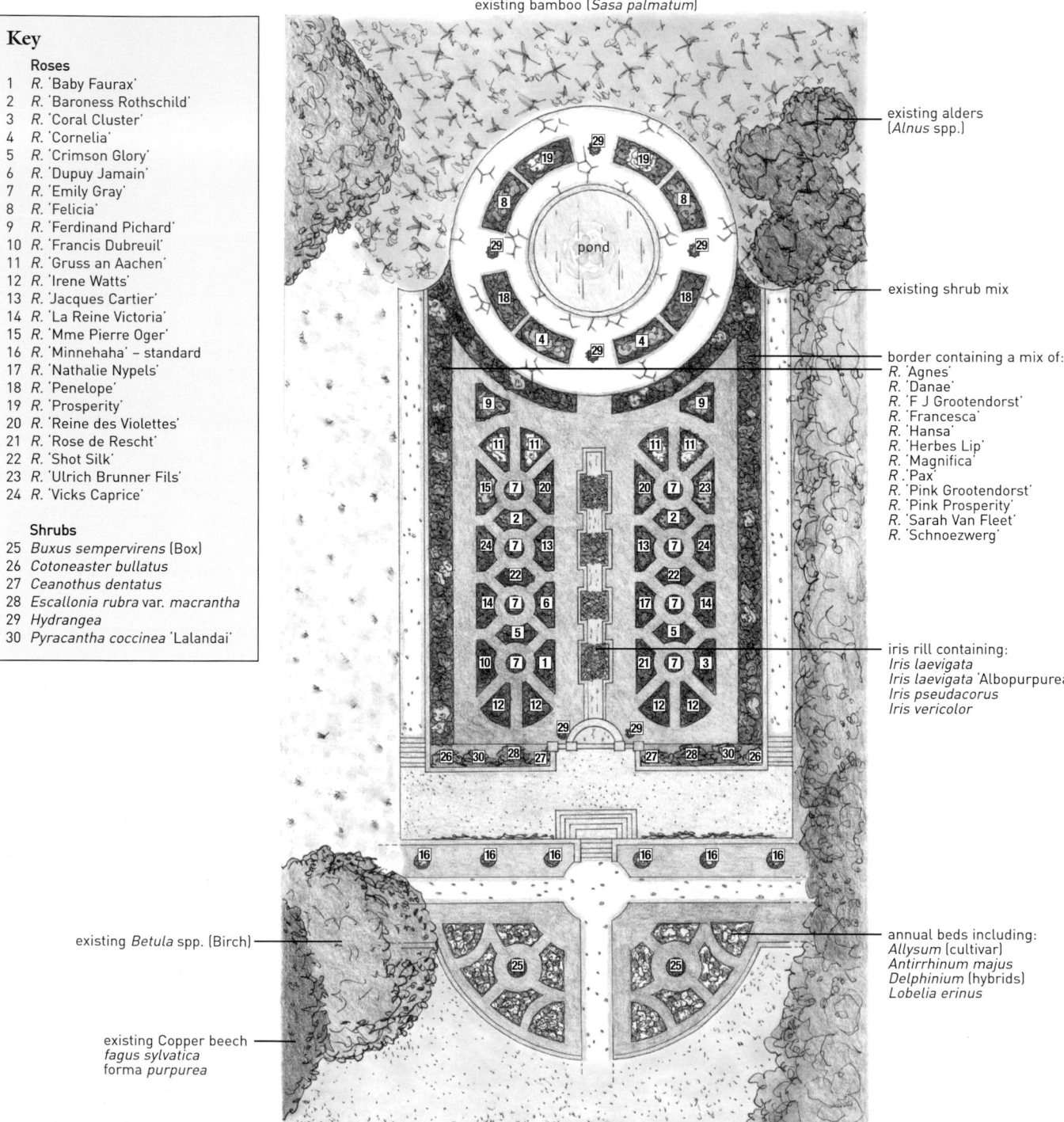

existing bamboo (*Sasa palmatum*)

Key

Roses
1 *R.* 'Baby Faurax'
2 *R.* 'Baroness Rothschild'
3 *R.* 'Coral Cluster'
4 *R.* 'Cornelia'
5 *R.* 'Crimson Glory'
6 *R.* 'Dupuy Jamain'
7 *R.* 'Emily Gray'
8 *R.* 'Felicia'
9 *R.* 'Ferdinand Pichard'
10 *R.* 'Francis Dubreuil'
11 *R.* 'Gruss an Aachen'
12 *R.* 'Irene Watts'
13 *R.* 'Jacques Cartier'
14 *R.* 'La Reine Victoria'
15 *R.* 'Mme Pierre Oger'
16 *R.* 'Minnehaha' – standard
17 *R.* 'Nathalie Nypels'
18 *R.* 'Penelope'
19 *R.* 'Prosperity'
20 *R.* 'Reine des Violettes'
21 *R.* 'Rose de Rescht'
22 *R.* 'Shot Silk'
23 *R.* 'Ulrich Brunner Fils'
24 *R.* 'Vicks Caprice'

Shrubs
25 *Buxus sempervirens* (Box)
26 *Cotoneaster bullatus*
27 *Ceanothus dentatus*
28 *Escallonia rubra* var. *macrantha*
29 *Hydrangea*
30 *Pyracantha coccinea* 'Lalandai'

existing alders (*Alnus* spp.)

existing shrub mix

pond

border containing a mix of:
R. 'Agnes'
R. 'Danae'
R. 'F J Grootendorst'
R. 'Francesca'
R. 'Hansa'
R. 'Herbes Lip'
R. 'Magnifica'
R. 'Pax'
R. 'Pink Grootendorst'
R. 'Pink Prosperity'
R. 'Sarah Van Fleet'
R. 'Schnoezwerg'

iris rill containing:
Iris laevigata
Iris laevigata 'Albopurpurea'
Iris pseudacorus
Iris vericolor

existing *Betula* spp. (Birch)

annual beds including:
Allysum (cultivar)
Antirrhinum majus
Delphinium (hybrids)
Lobelia erinus

existing Copper beech
fagus sylvatica
forma *purpurea*

In style, a typical Edwardian garden married a formal layout with informal planting, as in the Arts and Crafts gardens championed by architect Sir Edwin Lutyens and plantswoman Gertrude Jekyll. Their gardens had a strong architectural backbone, often in vernacular materials, softened by exuberant planting in exquisitely graded colours. Other gardens (sometimes called 'beaux-arts style') were more influenced by French and Italian models, with strong central axes, terracing, clipped hedges and patterned flower beds projecting into the landscape.

Adept at interpreting the needs of his clients, Thomas Mawson could happily mix-and-match elements from different styles, using stock elements like fountains, rills and a whole geometry of circles and rectangles. This could lead to accusations of plagiarism. Dunira's wall fountain and planted rill are strongly reminiscent of Sir Edwin Lutyens' at Hestercombe in Somerset, a garden Lutyens created with Gertrude Jekyll in *c*.1904. 'The planted rill may be considered the invention of Sir Edwin Lutyens,' wrote Gertrude Jekyll firmly. 'The one in the garden at Hestercombe shows the most typical form.' But Mawson at Dunira was also copying his own work: he had used just such a combination of wall fountain and planted rill at a garden in Ashton-on-Trent. If Mawson lacked the clarity and genius of Jekyll and Luytyens at their best, a few of his gardens achieved real greatness, notably the Hill Garden in Hampstead (now restored by English Heritage) for soap manufacturer Lord Leverhulme. Dunira doesn't quite scale those heights but it does show Mawson's skill in tying the ambitions of his garden to the splendour of its site.

Transforming and restoring

The restoration at Dunira was more straightforward than most. At least we had more information about this garden than for any other. Plans, descriptions, designer's notes, before-and-after photographs, memories – all would help in its recreation. But the gardens were far too large for us to tackle in full, so the first task was to decide which part would be our special focus.

The rose garden was an obvious choice: self-contained, a clear Mawson favourite and just about a manageable size. Our aim was to restore this part of the garden back to Mawson's original design as far as possible, disregarding any later changes. Realistically, we could not replace the stone balustrading that had been removed sometime after the estate was sold in the early 1950s. Real stone was beyond our budget and although Mawson used reconstituted stone in some of his gardens, modern examples would not match the beauty of the original. We also would not be able to replace the plundered pilasters from the terrace walls but we

Clearing starts on the pond.

would tackle all the other elements of hard landscaping, such as the stone paving around the lily pond. All the same, it was a daunting programme of work.

On site, the first tasks involved surveying and clearance. The terrace walling and coping around the side ramps had suffered during the garden's half century of neglect but at least the central water features were basically intact, though stones had naturally collapsed into the rill. Repair work involved resetting the edging stones in a pleasing chequer-board effect that alternated rectangles of stone, planting area and grass. We also needed to construct a self-contained

water system to get the fountains working again. Macbeth's original solution had involved diverting water from a stream at the top of the hill; the garden's water supply was gravity-fed and controlled by an old stopcock at the fountain. In its place, we used a pump in the burn, underground piping and some 200 metres of armoured cable. In this way, we would be able to turn the waterworks on and off.

With typical Scottish spring rain much in evidence, one of the trickiest jobs to accomplish was painting surfaces with pond sealant – three coats for the rill, four for the pond and fountain. The sealant had to dry properly between each coat, so we resorted to bottled-gas burners and a makeshift plastic tunnel to keep off the rain.

The hardest job of all, though, was to plot Mawson's intricate panelled rose beds down each side of the main rose garden and up on the semicircular terrace. First the ground had to be cleared, the old turf stripped off and the soil thoroughly prepared. We could then have laid turf over the

(opposite) *Argyranthemum frutescens.*

(left) The landscape team begins to peel back the old turf.

(below) Here the restored pond is viewed through a clump of alders.

whole area and cut out the shapes of the beds but this would have been extremely wasteful. Instead, our landscaper decided ambitiously to mark out the plan on the prepared soil, laying turf to fit around the beds exactly. It soon turned into a nightmare. The problem was that Mawson's original plan had been incorrectly measured, so we couldn't simply scale up the design to fit the site. Every angle had to be measured independently to create his intended pattern, starting with the five standard roses along each side and working back from that. It took our landscaper at least a day and some complicated trigonometry simply to mark out the plan using pegs and spray markers.

Another major job involved laying some 200 square metres of stone paving around the pond, in the neat, triangular crazy-paving style shown in the 1920s photographs, leaving cut-out beds for planting. Around the pool and the fountain we placed big white hydrangeas in wooden planters, as shown in Mawson's book and later photographs.

To help with our planting plans, we were able to draw on an extensively illustrated article about Dunira that appeared in *Country Life* on 21 March 1931, as well as photographs from the 1920s and 1930s. Written by G. C. Taylor, the article described the rose beds as being of sensible size and laid out on simple lines. Each bed was planted with one variety only to give a massed display within a strong overall colour scheme. At the centre of each side-panel, a row of standard rose trees relieved the 'monotony of level'. Photographs showed sentinel hydrangeas in square wooden planters on either side of the wall fountain; and more roses in the long side-beds from the terraced wall to the lily pond (where Mawson's simple jet fountain had given way to a cherub with a swan).

For help with choosing the different rose varieties, we turned to rose expert Peter Beales for period-correct stock. Virtually all the roses selected would have been available to Mawson in the early 1920s – more than 600 in all, of thirty-six different varieties. They were a glorious mix of shrub, rugosa, bourbon, bush and hybrid perpetuals, in a palette ranging from pinks, through crimsons and violet-purples to creams and white. Down the centre of each panel were weeping standards of *Rosa* 'Emily Gray', with its butter-yellow scented flowers set in mop heads of dark green leaves. More roses and rose standards went into the semicircular terrace, and two clipped box specimens (*Buxus sempervirens*) with 70-centimetre domes. The wet weather meant that much of the planting remained unfinished at the end of filming, however, leaving much for the owners to complete.

For the rill, we could again turn to the *Country Life* article of 1931 and the many charming photographs. 'Set in the symmetrical recesses of the water channel,' wrote G. C. Taylor, 'with its formal edge of paving sunk in grass, are groups of reeds and other handsome aquatics, including Siberian irises, lysimachias, alisma, cyperus and various grasses whose elegant leafage provides an attractive setting to the canal which gives the garden a note of distinction and beauty and a greater variety of interest.' Our plan included several iris species (some of which still survived on site): the yellow flag iris, *Iris pseudacorus*, the blue flag, *I. versicolor*;

and the varied colours of *I. laevigata* (in rich purple-blues) and *I. laevigata* 'Albopurpurea' (predominantly white). Mixed in with the irises were slender spikes of the small bull-rush, *Typha minima*.

Against the retaining terrace walls, we planted shrubs exactly as described in the *Country House* article: ceanothus, escallonia, pyracantha, cotoneaster; and two climbers: *Clematis montana* var. *rubens* and *C. alpina*.

A late golden age

Returning to Dunira after the restoration was a shock. Extravagantly formal gardens of the kind Mawson created to match the status (and wallets) of his wealthy clients are hopelessly ill suited to today's economics. Yet Dunira's rose garden looked so *right*. Framed between the distant hills, it had slipped back into the proud Scottish landscape as if it had never vanished.

The garden's strong lines created plenty of visual movement. Looking down the garden, the rill opened into the smooth circle of the lily pond like the head of a rose. From the pond looking back, the garden's central spine drew the eye along the angular rill to the rounded shapes of the wall fountain with its neatly creased tiles and benevolent lion. Above the fountain, tapering steps led back towards the precarious roofline of the burnt-out house.

Certainly the constant mowing, weeding, clipping and cosseting required will create much extra work for Dunira's current owners and estate staff. And certainly there is still much to restore – the walls need attention, and drainage remains a problem. But given the owners' genuine love for this absurdly brave recreation of a vanished era, Dunira's flamboyant rose garden will flower again long into the twenty-first century.

(left) Planting on the semicircular terrace provides a respite from roses.

(opposite) Yellow flag iris flower along the restored rill.

SOURCES AND FURTHER READING

GENERAL

Amherst, Alicia M. T. (1895) *A History of Gardening in England*.

Coats, Alice M. (1968) *Flowers and Their Histories*, 2nd edn. London: A. & C. Black.

Coats, Alice M. (1992) *Garden Shrubs and Their Histories*. New York: Simon & Schuster.

Elliott, Brent (1986) *Victorian Gardens*. London: B. T. Batsford.

Harvey, John (1993) *Restoring Period Gardens*. Princes Risborough, Buckinghamshire: Shire Garden History.

Jackson, J. B. (1980) *The Necessity for Ruins and Other Topics*. Amhurst, MA: University of Massachusetts Press.

Jellicoe, Geoffrey and Susan, Goode, Patrick, and Lancaster, Michael (eds) (1991) *The Oxford Companion to Gardens*. Oxford: Oxford University Press.

Ottewill, David (1989) *The Edwardian Garden*. New Haven, CT: Yale University Press.

Royal Horticultural Society (1956) *Dictionary of Gardening*, 2nd edition. Oxford: Clarendon Press.

Thacker, Christopher (1994) *The Genius of Gardening*. London: Weidenfeld & Nicolson.

CHAPTER 1: WARWICK

Contemporary sources

Glenny, George (1862) *Gardening for the Million*.

Hibberd, Shirley (1859) *The Town Garden*, 2nd edn.

Hibberd, Shirley (1877) *The Amateur's Kitchen Garden*.

Hibberd, Shirley (1878) *The Amateur's Flower Garden*, 2nd edn.

Kelly's Directory of Warwickshire (1880).

Paul, William (1865) *Villa Gardening*, 3rd edn.

Contemporary journals

Gardeners' Chronicle (1875–1900)

Gardeners' Magazine (1875–1900)

Warwick and Warwickshire Advertiser and Leamington Gazette (1875–1900)

Loudon, J. C. (1831) 'General results of a gardening tour', *Gardener's Magazine*, 7, August, pp.409–10.

Modern works

Berger R., Hodgetts, Dr C., Parkin, I., Brookes, A. (1995) *A New Life for Hill Close Gardens, Warwick*. Lammas: Lammas and District Residents Association.

Crouch, David, and Ward, Colin (1988) *The Allotment: Its Landscape and Culture*. London: Faber & Faber.

Harding, Jane, and Taigel, Anthea (1996) 'An air of detachment: town gardens in the eighteenth and nineteenth centuries', *Garden History*, Winter, 24 (2).

Hyams, Edward (1970) *English Cottage Gardens*. Walton-on-Thames: Nelson.

Lambert, David (1994) *Detached Town Gardens*, theme study. London: English Heritage.

Wilkinson, Anne (1998) 'The preternatural gardener: the life of James Shirley Hibberd (1825–90)', *Garden History*, Winter, 26 (2).

CHAPTER 2: SHELLEY HALL

Contemporary sources

College of Arms, Howard, J. J. (ed.) (1866) *The Visitation of Suffolk, Made by William Hervey in 1561*.

Hill, Thomas (1577) *The Gardeners Labyrinth*.

Tusser, Thomas and William Mavor (ed.) (1812) *Five Hundred Points of Good Husbandry*.

Modern works

Currie, Christopher K. (1988) 'Fishponds as garden features, c.1550–1750', *Garden History*, Summer, 18 (1).

Dymond, David, and Martin, Edward (eds) (1989) *An Historical Atlas of Suffolk*, 2nd edition. Suffolk: Suffolk County Council Planning Department & Suffolk Institute of Archaeology and History.

Harvey, John H. (1987) 'Garden plants of around 1525: the Fromond list', *Garden History*, Winter, 17 (2).

Harvey, John (1981) *Medieval Gardens*. London: B. T. Batsford.

Landsberg, Sylvia (1998) *The Medieval Garden*. London: British Museum Press.

Jacques, David (1999) 'The *compartment* system in Tudor England' and other articles in *Garden History*, Summer, 27 (1), issue on Tudor gardens.

Martin, Edward (1998) 'Shelley Hall and Church: the buildings of Sir Philip Tilney (d.1533)', *Suffolk Institute of Archaeology*, 38 pt 2, pp.260–2.

Putnam, Clare (1972) *Flowers and Trees of Tudor England*. London: Hugh Evelyn.

Whalley, Robin, and Anne Jennings (1998) *Knot Gardens and Parterres*. London: Barn Elms.

Wilson, D. (1985) *Moated Sites*. Princes Risborough, Buckinghamshire: Shire Archaeology.

CHAPTER 3: GATTON PARK

Contemporary sources

Colman, Sir Jeremiah (1932) *Hybridization of Orchids: The Experiences of an Amateur*.

Conder, Josiah (1893) *Landscape Gardening in Japan*.

Dresser, Christopher (1882) *Japan: Its Architecture, Art and Art Manufactures*.

Du Cane, Florence (1908) *The Flowers and Gardens of Japan*, painted by Ella Du Cane and described by F. Du Cane.

Fox, Edwin, and Bousfield, (1888) *Particulars and Conditions of Sale of the Gatton Estate*.

Freeman-Mitford, A. B. (1896) *The Bamboo Garden*.

The Golden Wedding of Sir Jeremiah and Lady Colman (1935).

Gauntlett & Co., V. N., undated nursery catalogues in the collection of the RHS Lindley Library.

Henslow, T. G. W. (1914) *Gatton Park, Seat of Sir Jeremiah Colman, Bart.*

Henslow, T. G. W. (1926) *Garden Architecture*.

Milner, H. E. (1890) *The Art and Practice of Landscape Gardening*.

White, John P. (undated) *Garden Furniture and Ornament*. The Pyghtle Works, Bedford, catalogue in the collection of the RHS Lindley Library.

Contemporary journals

Gardeners' Chronicle, 15 December 1860, pp.1103–4; 17 March 1866 p.243; 11 July 1896, 16 April 1910, p.243; 24 September 1910, pp.227–8; 31 January 1914, pp.65–7; 11 September 1915, pp. 161–3.

Gardeners' Magazine, 9 July 1910, pp.530–2; 15 March 1902, p.160.

Hudson, James (1907) 'A Japanese garden in England', *Journal of the Royal Horticultural Society*, XXXII, pp.1–10.

Journal of Horticulture and Home Farmer, 6 November 1913, pp.451–3.

Surrey Mirror and County Post, 20 May 1910, p.5.

Modern works

Couch, Sarah (1997) *Gatton Park, Reigate, Surrey, Historic Landscape Survey and Management Plan*. Cazenove Architects Co-operative for the Royal Alexandra and Albert School.

Keane, Marc (1996) *Japanese Garden Design*. Tokyo: Tuttle Publishing.

CHAPTER 4: ELLER HOW

Contemporary sources

Boyle, Clara (1938) *A Servant of the Empire*.

Bulmer, T. F. (ed) (1885) *History, Topography and Directory of Westmoreland*.

Clough, Blanche Athena (1897) *A Memoir of Anne-Jemima Clough*.

Holme, Charles (ed.) (1911) *The Gardens of England in the Northern Counties*.

Hibberd, Shirley (1856) *Rustic Adornments for Homes of Taste*.

Hibberd, Shirley (1869) *The Fern Garden*.

Kelly's Directory of Cumberland and Westmorland (various dates).

Martineau, Harriet (1855) *A Complete Guide to the English Lakes*.

Moore, Thomas (1848) *A Handbook of British Ferns*.

Robinson, John (1875) *Ferns in Their Homes and Ours*.

Robinson, William (1870) *The Wild Garden*.

Williams, B. S. (1852) *Hints on the Cultivation of British and Exotic Ferns*.

Contemporary journals

Abbey, George (1861) 'Ferns under glass', *Journal of Horticulture and Cottage Gardener*, 2 July, pp.260–2.

Harland, Henry (1876) 'Magic grottoes and show ferneries', *Gardener's Magazine*, 23 December, p.700.

Gardeners' Chronicle, 25 October 1879, pp.523–4; 12 February 1881, pp.205–6.

Kendal Mercury, 4 September 1869, p.5; 28 December 1900.

Westmorland Gazette, 9 October 1880; 29 December 1900; 25 April 1914.

Modern works

Elliston Allen, David (1969) *The Victorian Fern Craze*. London: Hutchinson.

Carnie, John M. (undated) *Harriet Martineau 1802–1876, with Particular Reference to Her Years in Ambleside: 1846–1876*.

Jay, Eileen (1998) *The Armitt Story, Ambleside*. Ambleside: The Loughrigg Press for the Armitt Trust.

Viljoen, Helen Gill (ed.) (1971) *The Brantwood Diary of John Ruskin*. New Haven, CT: Yale University Press.

CHAPTER 5: CHATHAM

Contemporary sources

Fairchild, Thomas (1722) *The City Gardener*.

Furber, Robert (1734) *The Flower Garden Display'd*, 2nd edn.

Mawe, Thomas, and Abercrombie, John (1782) *Every Man His Own Gardener*, 9th edn.

Miller, Philip (1768) *Gardeners Dictionary*, 8th edn.

Swinden, Nathaniel (1778) *The Beauties of Flora Display'd*.

Modern works

Bell, R. D. (1990) 'The Discovery of a Buried Garden in Bath', *Garden History*, 18 (1), pp.1–21.

Coad, Jonathan (1982) *Historic Architecture of Chatham Dockyard, 1700–1850*. London: National Maritime Museum with The Society for Nautical Research.

Coad, Jonathan (c.1989) *The Royal Dockyards, 1690–1850*. Aldershot: Scolar for Royal Commission on the Historical Monuments of England.

Cruickshank, Dan, and Burton, Neil (1990) *Life in the Georgian City*. London: Viking.

Galinou, Mireille (ed.) (1990) *London's Pride: The Glorious History of the Capital's Gardens*. London: Anaya Publishers.

Hall, Elisabeth, and Lear, Jean (eds) (1992) 'Chatham Dockyard Gardens', *Garden History*, 20 (2), pp.132–52.

Harvey, John (1974) *Early Nurserymen*. Chichester: Phillimore & Co.

Henrey, Blanche (1975) *British Botanical and Horticultural Literature Before 1800: Vol II: The Eighteenth Century*. Oxford: Oxford University Press.

Howes, Lesley (1995) 'The Archaeology and Excavation of Town Gardens in England', paper presented to garden archaeology conference in Gratz, Austria, 1994, *Die Gartenkunst*, 7 Jahrgang, Heft 1.

Laird, Mark (c.1999) *The Flowering of the Landscape Garden: English Pleasure Grounds 1720–1800*. Philadelphia, PA: University of Pennsylvania Press.

Laird, Mark, and Harvey, John (1997) 'The garden plans for 13 Upper Street, London: a conjectural review of the planting, upkeep and long-term maintenance of a late eighteenth-century town garden', *Garden History*, 25 (2), pp.189–211.

Longstaffe-Gowan, Todd (1990) 'Private urban gardening in England, 1700–1839: on the art of sinking', in *The Vernacular Garden*. Washington DC: Dumbarton Oaks Research Library and Collection.

CHAPTER 6: COVENTRY

Contemporary sources

Bernard, Thomas (1797) *An Account of a Cottage and Garden near Tadcaster*.

Forsyth, William (1824) *A Treatise on the Culture and Management of Fruit Trees*.

Loudon, Jane (1849) *The Ladies' Flower-Garden of Ornamental Perennials*, 2nd edn.

Loudon, J. C. (1822) *An Encyclopaedia of Gardening*.

Loudon, J. C. (1830) *A Manual of Cottage Gardening, Husbandry, and Architecture*.

Lindley, George (1831) *A Guide to the Orchard and Kitchen Garden*.

M'Intosh, Charles (1853–55) *The Book of the Garden*.

Rennie, James (1834) *The Hand-Book of Gardening in Principle and Practice*.

Contemporary journals

Errington, R. (1849) 'The Fruit Garden', *Cottage Gardener*, 1, pp.107–8.

Davis, Hewitt (1849) 'Cottage Farming', *Cottage Gardener*, 1, pp. 193–4.

Appleby, T. (1849) 'The Flower-Garden', *Cottage Gardener*, 2, pp.5–6.

Robertson, John (1827) 'On the Importance of Liquid Manure in Horticulture', *Gardener's Magazine*, pp.18–19.

The Florist (1849) 'Carnations and Picotees', pp.25–7; 'The Ranunculus', pp.57–8; 'A Few Remarks on Hardy Border Plants', pp.62–5; 'The Carnation', pp.257–9.

Modern works

Crowe, Nigel (1994) *Book of Canals*. London: B. T. Batsford/English Heritage.

Lewery, Antony (1996) *Flowers Afloat*. Devon: David & Charles.

Longden, Robert, compiled by Rolt, Sonia (1997) *Canal People: The Photographs of Robert Longden of Coventry*. Gloucestershire: Sutton.

Scott-James, Anne (1981) *The Cottage Garden*. London: Allen Lane.

CHAPTER 7: PENJERRICK

Contemporary sources

Collins, J. H. (1878) *A Catalogue of the Works of Robert Were Fox FRS with Notes and Extracts and a Sketch of his Life*.

Hooker, Sir Joseph Dalton, Hooker, Sir W. J. (ed.) (1849–51) *The Rhododendrons of Sikkim-Himalaya*.

Lowe, E. J. (1860) *Ferns: British and Exotic*, VIII.

Millais, J. G. (1917) *Rhododendrons and the various hybrids*.

Robinson, William (1871) *The Subtropical Garden*.

Veitch, James H. (1906) *Hortus Veitchii*.

Contemporary journals

Davey, F. Hamilton (1897) 'Acclimatisation of exotics in Cornwall: the Falmouth–Truro District', *Journal of the Royal Institution of Cornwall*, 13, pp. 313–42.

Davey, F. Hamilton (1899) 'Penjerrick', *Cornish Magazine*, pp. 275–84.

Meyer, F. W. (1899) 'Penjerrick, Cornwall', *Garden*, 21 January p.31.

Gardeners' Chronicle, 18 November 1871, p.1490; 7 March 1874, pp 308–9; 21 March 1894; December 1889 p.749; 3 December 1898 pp.399–400; 18 May 1901, p.309–10.

Gardeners' Magazine, 7 March 1908, p.183.

Modern works

Brett R. L. (ed.) (1979) *Barclay Fox's Journal*. London: Bell & Hyman.

Cornish Garden, especially articles by V. Challinor Davies, Bridget Graham, Shirley Heriz-Smith, Ivor J. Herring, Walter Magor, Tim Miles, Douglas Ellory Pett and Roger Trenoweth in volumes 15 (1972), 23 (1980), 24 (1981), 25 (1982), 26 (1983), 29 (1986), 30 (1987), 32 (1989), 34 (1991), 35 (1992), 36 (1993), 37 (1994), 39 (1996), 40 (1997), 41 (1998).

Monk, Wendy (ed.) (1972) *The Journals of Caroline Fox: 1835 –71*, Elek.

Pett, Douglas Ellory (1998) *The Parks and Gardens of Cornwall*. Cornwall: Alison Hodge.

Rickard, Martin (1998) 'Ferns as Big as Trees', *Country Life*, 15 September.

CHAPTER 8: DUNIRA

Contemporary sources

Hunter, Thomas (1883) *Woods, Forests, and Estates of Perthshire*. Robertson & Co.

Jekyll, Gertrude (1901) *Wall and Water Gardens*. Country Life.

Jekyll, Gertrude, and Weaver, Lawrence (1912) *Gardens for Small Country Houses*. Country Life.

Kemp, Edward (1864) *How to Lay Out a Small Garden*, 3rd edn.

Mawson, Thomas H. (1926) *The Art and Craft of Garden Making*, 5th edn. B. T. Batsford.

Mawson, Thomas H. (1927) *The Life and Work of an English Landscape Architect*. Richards Press.

Trollope, George, & Sons (1937) *'Dunira', Comrie, Perthshire: Illustrated Particulars and Plan*.

Contemporary journals

Gardeners' Chronicle, 17 November 1934, p.347.

Strathearn Herald, 1 March 1919; 28 July 1919; 21 February 1920; 17 April 1920; 28 April 1937; 27 December 1947; 23 October 1948; 4 March 1950.

Taylor, G. C. (1931) 'The Garden at Dunira', *Country Life*, 21 March, pp.379–82.

Modern works

Beard, Geoffrey, and Wardman, Joan (1976) *Thomas H. Mawson, 1861 –1933: The Life and Work of a Northern Landscape Architect*. Bailrigg, Lancaster: University of Lancaster.

Brown, Jane (1994) *Gardens of a Golden Afternoon: The Story of a Partnership, Edwin Lutyens and Gertrude Jekyll*. London: Penguin.

Mawson, David (1984) 'T. H. Mawson (1861–1933) – Landscape Architect and Town Planner, The Reflection Riding Lecture, 16 November 1983', *Journal of the Royal Society of Arts*, February, pp.184–99.

INDEX

PICTURE CREDITS

While every effort has been made to provide accurate
picture credits, the publisher apologises for any omissions.

© Andrea Jones: 2, 4, 5, 8 (*both*), 9 (*bottom*), 10/11, 14/15, 17 (*bottom*), 18, 19 (*both*), 20, 21,
23 (*both*), 24, 25, 26, 27, 29, 31, 32/33, 34/35, 36, 37, 38/39, 39, 40, 41 (*all*), 43 (*bottom*), 44, 46,
47, 48, 49, 50, 51, 52, 53 (*both*), 54/55, 57, 60, 63, 64, 66, 70, 71, 72/73, 73 (*all*), 75 (*both*), 76/77,
79, 80, 81 (*bottom*), 82, 84, 85 (*both*), 86, 87, 88 (*all*), 88/89, 81 (*bottom*), 82, 84, 85 (*both*), 86, 87,
88 (*all*), 88/89, 90, 93, 94 (*both*), 95 (*top*), 96, 97, 98/99, 100, 101, 102 (*bottom*), 104, 105, 107,
108 (*all*), 109, 120/121, 122/123, 124, 127 (*bottom*), 128/129, 130, 132, 134 (*bottom*), 135 (*all*),
137, 138, 139, 140 (*all*), 140/141, 142/143, 144, 145, 147, 148/149, 151, 153 (*both*), 154,
155, 157, 158 (*top*), 159, 161 (*both*), 162 (*top*), 163, 164/165, 166, 167 (*top*), 168, 170,
172, 174, 175 (*right*), 176, 177, 178, 179, 181, 182 (*both*), 183, 184, 185.

Andrea Jones © Garden Exposures Picture Library: 58 (*right*), 67, 74 (*both*), 91, 162 (*bottom*).

British Waterways Archive: 123, 127 (*top*).

Flashback Television: 16, 94 (*top*).

From Clara Boyle's *A Servant of Empire*: 83.

Jennifer Potter: 9 (*top*), 12, 56, 78.

Macbeth Family: 169, 173, 175 (*left*).

Michael Kerr: 28, 45, 69, 92, 105, 133, 160, 180.

Mr and Mrs E.W. Bacon supplied by Mrs F. Philbrook: 83, 95.

Mr J.E. Durrant: 17 (*top*).

National Maritime Museum: 102 (*top*).

Ordnance Survey: 13, 35, 58 (*left*), 81 (*top*), 146.

Pat Trevett: 61.

The British Library: 103.

The Royal Horticultural Society, Lindley Library: 30, 43 (*top*), 59, 65, 68,
108, 113, 131, 134 (*top*), 136, 152, 156, 158 (*bottom*), 167 (*bottom*).

AUTHOR'S ACKNOWLEDGEMENTS

This book would not have been possible without help from an enormous number of people. Ros Franey helped it to happen. Of the *Lost Gardens* production team, series producer Ann Booth-Clibborn advised and encouraged at every stage: I would like to thank her for her patience, good humour and sharp eye. Researchers on the two television series dug up a wealth of information for each garden and helped to untangle the gardens' stories: special thanks go to Emma Geary, Edwina Cooper and Alan Boyle for historical research; Laurence Pattacini, Barbara Simms and Lynne Vinton for garden history research; Michael Kerr, Annabel Turner and Andy Vernon for botanical research; and Richard Burton for help with landscaping. Thanks also to Tim O'Connor, Penny Heard and Samantha Goodwin who chased elusive information, and to everyone at Flashback Television who contributed so much to the programmes and the book.

Most of this material was first gathered together for the television series and I am indebted to Ben Frow at Channel 4; executive producer David Edgar; directors Claire Whalley, Lynda Maher, Peter Norrey and Ben Warwick; and the presenters who stamped their mark on the gardens: Monty Don, Toby Musgrave, Ann-Marie Powell and Twigs Way.

Dr Brent Elliott at the Royal Horticultural Society's Lindley Library was unfailingly generous with his time and advice, as were his staff: Elizabeth Gilbert, Jennifer Vine and Helen Ward. Archivists, librarians, and county record offices from Cornwall to Scotland responded to our many calls for help with great tolerance and skill – thank you all.

We owe a large debt to owners and occupiers of the eight gardens: staff and pupils of the Royal Alexandra and Albert School and especially Pat Pay (Gatton Park), Mr and Mrs Andrew Scott (Shelley Hall), Laing Homes (Linen Street, Warwick), Mr and Mrs Jim Philbrook (Eller How), Mrs Rachel Morin (Penjerrick), British Waterways, Phillip Prior-Pitt and residents Mr and Mrs Steve Faulkner (Coventry), Mr and Mrs James Brosnan (Chatham), and Mr and Mrs George Gordon (Dunira).

Experts in conservation, plants and garden history generously shared their knowledge and enthusiasm. Special thanks go to Peter Beales, Sally Beamish, Robert Bell, Jonathan Coad, Sarah Couch, Christopher Dingwall, Edward Fawcett, David Jacques, Dr Christine Hodgetts, Lesley Howes, David Lambert, Brian Lavery, Jean Lear, Tony Lewery, Brenda Lewis, Todd Longstaffe-Gowan, Edward Martin, Dr Chris Page, Rev Douglas Ellory Pett, Clive Powell, Jamie Quartermaine, Jill Raggett, Martin Rickard, Robin Savill, Chris Sumner and Sally Walker. The Association of Gardens Trusts and individual county gardens trusts were a mine of information and contacts, as were English Heritage, Historic Scotland and the Garden History Society.

At Channel 4 Books, commissioning editor Emma Tait skilfully held everything together. Landscape photographer Andrea Jones brought the gardens back to life in her sharply evocative images of their transformation. Michael Kerr put his passion for plants into the planting plans he drew for the programmes and the book. Designer, Jonathan Baker sensitively blended past with present.

As well as owners and caretakers, photographer Andrea Jones would especially like to thank: David Cummings, Gib Gall, Joan and John Murdock and family, Ken Murrell of Dobbies Garden Centre in Perth, Messrs Ritchley and son, Clive and Julie Shilton of Hardy Exotics Nursery in Penzance, Wallace and Katherine Fyfe and Alliance Mutimedia Insurance for replacing not one but two Nikons dropped in the lake at Penjerrick.

And finally, a big thank-you to all the people who shared their memories of the lost gardens we had set out to rediscover. Their joy at witnessing the transformation made all the striving and the sweat worthwhile. We remember especially Arthur Measures who passed on his remarkable memories of Warwick but sadly did not live to see the programme finished.